Collecting SWAROVSKI

Identification & Price Guide

Dean A. Genth

Published by

700 East State Street • Iola, WI 54990-0001
715-445-2214 • 888-457-2873
www.krause.com

Our toll-free number to place an order or obtain a free catalog is (800) 258-0929.

Library of Congress Catalog Number: 2004105838

ISBN: 0-87349-775-9

Edited by Tracy L. Schmidt
Designed by Elizabeth Krogwald

Printed in the United States

CONTENTS

Malachite Kingfishers, CRV ***$160***

FOREWORD

This book represents a tremendous labor of love over many years. Having worked with M. I. Hummel Figurines for many years and seeing the importance of a price guide for collectors through my involvment with *Luckey's Hummel® Figurines & Plates Identification and Price Guide,* I wanted to publish a book for collectors of Swarovski Silver Crystal.

The Crystal Report, which was published by myself, for so many years, served as a foundation for this book. As a collector interested in Swarovski Silver Crystal, I have enjoyed compiling as many interesting details as possible related to the collecting of Swarovski. It has been my desire to put forth a book for collectors that will benefit both the novice and the elite collector alike.

Should you have an important discovery to share, or need guidance with your collection, feel free to write or e-mail me.

Happy Collecting!

Dean A. Genth
5 Creekside Court
Mason City, Iowa 50401
E-mail: figfinesse@yahoo.com

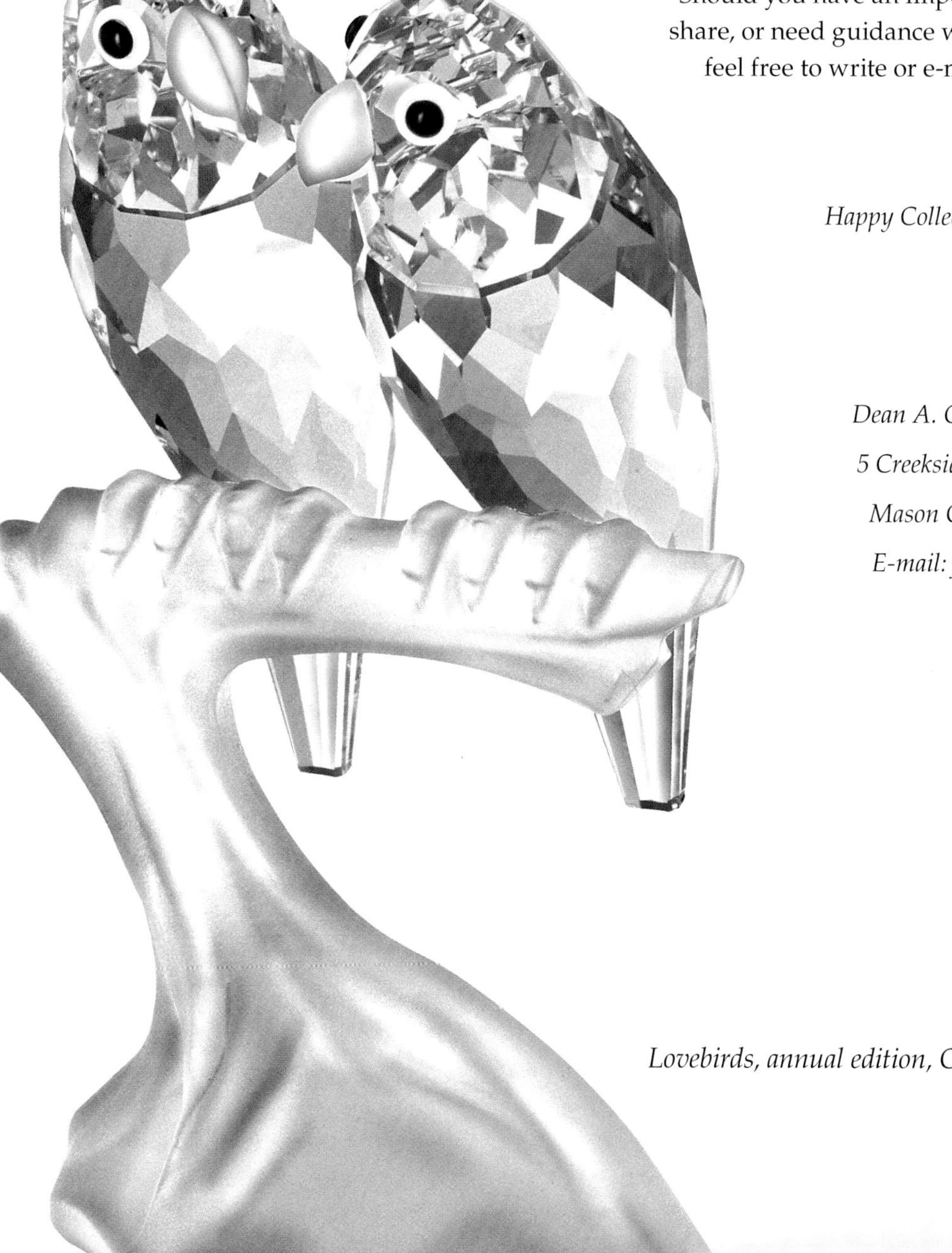

Lovebirds, annual edition, CRV ***$4000-$5000***

ACKNOWLEDGMENTS

No project of this size and magnitude can be accomplished without the assistance and collaborating of many individuals. First of all I would like to thank Paul Morton of Swarovski USA who believed that collectors deserve the best possible information to aid in their search for Swarovski collectibles.

A special thanks to Paul Kennedy of Krause Publications, who early on saw the possibilities for this book. My gratitude goes out to Mary Sieber, editor of *Collectors Mart Magazine,* who has been a steadfast rock of support and encouragement through the years.

This book is a culmination of years of Swarovski research that was first published by Dean A. Genth under the title of *The Crystal Report,* a publication for and about the Swarovski Silver Crystal Secondary Market. For over 10 years that publication served as a collectibles guide for subscribers. Douglas Gabbard was a constant help with that project. Vickey Washington and her staff were always an important part of the research process.

A special thanks to my assistant, Michelle Foster, without whose help these words may have never made it onto a separate computer disk.

I would like to especially acknowledge the outstanding effort by Richard Hill of Florida in providing photographs of his retired Swarovski Silver Crystal pieces. Without Richard's dedication and love for sharing his collection with the public, this book would not have been complete.

No book ever comes about without the loving support of many, many people. Thousands of collectors have helped to encourage me to keep working on their behalf. Family and friends have encouraged and supported this effort. So a special thanks to all you collectors who inspire me to learn something new each day about the wonderful world of collecting Swarovski Silver Crystal.

Butterfly, version 3, CRV ***$90***

DEDICATION

I would like to dedicate this book to my loving parents, Dale and Erma Genth.

To Dad for his unwavering devotion to 4-H leadership for over 40 years, and his love of the land.

To Mom for her ever present faith, unconditional love, and the ability to live one day at a time.

Dean A. Genth

CHAPTER 1

Clockwise from upper left: limited editions; Eagle, Peacock, and Wild Horses.

Daniel Swarovski Corporation History

Swarovski Background

In 1895, Daniel Swarovski founded Daniel Swarovski & Co. in the Austrian village of Wattens. As a crystal stonecutter, Swarovski was inspired by a visit to Vienna's "First Electric Fair" in 1883, and subsequently invented an electric machine to precision cut high-quality crystal jewelry stones in large quantities. He situated his company in the Tyrolean village of Wattens, Austria, as the mountain stream provided an abundance of waterpower for the machinery.

Precision cutting remains a hallmark of Swarovski today. As the leading manufacturer of cut crystal for the jewelry, fashion, collectibles, and gift industries, the name Swarovski has become synonymous with the perfect brilliance of crystal. That brilliance begins in the quality of the raw materials, which are blended by master craftsmen and melted to create crystal of flawless purity.

Each product from Swarovski—whether a figurine from the immensely popular Silver Crystal collection or a bracelet from the exquisite Swarovski jewelry—combines the quality of fine raw materials, the vision of talented designers, and the faceting of skilled craftsmen. The superior quality and enchanting spirit of Swarovski collectibles have inspired more than 450,000 people worldwide, with more than 100,000 in the United States alone, to join the Swarovski Collectors Society. The range of colors and gem-like faceting of Swarovski crystal stones bring designers' visions to brilliant fruition—whether on a lariat necklace or a ballroom dance costume.

Swarovski, Wattens, Austria, is the world's leading manufacturer of full-cut crystal stones for the giftware, fashion, jewelry, and lighting industries. Swarovski North America Limited's labels include Daniel Swarovski Paris, Swarovski Crystal Moments, Swarovski Crystal, Swarovski Crystal Home Accessories, and Swarovski jewelry. The Swarovski Collectors Society boasts more than 450,000 members worldwide.

Swarovski represents the height of unmatched quality, unique variety, crystalline brilliance, latest trend information, and cutting-edge innovations. Discerning consumers value Swarovski products and services. Exceptional crystal purity and cutting precision guarantee exclusivity and quality beyond compare. With its unsurpassed variety and brilliance, the broad crystalline spectrum gives customers free creative rein. Crystal enthusiasts throughout the world succumb to the magic of fascinating crystal creations. The Swarovski brand follows the principle of "crystal to create new worlds—worlds of glitter, worlds of amazement, worlds of magic and worlds of enjoyments."

Swarovski is the global market leader in:

- Crystal jewelry stones and crystal components
- Crystal objects, crystal jewelry and accessories
- Grinding and dressing tools (Tyrolit)
- Precision optical equipment (Swarovski Optik)
- Reflectors for road safety (Swareflex)
- Synthetic gemstones (Signity)

Top: Belle Epoque Clock; bottom: Colosseum Clock.

Swarovski Fact Sheet

With world manufacturing headquarters in Wattens, Austria, Swarovski is the world's leading manufacturer of full cut crystal for the giftware, fashion, jewelry, and lighting industries. Swarovski North America's labels include Swarovski Silver Crystal, Swarovski Crystal Moments, Swarovski Crystal Home Accessories, Swarovski Crystal Paradise, Swarovski Jewelry, and Daniel Swarovski Paris.

Swarovski Silver Crystal: Swarovski Silver Crystal consists of more than 150 figurines and decorative items inspired by themes such as "African Wildlife," "Woodland Friends," "When We Were Young," and the "South Sea." The popularity of the Silver Crystal collection led to the creation of the Swarovski Collectors Society in 1987. The Society now boasts more than 450,000 members worldwide.

Swarovski Crystal Moments: Swarovski Crystal Moments is a collection of more than 70 adorable miniatures and ornaments created to symbolize life's special moments. They're perfect as small gifts to celebrate joyous occasions, table setting enhancements or spontaneous treats. Each miniature unites brilliantly faceted crystal with meticulously designed 18-karat gold or rhodium plated details.

Swarovski Crystal Home Accessories: Since 1992, Swarovski has commissioned acclaimed artists and architects such as André Putman, Joel Desgrippes and Bořek Šípek for the creation of this unique collection of tabletop objects. They unite state-of-the-art Swarovski crystal cutting technology with natural and manmade materials in functional works of art for the home. Each piece carries its designer's signature. Additionally, in 2002, Swarovski launched its own take on the fascinating mid-sixties art genre, Op Art (Optical Art), a movement utilizing graphic elements to create optical illusions and actively involve the viewer in the art process. The collection introduced six modern crystal objects, consisting of four boxes, a compass, and a table clock, by Milanese designer Anna Gili.

Swarovski Crystal Paradise: Swarovski embraces its passion for high-style and uniqueness with Crystal Paradise—a colorful line of bird and insect-related crystal pins, brooches, and objects. A homage to nature, this enchanting and creative collection fuses Swarovski's expertise and innovation to create whimsical crystal creatures.

Swarovski Jewelry: A line of opulent crystal jewelry using pavé settings and colored stones for day-into-night dressing, the collection includes earrings, necklaces, bracelets, pins, rings, watches, and crystal tattoos. Bold silhouettes and exceptional design are trademarks of this contemporary collection. Four collections are created each year.

Daniel Swarovski Paris: Launched in July of 1989 by Creative Director, Rosemarie Le Gallais, the Daniel Swarovski Paris collection is an innovative line of haute couture accessories that celebrate the versatility of crystal. Combining creativity, French traditional craftsmanship and Swarovski's advanced technology, the Daniel Swarovski Paris collection offers elegant and refined handbags for day and night, as well as unique costume jewelry pieces at the forefront of design and fashion. In addition, Daniel Swarovski Home Accessories, an upscale line of crystal-driven, functional home décor objects such as lamps, candleholders, and paperweights, was launched in 2002, further enhancing the brand's luxury image.

Mini Chicks, CRV **$46.50**

Daniel Swarovski I Biographical Timeline:

10-24-1862 to 1-23-1956

Daniel Swarovski I was born in Georgenthal, Bohemia—at that time part of the Habsburg Monarchy. The region had centuries old tradition of glass manufacturing and engraving. He was trained in his father's glass cutting factory, and soon realized that the manual cutting of glass was inadequate to meet the growing demands of the market. He began devising methods of making this handicraft into an automatic process.

1883 Daniel Swarovski I visited the "First Electrical Exhibition" in Vienna. He was fascinated by what he saw and even as a young man, foresaw the great potential in this new source of energy.

1892 Daniel Swarovski I was just 30 years old, but already a father of three sons, when he applied for a patent on his first invention; a machine capable of cutting glass jewelry stones with perfect precision. This innovation gave him a decisive advantage over companies using traditional methods. Anticipating the long-term implications, he looked for a suitable site to further develop his ideas, away from prying eyes!

1895 After an extensive search in the Austrian part of the Monarchy, he finally found what he was looking for in the Tyrol. He and his family left their Bohemian homeland on October 1, 1895 to set up a new company. He had leased an empty factory with a small water power plant in Wattens, a village with 744 inhabitants, lying approximately 15 kilometers east of Innsbruck, the capital of the Tyrol. This picturesque alpine setting provided the most important element for his intended project: energy, in the form of waterpower. At first, the Wattens mountain brook supplied the mechanical energy required, but also later, the newly discovered "white coal," meaning the energy was harnessed into electricity from the flowing waters. This source of power allowed the precision grinding and polishing of hundreds of glass jewelry stones in one working process, which is still used to a large extent today. Wattens was also conveniently situated. The recently constructed, over 10 km long Arlberg railway tunnel was close by, meaning that transport facilities were available to the West. The door was open to the major fashion center, Paris, and beyond.

1899 Within a short time, the "Tyrolean cut stones," as they were named by the people in the trade, became an international byword for quality. They were in great demand not only in the well-known jewelry manufacturing centers in France, England, and Germany, but also in America. With pride, Daniel Swarovski I chose a trademark to symbolize the beauty of the products—the finest flower of the alpine world, the Edelweiss.

1900 The factory and some additional land was bought for 24,000 gilders. Business was thriving and already 100 workers were employed. The installation of electric lighting in the workshops ensured the precision cutting of glass, even when visibility was poor. The improvements in factory conditions were accompanied by concerted efforts to enrich the workers' leisure time. Daniel Swarovski I esteemed the value of life, advocated the pursuit of hobbies, and supported the founding of cultural and sport clubs.

1906 To increase production capacity, a larger factory with modern installations was required. Full concentration was given to this objective, including the planning of a water power station higher up in the valley, which would provide a more powerful source of energy.

1907 The water power station was in operation by the end of the year, and could supply the new factory building with electricity by direct cable. However, to keep abreast with the continuing demand for more products, the infrastructure had to be extended, and the provision of housing for employees was introduced.

1908 Up to date, the crystal used for the manufacture of the jewelry stones was processed from Bohemian-made raw glass. This did not satisfy Daniel Swarovski I who was a perfectionist by nature, and self-sufficient by choice. He began to experiment in glass manufacturing assisted by his sons, Wilhelm, Friedrich, and Alfred, in a workshop next to their own villa.

1911 The success of the experiments led to the construction of the so-called laboratory and the establishing of their own glass works. They were able to manufacture crystal themselves, using self-designed glass-melting furnaces and new production processes. This gave them the means to refine crystal to a state of perfect brilliance. Swarovski was now independent as far as the supply of raw glass was concerned, and in addition, had the advantage of being able to produce colored glass using self-devised methods. Thus, the foundations were laid for a large-scale industry of a type hitherto unknown in this particular manufacturing sector.

1914 The outbreak of World War I brought the manufacture of glass jewelry stones to a standstill, as most of the workers were conscripted for military service. The consolidation and growth of the company was interrupted. In order to avoid the confiscation of machines and tools for the armaments industry, Daniel Swarovski I was forced to produce military equipment. Quite a contrast to jewelry stones, but at least by the end of the war in 1918, he had salvaged a workforce and provided security for the families of 600 workers.

1918 After two years of trial and effort, grinding wheels, essential for the cutting of crystal jewelry stones, were produced on the premises. Daniel Swarovski I had initiated this tactic because of the acute shortage of abrasives during the war years. He recognized the necessity to have an independent source of supply.

1919 The excellent quality of the grinding tools attracted outside interest, and with a view to diversification, a decision was made to sell them on the open market. The brand name "TYROLIT" was entered into the commercial register of the Chamber of Commerce and Trades in Innsbruck. These Tyrolit wheels were not only sold in Austria, but also exported to customers abroad. Today, 80% of the production is exported to over 80 countries in the world.

1920 The fashion crazes of the "Roaring Twenties" led to a boom in the imitation jewelry business. Daniel Swarovski I developed new types of cutting machines to work more efficiently and a grindery was installed in the laboratory for the mass-production of precision-cut jewelry stones.

1925 Daniel Swarovski I made the first attempts to produce reflecting elements out of glass using the experience he had gained in the manufacture of precision glassware. These glass reflectors were later applied to articles specially designed to increase the safety of rail, road, and harbor traffic at night and in poor visibility. They were introduced to the market under the trade name of "SWAREFLEX" in 1950. From the mid-twenties on, Daniel Swarovski I's three sons presumed greater responsibility in the factory's management. Wilhelm specialized in the field of optics and glass, Friedrich in the technical, and Alfred in the commercial side of the business. This gradual transition from one generation to the next was to become a Swarovski family tradition.

1930 The Great Depression, following the crash of the U.S. economy in 1929, seriously affected the Swarovski turnover. A drastic cutback in production resulted in the unavoidable dismissal of many workers. To combat the crisis and survive the difficult times, Daniel Swarovski I and his sons continued on a course of further diversification, with success.

1931 A new area of production was established—Swarovski trimmings. These were jewelry stones processed into decorative bands and laces, ready for application to garments or accessories.

1935 Wilhelm Swarovski, whose particular interest lay in the research of optical precision instruments, introduced the first prototype binoculars.

1939 The outbreak of World War II forced the Swarovski management once again to make a decision: either to accept military commissions or close down. The manufacture of glass jewelry stones was prohibited during wartime. Fortunately, the emerging optics program, in combination with the production of abrasive and technical products, secured the factory from closure.

1940 The Swarovski glass works received the first order to produce binoculars and optical instruments for the armed forces. This was a sector of production, but by the end of the war 183,000 top-quality binoculars (ca. 6000 per month) had been produced.

1945 On May 3rd, Wattens, having miraculously just escaped one of the final Allied bombing raids, was occupied by the American troops. The war was over, but the economically depressed times in Austria continued with rampant inflation and high unemployment. Through a business connection in America, the Swarovski management was able to organize emergency food parcels for the workers and their families in Wattens.
At the same time an important export drive was launched which resulted in the company emerging in the late 40s, early 50s, as the largest earner of foreign currencies in Austria. This was the beginning of a new era of prosperity for Swarovski, with an ensuing stability that the people of Wattens were to appreciate for years to come. Daniel Swarovski I had always been sincerely interested in the welfare of his workers. Already in the period between the two wars, he had promoted a housing program and received municipal backing. After World War II, his grandson, Daniel II, with the full support of the family, continued his pioneer work and further developed the scheme using Swarovski funds.

1946 The third generation brothers, Daniel II and Manfred Swarovski, were named members of the board of the family company. Daniel I and his sons wanted to invest their valuable experience in optics acquired during the war years, in peacetime projects. Consequently, they began manufacturing spectacle lenses.

1947 In the West, particularly America, the enormous postwar demand for the brilliant crystal jewelry stones made by Swarovski remained constant. Space to expand the production departments became a requisite. It was decided to move the optics department from Wattens to the nearby village of Absam-Eichat.

1948 The SWAROVSKI OPTIK factory was founded and the independent development and manufacture of precision optical instruments was established.

1950 The manufacture of TYROLIT grinding wheels and abrasive products was transferred to Schwaz, where a rapid production development took place.

1952 The first Swarovski Sales Office was founded in Linz, in Upper Austria. This organization set the precedent for the 42 sales subsidiaries, which have since been established around the world.

1953 The first experiments were made to coat the cut and polished crystal jewelry with a color effect. A new and highly sophisticated technique was developed which vaporized a thin layer of metal onto the stones.

1956 Swarovski was ready to distribute crystal jewelry stones and beads enhanced with an iridescent coating effect, on a mass scale. The most famous of which, known as the "Aurora Borealis" effect, triggered off a boom in the crystal bead market.

Daniel Swarovski I died on January 23rd, 1956 at the age of 94. He left behind one of the important enterprises in Austria. But to his inheritors, his most important legacy was his attitude towards his fellow beings, and his will to succeed in the face of adversity. These distinctive characteristics form the basis of the company's philosophy today.

CHAPTER 2

From upper left, the Elephant, Kudo, and Lion.

Swarovski Designers

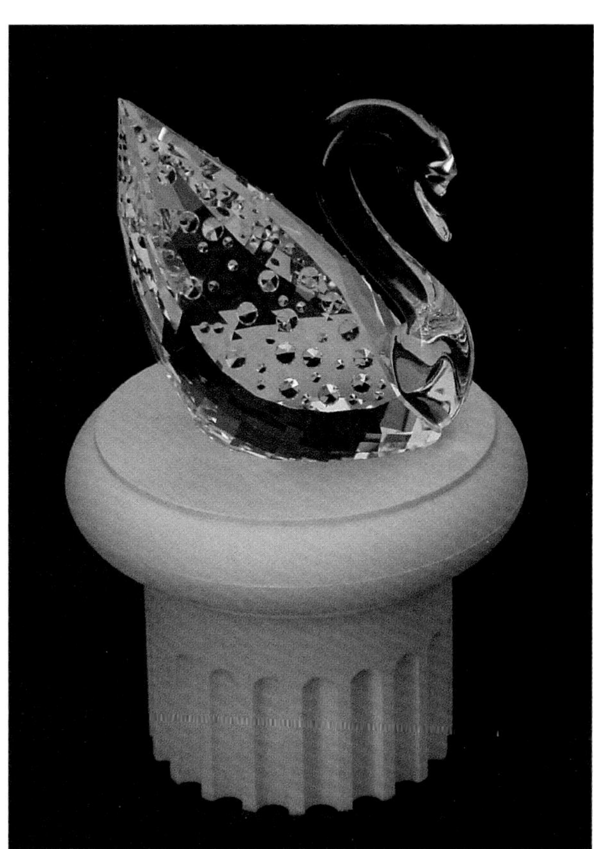

The Centenary Swan, CRV **$175**

Anton Hirzinger

Anton Hirzinger has lived in Kramsach in the Tyrol since he was born in 1955. The reputation of this idyllic small town for its achievements in the field of glass production, and in particular for the College of Glass and Design, has spread far beyond its regional borders. "Even as a child, I was fascinated by this material like no other and I knew at a very early age that when I grew up I wanted to make it my career," says the designer who learned his craft at the Kramsach College of Glassmaking. He initially worked as a hollow glass craftsman at a small company in his hometown.

The father of two small children has now been working for Swarovski for more than eight years. He initially started work in the Swarovski Crystal Shop in Wattens, spending a period of five years providing the countless visitors from all over the world a closer insight to glass and crystal craftsmanship. Ready to move on to new challenges, Anton Hirzinger was then transferred to the Design Center where designs are developed for the wide variety of Swarovski products.

We have the creativity of Anton Hirzinger to thank for the Swarovski Silver Crystal *Pelican* and the *Owlet*. His latest works are the *Centenary Swan,* a commemorative edition for the company's 100th anniversary in 1995, and the *Maxi Swan.*

In his spare time, Anton Hirzinger spends as much time as possible with his family. The four of them go for family walks through the beautiful countryside of the Tyrol or skiing in the winter. He follows his interest in art and culture primarily when on holiday, preferring to spend his holidays in neighboring Italy as he has done for years.

Anniversary Squirrel, CRV **$150**

Tao Ho's mission is to breach the gap between the cultures of East and West, the Orient and the Occident. The declared aim of the artist, deeply rooted in his native Chinese culture, is to achieve a state of harmony and balance between two very different cultural heritages—an aim uniquely expressed and visualized in his Yin Yang *candleholder for Swarovski Selection.*

Tao Ho

Tao Ho, born in Shanghai in 1936 and educated in the USA, was the personal assistant of Walter Gropius and Siegfried Giedion. He is an internationally renowned architect and recipient of numerous awards, including the prestigious 1997 Crystal Award from the World Economic Forum in Davos for his outstanding and successful efforts to bridge Western and Chinese culture. Tao Ho, whose studies included art history, philosophy, and music, has also made a name for himself in the world of design.

In 1968, Tao Ho, who returned from the USA to Hong Kong in 1964, founded his own TAOHO design company, in which he combines architecture, town planning, interior and graphic design. In 1984 he co-founded the Great Earth Architects & Engineers International in Beijing, the first, and at that time, only private architectural joint venture recognized by the Chinese government. Since then, he has been commissioned to design several Chinese cities including Xiamen, Qingdao, and Hangzhou. His activities, however, are not restricted to his native country. His name appears in the *Who's Who* lists of architecture and design all over the world.

One would be quite right to call Tao Ho an all-round talent. Painting, sculpture, photography, music, poetry, the study of the universe, Carl Jung, and Huang Binhong—this short summary of the artist's interests gives us an insight into the diversity of his works, works which includes his *Yin Yang* candleholder for Swarovski Selection.

In 2000 Tao Ho completed a light object depicting the "Big Bang" made of over 22,000 pieces of Swarovski crystals and 575 of fiber optic points for the new headquarters of the World Economic Forum in Geneva. The Swarovski Light Laboratory produced this fascinating creation.

In all of his designs and ideas, we are very aware of his Chinese roots—that great cultural heritage whose future he wants to help shape. That is his mission, the idea that underlies his lectures, publications, and his artistic oeuvre. Tao Ho's 21st century will be marked by the gradual merging and mutual enrichment of the cultures of Orient and Occident, harmony and balance, his vision of the world of tomorrow, as expressed and visualized in the ancient Chinese symbol of Yin and Yang.

Her designs have an "unmistakably feminine touch," say Edith Mair's fans. And it is true that her creations, such as the endearing Fawn and the cheerful Snowman, tend to appeal particularly to women and children.

Edith Mair

Edith Mair, who was born in Brixlegg, Tyrol, Austria in 1966, is a representative of the new generation in the Swarovski designer team. Her spontaneous, sensitive, and inspired designs for Swarovski Silver Crystal make use of unusual contrasts and material combinations in an ongoing search for new forms of expression.

Edith Mair discovered her creative and artistic abilities as a child, and went on to develop her talent at the College for Glass Making and Design in Kramsach, Austria. Her first area of specialization was in the area of lead glazing and glass painting, and was followed by studies in graphics as well as much experimentation.

The main motivations of the artist are inquisitiveness and openness. It was in her search for new creative challenges that she joined Swarovski, where she has been able to acquire extensive experience. She has been a permanent member of the design team at the company's headquarters in Wattens since 1990, and soon began to attract the attention of the public with such sensitive interpretations as *Fawn* and *Ladybird*.

Edith Mair's interest in art and architecture is not solely professional in nature. She is also fascinated in her private life by the Gothic, Renaissance, Baroque, and art nouveau eras, from which she takes much of her inspiration. The same applies to modern and contemporary art.

Edith Mair lives entirely for her work—to the extent that she regards it as her hobby. However, it is a hobby that demands much strength and inspiration. Luckily, she is able to find both in the nearby Tyrolean Alps, where she spends every minute of her spare time. Indeed, it is in the pursuit of her three favorite outdoor pastimes—mountaineering, climbing, and skiing—that the artist is able to not only invigorate body and soul, but also restore her creative energies.

Baby Snails on Vine Leaf, CRV **$49.50**

Gabriele Stamey was born in the small Tyrolean town, Wörgl, in 1956. Already as a young child, she was drawn to artistic and creative experimentation in various forms and colors. At the tender age of 14, Gabriele decided to broaden her budding talents by enrolling at the Kramsach College of Glass and Design.

Gabriele Stamey

Upon completion of the four-year program at this world famous art school, Gabriele began her professional career designing aesthetic, hand-blown stemware. As a freelancer, she later created stained glass objects and glass paintings, which were displayed at a number of successful exhibitions.

Gabriele's designs are inspired by her two favorite hobbies: art and music, to which she would like to devote more time than her commitments allow. After her marriage to Michael Stamey—also a famous Swarovski designer—and the birth of their two sons, however, Gabriele's leisure time was even more reduced.

In 1986 Gabriele accepted a full-time position for the Swarovski Silver Crystal line. Her professional skills and lively imagination were immediately evident in her first Swarovski Silver Crystal figurines comprising a whimsical cockerel, hen, and three chicks in faceted full-cut crystal.

Gabriele expanded her designs based on her own artistic interest and ideas. Inspired by her family life, she created a completely new Swarovski Silver Crystal product group, "When We Were Young," which features the recently launched flagship *Santa Maria*. Her most popular design in this series, which is dedicated to man's fascination with flight and travel, is the *Silver Express*. This is a lovingly crafted, cut-crystal train complete with locomotive, tender and two wagons. Another of her new series is "Silver Crystal City," a set of miniature ancient buildings, which debuted in the autumn of 1990.

Anniversary Vase of Roses, CRV ***$150***

Michael Stamey is no stranger to Swarovski Collectors Society (SCS) members. His designs for the three annual editions in the "Mother and Child" series—the Dolphins (1990), the Seals (1991), and the Whales (1992)—have made his name a household word with collectors and turned him into a much sought-after celebrity at SCS events all over the world.

Michael Stamey

Modest and unassuming, with an engagingly boyish charm, Michael would probably be the last to admit that he is one of a small group of Swarovski Crystal designers who have revolutionized the genre of the animal figurine. Bursting with naturalistic strength and energy, the new pieces evoke a deep-seated response that transcends the largely sentimental appeal of many earlier models.

Now, in the *Kudu*, Michael has created what some connoisseurs claim is the most elegant piece ever manufactured by Swarovski. While expressing all the Kudu's grace and agility, his interpretation also conveys a tangible sense of its vulnerability. The magnificent spiral horns, for example, fashioned in opaque crystal, not only represented an immense challenge but will also demand careful handling from owners.

Michael admits that the *Kudu* posed problems. For a start, kudus are only found in Africa, which meant relying on drawings, photographs, and videos. Even then, it wasn't easy to find a picture of a kudu with its horns in the required position, i.e. with its head pointing slightly backwards. To get the proportions right, Michael studied the anatomy of other members of the antelope family from nearer home. After making a few rough sketches, he immediately started working in crystal. He finds that other materials are simply unable to give him a true sense of the finished item.

No doubt many collectors flocked to have their copy of the Kudu personally signed by Michael while he was on the road with Swarovski in 1994. His itinerary included the USA, Canada, the UK, and Germany, with a possibility of a visit to the Asian markets later in the year—a prospect he found extremely exciting.

When not traveling with SCS, Michael works mainly from his studio at home in Orlando, Florida. His wife, Gabriele, who designs Silver Crystal giftware and collectibles for Swarovski, also has her studio at home. She is best known to collectors for the Swarovski Silver Crystal train and her outstanding interpretation of Christopher Columbus' Santa Maria.

When Michael Stamey finds time for himself, he spends it with his two sons or tending his impressive collection of cacti and succulents. Nature is central to Michael's life and art: as he says, if you consider anything beautiful or complex for long enough, parallels with Nature are bound to appear eventually. And it is these Michael Stamey distils with such mastery into the full-cut crystal pieces he designs for Swarovski.

A fascination for foreign cultures and a deep love of nature provide the inspiration for Adi Stocker's crystal designs. This source of inspiration finds its crystal embodiment in his two most recent designs, the Pierrot (1999) for the Swarovski Collectors Society and the Silver Crystal Eagle.

Adi Stocker

To Adi Stocker, home is the mountains of the Austrian Tyrol. From his early youth the challenge of rock climbing has had a formative influence on his character, and today still provides the energy and concentration he needs in his work. In the mountains, where he spends his leisure time, he seeks to experience both nature and his inner self. Born in St. Johann in the Austrian Tyrol, Adi Stocker returned there in 1992 to start a family with his wife, Johanna.

Anteater, MSRP ***$60***

Before this his wanderlust had led him all over the world: first he left the famous Technical College of Glassmaking in Kramsach in 1977 to go to the P. Herrmann glass studio in New Hampshire. After working there for four years, he continued on his journey around the world. Among the countries he visited on his travels were India, Nepal, Thailand, China, and Japan. It was a year packed full of impressions, and, as he says himself, an extremely valuable year for him personally.

The experience of foreign cultures and, at the same time, an almost intimate communion with nature—these are the sources of inspiration reflected in Adi Stocker's crystal designs for Swarovski. In 1983 Adi Stocker returned to the mountains of his native country. It was a return, not only to the country, but to crystal, the material, which exerts an equally strong fascination on the artist Adi Stocker as do the mountains: "For me crystal is as multi-facetted and beautiful as nature itself. It provides a never-ending challenge."

His answer to this challenge can be seen in his uniquely innovative and diverse creations. Adi Stocker's designs for the various Swarovski lines have, on more than one occasion, displayed the full spectrum of his creative talent. *The Eagle* and the Silver Crystal *Polar Bear* are highlights of the Swarovski collection. He is highly regarded by the members of the Swarovski Collectors Society for his *Turtle Doves*, the *Lion*, and the *Pegasus*. His design objects for Swarovski Selection, such as the *Jewel Box* or the *Penholder* are impressive proof of his artistic potential.

Creativity and technical prowess, sensitivity and empathy, communion with nature and the experience of foreign cultures—all of these are reflected in Adi Stocker's creations. They are characteristic of his work, which has made him one of Swarovski's top designers.

This talented designer is particularly well known for his natural-looking animal designs. With his German Shepherd, the Siamese Fighting Fish, the Cobra, the Camel, the Grizzly Bear and the Cockatoo, he has enriched the collections of lovers of Swarovski crystal all over the world.

Heinz Tabertshofer

Many collectors of Silver Crystal have Heinz Tabertshofer to thank for some of their most treasured pieces; although, for a long time they had never even heard his name. Until he became known for his own Swarovski designs, Heinz Tabertshofer remained very much in the background for almost twenty years. There he played a leading role in the production of Silver Crystal, making machine tools for the production of the Swarovski models and engravings. During all these years his love of creative design accompanied him in all his work. Sculpture has always been one of his great passions. Painting and drawing, too, are his favorite leisure activities; and to further his education in these subjects, he took courses at the Technical College in Jenbach. Since 1997 his name has become known to more and more collectors of Silver Crystal, for in that year he joined the Swarovski design department and started creating his very own crystal designs.

Born in the Austrian Tyrol in 1962, Heinz Tabertshofer is firmly rooted in the country of his childhood. He lives in Wattens, the home of Swarovski's creative centre, with his wife and two children. He likes to spend his leisure time in the beautiful mountain scenery of the Tyrol, which provides him with a constant source of strength and inspiration. Among his favorite leisure activities are cycling and hiking, though he admits to mountain climbing being one of his greatest passions. However, his activities are by no means limited to the great outdoors—his creative side is in constant touch with the world of art and culture: all this combining to influence his artistic creations, lending them his typical signature.

For relaxation, Heinz Tabertshofer likes to design and build wooden furniture. At Swarovski, however, it is his many animal designs with which he has made a name for himself. His contributions to the collections of Silver Crystal lovers all over the world include the German Shepherd, the Siamese Fighting Fish, the Cobra, the Camel, the Grizzly Bear, and the Cockatoo. Each of Heinz Tabertshofer's creations impresses the beholder with its exceptionally natural appearance in which he manages to capture the very essence of the animal and express it in his crystal design. However, his creations are not merely a mirror image of reality. His close observation of his subjects and his great empathy with them, combined with a wealth of technical knowledge and experience, enable him to create impressive designs which are new and absolutely individual.

The designer with a passion for deep-sea diving has contributed a number of very different designs to the Swarovski product range. His creations include not only the popular Kris Bear family, the Bambi, and the Ballerina, but also the Elephant (1993) and the Unicorn (1996) for the Swarovski Collectors Society. With ANTONIO—Magic of Dance, the 2003 annual edition and second piece in the SCS "Magic of Dance" trilogy, Martin Zendron has created yet another masterpiece.

Martin Zendron

Unlike many people who realized at a young age that they were predestined for a creative profession, Martin Zendron never seriously considered the idea of becoming a designer. Nevertheless, he displayed an aptitude for drawing, painting and modeling in clay early on; and when the family moved to Wattens because of his father's job at Swarovski, the creative boy, more or less, grew up in the world of crystal design.

Martin Zendron's second stroke of luck was the fact that he attended the College for Glass Making and Design in Kramsach, Austria. He subsequently specialized in glass cutting and engraving—a decision indicative of his further path through life.

This began to take on shape at his first job, which was at a noted Tyrolean store specializing in glass objects. He was soon made responsible for special engraving commissions, and his growing talent as a designer was proved by the goblets, drinking-cups, and vases he embellished. An offer from the house of Swarovski was not long in coming, and in 1988 Zendron, joined the design team in Wattens.

At Swarovski, the new staff member soon became known for skilled workmanship, artistic talent, and elegant variations; and it was in this respect that he began to provide cut crystal design with new impulses. The reward for his input was a real challenge, namely to design the elephant for the Swarovski Collectors Society's (SCS) African

Kris Bear with Honey Pot, CRV $85

Wildlife trilogy. The work involved took two years, and during this time Martin Zendron never used a sketchpad. After considering his subject from many different angles and observing it in life, his first step was to craft a model in plasticine—an approach that he always takes. And all this is part of a creative process that requires the utmost concentration.

For *ANTONIO—Magic of Dance,* the second piece in the SCS "Magic of Dance" trilogy, Martin Zendron turned to guitar music for inspiration and guidance. This strategy has been successful, judging by the superb way in which he has managed to interpret the feelings and emotions of flamenco in his work. With innumerable facets and great precision. Perfect in every detail, ANTONIO symbolizes grace, pride and concentration, and represents a fleeting flamenco pose captured forever in crystal.

He finds the creative energy he requires for his work in deep-sea diving, which is more a passion than a hobby, for it is beneath the waves that he finds the deep silence that is "the most special experience in the world," as he puts it. Naturally, the born Tyrolean also spends a lot of his spare time in the Alps, but his dream is to become a diving teacher. After all, no element resembles crystals closer than water.

Arabian Stallion, CRV **$265**

CHAPTER 3

No matter whether you're collecting fantasy pieces or wildlife, you must take the proper steps to insure your collection.

Insuring And Protecting Your Swarovski Collection

"Insurance after a theft is like taking medicine after death." This adage speaks pointedly to the problems that can occur when collectors fail to take the time to get their valuable collections properly insured and protected. I know many collectors who have spent countless hours making weekend trips to all parts of the country in pursuit of adding some very special items to their collection, yet they have not invested the few hours of time it might take to adequately protect that same collection.

Another very common problem that exists among collectors is the lacking awareness of the greatly increased replacement value of the entire collection. Collections, by their very nature, generally accumulate over a period of time with the collector not always aware of the inflation factor or the secondary market quotations for the pieces they have been acquiring. None of us are going to dwell on the prospect of having our collection stolen, broken, or lost in transit, but a few logical precautions can properly protect the collection that you have so lovingly assembled.

Security Devices Offer Peace Of Mind

An entire volume could be written on the subject of alarm protection devices. In today's society, electronic protection devices have become the locks of ultimate security. The first choice for any burglar is a home or site that has no electronic security system. Therefore, it is a wise and caring collector who will take the time and expense to have a home security system installed. There are many excellent companies now offering home systems that can be specially designed for your particular home and collection. These firms can be easily located by checking your local yellow pages under the "security" heading.

There are several points to consider when purchasing a security system. Some systems operate with batteries at the point of contact, and these batteries either need to be replaced on occasion or checked regularly by the security firm's employees. A system that relies primarily on batteries and constant maintenance by company employees may not be the most effective form of protection. The most effective systems ring into a central station where the local police are dispatched on a 24-hour basis. While having a burglar alarm installed, it is usually wise to also connect a smoke/fire alarm to the system, thereby offering yourself further protection against another type of loss that could occur. In any case, shop around and compare systems before making your selection. Speak with other collectors that you respect for their comments regarding the systems they have purchased to protect their own collections.

After securing your home with deadbolt locks and an electronic security system, take the time to review the options available regarding insurance for your collectibles. Several years of speaking on the subject of appraising and insuring collectibles have made me keenly aware of the lack of experience and understanding among collectors regarding insurance policy options for protection of their valuable collection. One of the most important aspects of shopping for a good policy is to make good resolutions to ourselves that somehow never seem to materialize, so I encourage you first of all, not to procrastinate.

Insuring Your Collectibles Is A Must

Once you have begun to make the search for insurance, you will find that insurance agents are generally exceedingly accommodating and essentially eager to help you obtain a "good" policy to protect your collectibles. It may be at this very point that the buyer must truly beware. Because the insurance sales system works like all other free enterprise, agents are competing with others for your business, and may not want to burden you with too many details about your collection, lest they drive you toward their competition. Therefore it is up to you, the collector, to retain proper documentation regarding your collection's value. For the moment, however, let's concentrate on the task of learning more about insurance.

Chubb Insurance with home offices in Warren, New Jersey, is a major insurer of all types of fine arts and collectibles. In a recent interview with Susan Mahon, a marketing specialist in Chubb's personal insurance division, I asked Susan what Chubb has to offer the collector in the way of protection. Ms. Mahon states that Chubb issues what is called Valuable Articles Coverage (VAC), which includes fine arts, jewelry, silver, figurines, furs, etc. The Chubb Valuable Articles Coverage Policy is an "agreed value" policy, meaning that when the policy is written, you, as the owner of the valuable items, place a value on the items at that time, and both parties agree that this amount is the stated value of the articles. "The really nice thing about Chubb's Policy is that breakage is included on fine arts and figurines, and this is not an insurance industry standard yet," says Ms. Mahon. "When we take and underwrite your collection, we ask you to tell us what you think it's worth. If we have any questions on it, or it's a particularly high value, we might ask you to go get an appraisal, but we don't generally require appraisals on items unless they're of greater value than $10,000."

Insurance agents will usually allow you to place the values on your items by using various reliable publications such as the *Price Index* by *Collector's Information Bureau, The Bradex* (complied by The Bradford Exchange), *Luckey's Hummel® Figurines and Plates Identification & Price Guide* by Luckey (updated by Dean A. Genth, published by Krause Publications), or in the case of Precious Moments, *The Greenbook.* Just remember to ask your agent what source he will accept when you are placing the value on your insurable items.

If you already have a homeowner's policy, the best place to begin your insurance search is with your existing agent. Ask him to check your policy's fine print to see if your collection is indeed covered as a part of that policy. It is important that you know exactly what is covered and what value will be paid in the event you will ever have to file a claim.

Replacement Value Or Fair Market Value

Generally, most collectors will want to insure their collections for current replacement value. Replacement value is the stated amount that it would take to replace the items if they were damaged, stolen, or lost. Fair market value is the value of the collection if it were to be sold suddenly at auction or by any other willing seller/willing buyer arrangement. This fair market value is usually used for reports to the Internal Revenue Service when a collection is donated to a museum or charity. However, some collectors may feel that if their collection were completely lost, current fair market value would make the most sense for a cash settlement by the insurance company. One consideration for this fair market value coverage would be the collector of advanced years who may not see the necessity for continuing the collection after a loss.

Documentation Is A Must

Having explained earlier that documentation is a must when a claim is filed with an insurance company, let me suggest some possibilities that can make this task much easier. You can free yourself from the burden of having to complete all the documentation for your collection alone by contracting for the services of a professional appraiser. Two outstanding appraisal organizations exist in the United States with members that are experts in various areas of collectibles. *The American Society of Appraisers* (ASA), P.O. Box 17265, Washington D.C. 20041, or *The International Society of Appraisers* (ISA), P.O. Box 726, Hoffman Estates, Illinois 60695, can give you the names of experts in various fields of interest.

What Is An Appraiser?

An appraiser is a person who determines the value of an item or items for insurance purposes and can supply the necessary information for the

Clockwise from upper left; Lovebirds, Turtledoves, and Woodpeckers.

settlement of damage claims. The professional appraiser is also the person who can determine the value of a collection at the time it is donated to a tax-exempt institution or charity.

We all should remember that appraising is not a casual matter. All expert appraisals must be accurate and precise, and should be updated annually to reflect market changes. Oftentimes an appraiser must be able to stand up in court if litigation arises from a dispute over valuation of the property. Therefore, I suggest that you select an appraiser in the same manner you would select your family physician or attorney. Don't be afraid to ask for credentials and what type of experience the individual has acquired. Be careful not to rely solely upon a shop owner purporting to be an "appraiser." It is also sometimes wise to check with collector friends as to whom they trust and feel confident with for appraisal opinions.

How Do I Choose an Appraiser?

- Documented accomplishments (experience)
- Professional Certification (education)
- Reputation
- Personal Interview (ask for credentials)
- Member of ASA or ISA

Detailed Inventory A Must

If you haven't already done so, begin to compile a listing of all items in your collections. While some companies may not request it, you should have an inventory for your own use to determine your collection's value. And with some policies, it may not be possible to receive reimbursement for the full value of your collection without such a list.

Record the following basic information for each item:

Manufacturer's Name

Edition Limit/Your Item's Number
If Numbered

Artist Name

Your Cost

Series Name

Added Expenses
(Shipping, Framing, Restoration, etc.)

Item Name

Special Markings (Artist's Signature, etc.)

Year Of Issue

Secondary Market History
(If Purchased On Secondary Market)

Size/Dimensions

Place Of Purchase

Location In Your Home (For Burglary Or Loss)

Date Of Purchase

Insurance Company/Policy Or Rider Number

Record each new item you buy at the time of purchase. Make a date with yourself to update this material periodically, possibly after you complete your taxes for the year. The pleasure of seeing how your collection is growing may offset the chore of preparing tax returns. Large index cards will handle the pertinent information, or you may prefer to invest in one of the published record books that look so official and orderly when placed on your bookshelf. Possibilities to consider include:

The Kovels' Organizer for Collectors by Ralph and Terry Kovel, (Crown Publishers, One Park Avenue, New York, New York 10016);

The Official Collector's Journal, (The House of Collectibles, Inc., 201 E. 50th Street, New York, New York 10022);

Collector's Inventory File (Collector's News, Grundy Center, Iowa 50638). These books may be available in your local bookstore.

Provide Video Documentation. Today, collectors have the opportunity to inexpensively make a complete, yet concise, pictorial record of their collections by means of the video camera. Begin with a general overview of the entire collection so the viewer can get a feel for the entire size of the particular collection, and where it is generally on display. After the introductory shots, detailed looks at each piece constitute a complete video document. Take each item and hold it up so that the markings on the underside of the bases can be seen. Close-ups should offer special views of details and any printed working on the items. After you have finished with your video record, replay the film to check the quality, then store it in a site off the premises, along with your copy of the detailed inventory. Make a copy of your video and written inventory so that one set can be kept at home, and another in your lockbox or other secure place away from your home.

Insurance Options

Once you have taken all the necessary steps for physically securing and recording your collectibles, you are now ready to shop around for appropriate coverage. It is a good idea to get two or three different companies to quote you a price, since different insurance companies specialize in certain types of policies. Be sure to ask exactly what is covered in the policy being quoted. For example, will it cover breakage, burglary, loss, damage, fire, etc.?

There are several types of coverage available today: valuable articles coverage (VAC), homeowner's or renter's, a separate endorsement to an existing policy, an endorsement to a business policy, or a completely separate policy.

Rates for insurance policies vary widely from company to company. Your best procedure is to talk once again with other collectors and find out what companies they have dealt with, how pleased they have been with their coverage, and how their rate compares to what you have been quoted. Once you have determined that your policy covers your collectibles for the proper values and the appropriate types of loss, you are then ready to bind your policy. If you are one of the persistent collectors who have taken the aforementioned steps in insuring and protecting your collection, you are well aware of the peace of mind that comes with knowing that you have done everything humanly possible to adequately protect your valuables.

Collector's Checklist

- Have I recently checked the cost of a good alarm system?
- Do I have my collectibles adequately insured?
- Do I have adequate appraisal support for my collection?
- Do I keep a complete and accurate listing and appraisal of my collection off premise?
- Have I considered videotaping my collection and keeping a copy of it in my lock box?
- Do I know the current replacement value of my collection?
- Have I received competitive quotations for my collectibles insurance?

If you answer NO to any of the above questions, your collection may not be adequately protected. Take the time to look at your collectibles from a fresh perspective now that you've learned how to go about fully protecting them. Don't delay...and don't put off until tomorrow what can be done today.

CHAPTER 4

Butterflies, bees, and hummingbirds in rhodium and gold finishes.

Puttting The Brakes On Breakage

It is every collector's nightmare to see a prized collectible break into a million pieces. Breakage is one of the greatest risks of collecting, but developing a little more figurine finesse in the ways we handle and display our cherished figurines can minimize the risk.

In my years in the collectibles business, I have heard countless stories from collectors who have regretted not properly protecting a figurine from its eventual demise. Some collectors lament that if they had only known that the cat could jump that high or that the grandchildren would be that careless, they certainly would have placed the item in a more secure location.

Often collectors damage their figurines in the process of caring for them. They accidentally knock over or drop a figurine during a periodic dusting. Or the figurine strikes the side or bottom of the sink during a routine washing and they see their expensive treasure shatter.

Many times I have wished that I could have helped one of my collector friends avoid an ugly breakage incident. To help prevent future such tragedies, I have prepared a list of prevention tips. Collectors who follow these precautions will continue to enjoy their flawless figurines for many years to come.

Figurine Finesse's Top 10 Breakage Prevention Tips

- Maintain adequate breakage coverage on your insurance policy.
- Anticipate what your children or grandchildren might do.
- Anticipate what your cat might do.
- Check curio shelves regularly.
- Clean your own collection.
- Line your sink with towels when you clean your figurines.
- Always double box figurines for shipping.
- Handle figurines with a firm grip.
- Remove figurines that may "walk" from any shelf that vibrates.
- Make sure wall units are securely fastened.

Transporting a figurine introduces new risks, but with proper packaging the figurine can be kept as safe as it would be at home. If an item must be shipped by commercial transport, it should be heavily wrapped, individually surrounded by foam chips and double boxed. Even a short trip with figurines requires careful packaging.

Collectors should consider adding breakage coverage as part of their fine arts' insurance policy. They might be surprised to find that breakage coverage is not as expensive as anticipated. No matter how carefully a collector handles and displays a collection, accidents will happen. Therefore, it only makes sense for conscientious collectors to provide themselves with the best insurance coverage available.

When an item breaks, another option for collectors is restoration. Whether or not your insurance company pays for the restoration, is one of several factors which should weigh heavily in your decision. Unless the item is irreplaceable, or a sentimental family heirloom, it is usually unwise for a collector to spend more than one-half of the item's current market value on restoration. Several reputable restoration firms around the United States specialize in ceramic restorations. To find the professional restoration firm best suited to handle your repair, ask your nearest collectibles retailer for a recommendation.

But remember, the old adage that "an ounce of prevention is worth a pound of cure" is nowhere more true than with figurines.

Printed with permission from *Collector's Mart Magazine.*

CHAPTER 5

A collection of Swarovski Silver Crystal candleholders.

Caring For Your Crystal

Swarovski—Clearly A Collectible

The market for retired Swarovski Silver Crystal continues to blossom. The older, retired items are becoming more difficult to find with each passing day. At the same time, collectors who appreciate the current designs and quality offered by Swarovski Silver Crystal are causing the demand to greatly exceed the available supply. Some retailers are reporting that their allocations of new pieces are sold before arriving at the store. This was especially true with *Butterfly Fish* and the *Ship.*

Several retired pieces in the Swarovski Silver Crystal line have recently risen in price so rapidly that even the most skeptical look with amazement at the prices paid. To date, the Swarovski Collectors Society has released six pieces to members of the Society. The premier piece in 1987, entitled *The Lovebirds,* was followed by *The Woodpeckers, The Turtledoves, The Dolphins, The Seals,* and *The Whales. The Lovebirds,* issued at $150, reportedly has been sold for as high as $4000 in recent months. Even *The Dolphins,* released in 1990, is selling around $1250 already.

Older retired Swarovski items are soaring in value as collectors seek out the most difficult-to-acquire figurines for their collections. In this category we find the *Carousel Paperweight, Shaving Brush, Snowflake Candleholder, Octagonal Dealer's Plaque, Beetle Bottle Opener,* and *The Orlando Elephant,* all of them more difficult to obtain on the secondary market than *The Lovebirds.* Prices for these items have not reached the level of *The Lovebirds* due to the fact that most collectors have not even seen these pieces to know they need them for their collections. It seems entirely likely that Swarovski pieces such as the *Octagonal Dealers' Plaque* and *Beetle Bottle Opener* will in time exceed even the extraordinary market price of *The Lovebirds.*

Caring For Your Crystal

A well-known brand not only owes its good reputation to the outstanding quality of its products, but also to a first-class customer service. Even though you may take all precautions to avoid any damages when handling and displaying your pieces at home, the necessity of repairs can never be excluded.

Swarovski Silver Crystal Repair Policy

Please do not attempt to repair your broken crystal piece by yourself. There are no commercial adhesives available for that purpose and any attempt at self-repair will only result in a mess (all commercial adhesives turn yellow with time and discolor the crystal), for which Swarovski cannot be responsible.

Examples of Swarovski paperweights.

Raw Swarovski crystal at top, Cone Paperweight below.

If it is a current piece, there should be o problem getting it repaired. Retired or discontinued items can be repaired only if replacement components are available. The customer care center should be called for a return authorization form.

The formal repair policy is listed inside the booklet that comes with each SC piece. It reads:

...Swarovski offers, for every piece purchased from authorized Swarovski retailers, a repair service for damages not covered by terms of Swarovski's warranty policy. Every piece found to be defective under this warranty by Swarovski's technical staff will be at Swarovski's option either repaired, pending repair feasibility and availability of parts, or replaced, or substituted with a piece of comparable value. In case of substitution, it cannot be guaranteed that the consumer will receive the same design but a piece of comparable value. Swarovki's obligation to repair, replace, or substitute shall not apply to any goods which have been, in Swarovski's opinion, subject to abuse, modification, attempted repair, negligence, misuse, or accident.

Cleaning Tips

Dust and air pollution quickly dim the crystal's brilliant surface and deprive your figurines of their sparkling beauty. Although crystal should be touched as little as possible with bare hands, you should clean your pieces regularly. As well as simply dusting your pieces, you can wash them in lukewarm water with a soft detergent. The cleaned pieces can be laid on a soft towel to drain and dry, or may be carefully polished using a lint-free cloth. For a perfect finish, we recommend the Swarovski Silver Crystal polishing cloth.

Here A Box, There A Box...

The issue for collectors on what to do regarding the storage of the collectibles' packaging continues to mount with every new box they have to store. When the closets and cupboards all become piled high with empty boxes, questions (and other things) begin to tumble out: What will I do with anymore BOXES? Do I really need to keep these boxes? Are these empty boxes really worth anything? A good starting point to answering these questions is an analysis of the "box-is-valuable" myth.

When did the myth begin? There's no certain answer, but one can easily imagine that some sales associates in retail settings have used the phrase, "By all means, save this original box, because it makes your figurine much more valuable." To whom would it make the figurine more valuable? I have never heard of a collector refusing to purchase a collectible because the box produced from storage was not pretty or collectible enough.

It is conceivable that perpetration of the "box-is-valuable" myth could reach ridiculous proportions for both collectibles dealers and collectors alike. For example, if boxes were considered important on the secondary market, what would determine each box's value? Would size of box relate to the price—small value for small boxes, greater value for larger boxes? And what about the box's condition? How much would you deduct for a scratch, a tear, a dent, or a cut somewhere on the box? And what happens if the box no longer has its original packaging papers or enclosures?

In checking with some retail collectibles dealers, I found no one who felt the packaging for a Swarovski piece needed to be saved to preserve value. Manufacturers of collectibles have provided the finest quality of packaging in order to get these items safely into our homes. That does not, however, justify our turning boxes into items to be "worshipped" or revered.

While a piece's original box may be helpful in sending an item back for repair, it may not be necessary to save the boxes for all of your pieces. Whether you should plan to keep an item's box really depends on whether you are solely collecting or planning to be involved with secondary market dealing. If you are going to ship a piece, save the box; if not, don't worry about recycling it.

Masquerade Series: Columbine, Harlequin, and Pierrot.

CHAPTER 6

A pair of Swarovski paperweights.

The Collector's Guide

Finding And Buying Swarovski Silver Crystal

Every collector should begin the process of collecting by becoming as knowledgeable as possible about the Swarovski Silver Crystal line. Having purchased this book you've made a good start. Now you must do your part to study and keep this book where you can refer to it often.

For the currently produced items, collectors have a good selection available from the many worldwide, authorized retailers. When you are looking for the older, retired items, the search becomes a bit more complicated. A good way to locate dealers that specialize in selling retired Swarovski is to look at the classified and display ads of the major antique and collectible publications. *Collector's Mart Magazine* is an excellent source for finding many of the major Swarovski dealers around the United States.

Using the Internet, the possibilities for expanding a collection, or selling one, now seem endless. Enter the search word Swarovski into your search field on your computer, and you will find a myriad of choices regarding sellers of old and new Swarovski Silver Crystal. See "More about E-Buying" for more details on Internet buying.

There are still bargains to be found when purchasing Swarovski Silver Crystal. Swarovski auctions or estate sales and tag sales often provide collectors with some real bargains. Many times heirs who have no interest in a particular item will offer collectibles at a significant discount off of the regular retail.

Understanding The Swarovski Trademarks

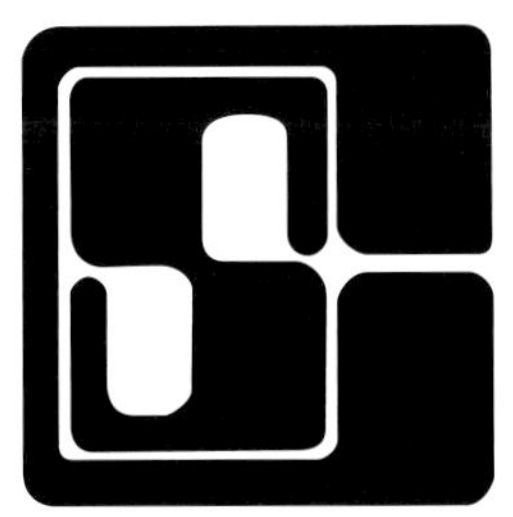

SC trademark

Swan trademark

Understanding the registered trademarks of the Silver Crystal items is quite simple due to the fact that basically only two distinct trademarks have been used on the product to date. The earliest trademark that is found on Swarovski Silver Crystal is the "SC" trademark designed in a block style. The SC trademark was used from 1976 until 1988. From 1988 until present day the Silver Crystal pieces have borne the "Swan" trademark in two different forms. For value purposes, we break apart the values only between SC and Swan periods.

The "Silver Crystal" name is a registered trademark by the Swarovski Company. Although Swarovski manufacturers and sells crystal components and pieces worldwide, only the Swarovski Silver Crystal line utilizes the crystal that makes up the company's signature collectible crystal.

In order for the Swarovski Company to protect their copyrights, you will find the SC or Swan logo on almost all Swarovski Silver Crystal items. The copyright symbol (©) is also etched near the Swan trademark today.

Oftentimes you will find the word "swarovski" etched onto a Silver Crystal piece. There seems to be no definite rule regarding the placement of the name, other than the fact that the stone must be large enough to accommodate the word length.

Understanding The Numbering System

In the early days of the Swarovski Silver Crystal production, the numbering system was not very formal or uniform. In fact, I developed a special subset of numbering devices for Swarovski Silver Crystal items that were never assigned an item number. These numbers were published for many years in *The Crystal Report* publication and were adopted subsequently by collectors worldwide. For example, many of the Dealer's Plaques that were found had no assigned number; therefore, I assigned the number SCDPNR1 to represent "Swarovski Crystal Dealer Plaque Number One". Likewise, Silver Crystal Ornaments take on the number SCO followed by the annual year number such as SCO 1981 for "Swarovski Crystal Ornament 1981."

Prior to the year 2000, Swarovski used an item number that included NR as a part of the number. Usually the item would be assigned a four-digit number followed by the NR, and then an additional series of numbers to designate the size in millimeters and the color. Since 2000, all Swarovski Silver Crystal items have been assigned a new six-digit number. For example, previously the Large Swan was 7633 063 000, now it is number 010 005.

I have attempted to use all known numbers assigned to the Swarovski Silver Crystal items in order to help you identify your crystal when looking at a particular number on a box or certificate.

Current Replacement Value (CRV)

The current replacement values quoted in this book are the result of years of intensive study and research from multiple secondary market sources. Collectors should realize that these higher values that are stated should be regarded as replacement value insurable prices.

Secondary market prices will vary from geographical region to geographical region within the United States. As is the case with any collectibles price guide, it is just that—a guide. The current retail/replacement values stated in this book act as a baseline for collectors and dealers for the effective pricing of Swarovski Silver Crystal items. In some retail secondary settings, the selling price will be a percentage of the book price. Likewise, some buyers may use the book price as a starting point and attempt to purchase at a percentage of that price.

The current replacement values stated in this book are subject to change due to market activity and Swarovski's determinations of current suggested retail prices.

E-Buying Swarovski Silver Crystal

People today are flocking to online Internet sites to shop for a wide array of collectibles. As more opportunities develop for making the best deal, collectors need to educate themselves on the proper methods of buying online, and by doing so, reduce the risk of possible abuse by an unscrupulous merchant.

In 1999, auction sales amounted to $2 billion, and the figures continued to grow into the new century. Although online auctions have tapered somewhat in today's tough economy, I interviewed Federal Trade Commission staff attorney Lisa Hone for the April 2000 edition of *Collector's Mart Magazine* and she indicated that auctions are popular because they give buyers and sellers wonderful opportunities to find each other.

"If I'm in Alaska, I can reach out all over the world and find a particular piece of Mission furniture or even a Beanie Baby," Hone said. "The vast majority of the times, it works out fine."

In the first half of 1998, the FTC's Bureau of Consumer Protection received about 300 complaints involving online auction fraud, according to Hone. In the first half of 1999, about 6,000 such complaints were recorded. The growth of exploitation is not surprising, given the phenomenal expansion of one-on-one trading through the Internet.

Collectors need to be aware of potential risks and apply a full measure of commonsense precautions to ensure the safety and reliability of any transaction. Some test of basic principles must be utilized: What is the seller's reputation? Is the seller willing to give me a valid street address where I can find him should something go wrong? Do I get a warranty? Do I have return privileges?

In order to finesse your collectibles buying online, review the "E-Buying Tips" provided for important considerations when you are shopping the 'Net.

With a few commonsense precautions, you should be ready to e-shop until your fingers drop.

E-Buying Tips

- Understand how the auction works.
- Check out the seller. For company information, contact the state or local consumer protection agency and Better Business Bureau.
- Be especially careful if the seller is a private individual.
- Get the seller's name, street address, and telephone number to check him/her out or follow up if there is a problem.
- Ask about returns, warranties and service.
- Be wary of claims about collectibles.
- Use common sense and ask yourself: Is this the best way to buy this item? What is the most I am willing to bid?
- Get free insurance through the auction sites whenever possible.
- For assistance, check out these web sites: www.fraud.com, www.ftc.gov, and www.bbbonline.com.

Selling Swarovski Silver Crystal Items

Attempting to be a seller of Swarovski Silver Crystal takes some patience, expertise and a good working knowledge of how the selling of collectibles works. One method of selling is to utilize an auctioneering firm or an auction house to sell your items. When selling at auction, you have the ability generally to place a reserve on the highest dollar value pieces. A reserve represents the lowest price at which the piece must reach in order to be sold. If the reserve is not met, then the piece remains in your possession.

Another option for sellers rests with the network of secondary market dealers. Many of today's leading secondary market dealers have Web sites where they can easily be reached making communication regarding your items very easy. The advantage of selling to a dealer is that you can dispose of your entire collection all at once. Selling to a dealer, however, represents selling at wholesale or below in order to move your items quickly.

Still a third method is selling your items directly to another collector via a classified ad. This is the most profitable way to market your collection. However, it involves your placing the ad, allowing multiple people to come into your home for inspection of the items, and risking exposure to thieves who "case the neighborhood" by this method. You do also reduce your risk of having to ship items by selling them directly from your home.

Flamingo, CRV **$265**

CHAPTER 7

The Swarovski Silver Crystal Collection

Abbreviations:

CRV: Current Replacement Value
MSRP: Manufacturer's Suggested Retail Price

Airplane

7473 NR 000 002/7473 000 002
Designer: Adi Stocker
Size: 2-7/16"/62mm
Trademark: Swan

The *Airplane* was introduced in 1990 as part of the "When We Were Young" grouping. The *Airplane* retired in 1999 at $155. A known variation is the inversion of the front propeller.

CRV: $160

Alligator

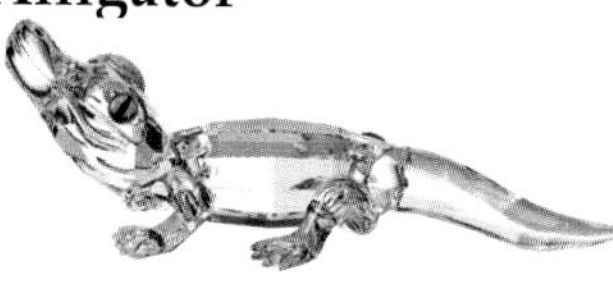

7661 000 005/221629
Designer: Michael Stamey
Size: 3"/75mm
Trademark: Swan

The *Alligator* was introduced in 1998 as part of the "Endangered Species" grouping.

MSRP: $75

Angel (Nativity)

7475 NR 000 009/7475 000 009
Designer: Team
Size: 1-3/8"/35mm
Trademark: Swan

This *Nativity Angel* was introduced in 1992 and was only produced for one year. It was retired in December 1993.

MSRP: $65
CRV: $195

Angel

7475 000 060/194 761
Designer: Adi Stocker
Size: 3-3/4"/95mm
Trademark: Swan

Note that the angel's hands and head are frosted. Introduced in 1995 as part of the "Exquisite Accents" grouping.

MSRP: $215

Anniversary Birthday Cake

003-0169678/169 678
Designer: Gabriele Stamey
Size: 2"/50mm
Trademark: Swan (SCS)

The *Anniversary Birthday Cake* was issued in 1992 to celebrate the Swarovski Collectors Society's first five years. The edition was closed in 1993.

MSRP: $85
CRV: $300

Anniversary Squirrel

7400 097 001/208 433
Designer: Anton Hirzinger
Size: 2-3/4"/69mm long
Trademark: Swan (SCS)

The *Anniversary Squirrel* was issued by The Swarovski Collectors Society to commemorate its 10th anniversary in 1997. When introduced, a mirror accompanied the piece to be used as a base for the squirrel to rest upon. The 10th *Anniversary Squirrel* became a closed edition in 1997.

MSRP: $140
CRV: $150

Anniversary Vase Of Roses

7400 200 204/283 394
Designer: Gabriele Stamey
Size: 2-3/4"/70mm
Trademark: Swan

The *Anniversary Vase of Roses* was first introduced in 2002 to commemorate 15 years of The Swarovski Collectors Society. The piece features a vase filled with 15 ruby red roses with silver stems. Available originally to Society members only by redemption certificate.

MSRP: $140
CRV: $150

Anteater

7680 000 001/271 460
Designer: Adi Stocker
Size: 2-1/4"/55mm
Trademark: Swan

The *Anteater* was issued in 2001 as part of the "Endangered Species" grouping.

MSRP: $60

Antonio

7400 200 300/606 441
Designer: Martin Zendron
Size: 8-1/4"/206mm
Trademark: Swan (Swarovski)

Antonio was issued in 2003 as the second piece in the "Magic of Dance" series. The edition closed December 2003. Annual edition for 2003 Collectors Society members.

MSRP: $370
CRV: $400

Antonio Plaque

626 472
Size: 2-1/2"/63mm

Produced by Swarovski Silver Crystal as a name plaque for the *Antonio* annual edition.

MSRP: $35

Apple

7476 NR 000 001/7476 000 001
Designer: Michael Stamey
Size: 3"/76mm
Trademark: Swan

The *Apple* was introduced in 1991 as a part of the "Sparkling Fruit" theme. It was retired in December 1996.

MSRP: $185
CRV: $325

Apple Photo Stand, King, Gold

7504 NR 060 G/7504 060 000 G
Designer: Max Schreck
Size: 3-1/8"/80mm
Trademark: SC

The *Apple Photo Stand* was first issued in 1983. The apple opens for functional use as a photo holder/display. The trademark is usually found on the metal leaf. It was retired in December 1988.

MSRP: $150
CRV: $675

Apple Photo Stand, King, Rhodium

7504 NR 060 R/7504 060 000 R
Designer: Max Schreck
Size: 3-1/8"/80mm
Trademark: SC

The *Apple Photo Stand* was first issued in rhodium finish in 1976. The apple opens for functional use as a photo holder/display. The trademark is usually found on the metal leaf. Originally distributed in European and British markets. It was retired in 1988 at a U.S. retail equivalent of $150.

CRV: $600

Apple Photo Stand, Large, Gold

7504 NR 050 G/7504 050 000 G
Designer: Max Schreck
Size: 2-5/8"/6mm
Trademark: SC or Swan

The large, gold *Apple Photo Stand* was first issued in 1980. The apple opens for functional use as a photo holder/display. The trademark is usually found on the metal leaf. It was retired in December 1990 at the suggested retail of $125.

CRV: $300

Apple Photo Stand, Large, Rhodium

7504 NR 050 R/7504 050 000 R
Designer: Max Schreck
Size: 2-5/8"/65mm
Trademark: SC

The large, rhodium *Apple Photo Stand* was first issued in 1980. The apple opens for functional use as a photo holder/display. The trademark is usually found on the metal leaf. It was retired in December 1986. The retirement price was $88.

CRV: $295

Apple Photo Stand, Small, Gold

7504 NR 030 G/7504 030 000 G
Designer: Max Schreck
Size: 1-7/8"/48mm
Trademark: SC

The small, gold *Apple Photo Stand* was first issued in 1983. The apple opens for functional use as a photo holder/display. The trademark is usually found on the metal leaf. It was retired December 1990 at $60.

CRV: $195

Apple Photo Stand, Small, Rhodium

7504 NR 030/7504 030 000 R
Designer: Max Schreck
Size: 1-7/8"/48mm
Trademark: SC

The small, rhodium *Apple Photo Stand* was first issued in 1980. The apple opens for functional use as a photo holder/display. The trademark is usually found on the metal leaf. It was retired in December 1986 at the suggested retail of $44.

CRV: $275

Arabian Stallion (see page 82)

Arch (Nativity)

7475 NR 000 010/7475 000 010
Designer: Team
Size: 3-5/8"/92mm
Trademark: Swan

The *Arch* was issued in the U.S. as part of the "Holy Family" group. In Europe, the *Arch* was sold separately when issued in 1991. It was retired in December 1993.

CRV: $200

Ashtray

7461 NR 100/7461 100 000
Designer: Max Schreck
Size: 3-15/16"/100mm
Trademark: SC or Swan

The *Ashtray* was issued in 1981. There are no known variations. It was retired in 1990 at a suggested retail of $170.

SC CRV: $350
Swan CRV: $310

Ashtray Gold/Rhodium

7501 NR 61/7501 061 000
Designer: Team
Size: 2"/50mm
Trademark: SC

The *Ashtray* was first issued in 1977 and is identifiable by the gold or rhodium metal band around the top, which holds the cigarette. The retail price at retirement was $45 in 1981.

CRV Rhodium $850
Gold $625

Athena Clock, Gold Or Rhodium

9280 NR 102
Designer: Team
Size: 2-1/4"/57mm

The *Athena Clock* is a working clock and can be found in both gold or rhodium finishes. Variations can be found with a moon dial and with or without date and alarm. The *Athena Clock* was introduced in 1987. The retail price at retirement in 1992 was $330.

CRV: $375

Automobile, Old Timer

7473 NR 000 001/7473 000 001
Designer: Gabriele Stamey
Size: 3-1/4"/83mm
Trademark: Swan

The *Old Timer Automobile* was introduced in 1989. The trademark is commonly found on the car's steering wheel. The retail price was $155 when it was retired in 1995.

CRV: $250

Baby Beaver, Lying

7616 NR 000 003/7616 000 003
Designer: Adi Stocker
Size: 1-1/2"/38mm
Trademark: Swan

The *Lying Baby Beaver* was issued in 1992 at a suggested retail of $49.50. The eyes are black and the large front teeth are frosted. It was retired in December 1995.

CRV: $100

Baby Beaver, Sitting

7616 NR 000 002/7616 000 002
Designer: Adi Stocker
Size: 1-3/4"/44mm
Trademark: Swan

The *Sitting Baby Beaver* has black eyes and large, frosted front teeth. It was issued in 1992 with a suggested retail of $49.50 when it was retired in December 1999.

CRV: $85

Baby Carp

7644 000 003/211 743
Designer: Michael Stamey
Size: 1-3/4"/44mm
Trademark: Swan

The *Baby Carp* was issued in 1997 and was subsequently retired in December 2001. The suggested retail when it was retired was $49.50.

CRV: $65

Baby Carriage

7473 NR 000 005/7473 000 005
Designer: Gabriele Stamey
Size: 2-1/8"/52mm
Trademark: Swan

The *Baby Carriage* was issued in 1996 and retired in December 1999 at a suggested retail of $140.

CRV: $150

Baby Frog

7642 000 002/286 313
Designer: Gabriele Stamey
Size: 3/4"/20mm
Trademark: Swan

The *Baby Frog* was issued in 2002 at a suggested retail price of $29.50. Collectors have noted various positioning of the frog's eyes.

CRV: $29.50

Baby Giraffe

7603 000 002/236 717
Designer: Michael Stamey
Size: 6"/150mm
Trademark: Swan

The *Baby Giraffe* was issued in 1999 at a suggested retail of $265. There are no known variations to date.

CRV: $265

Baby Lovebirds

7621 000 005/199 123
Designer: Adi Stocker
Size: 4-1/8"/104mm
Trademark: Swan

The *Baby Lovebirds* were introduced in 1996 with a current suggested retail of $160. The bird's beaks are frosted and in color.

CRV: $160

Baby Panda

7611 NR 000 002/181 081
Designer: Adi Stocker
Size: 7/8"/22mm
Trademark: Swan

The *Baby Panda* was issued in 1994 and is notable for the combination of black stones for feet, ears, and eyes. The suggested retail is $27.50.

CRV: $27.50

Baby Penguins (Set Of Three)

7661 000 003/209 588
Designer: Adi Stocker
Size: 15/16"/23mm
Trademark: Swan

The *Baby Penguins* were issued in 1997 as a set of three babies with an acrylic base. The suggested retail price is $75. There are no known variations.

CRV: $75

Baby Sea Lion

7661 NR 000 004/221 120
Designer: Michael Stamey
Size: 2-1/4"/56mm
Trademark: Swan

The *Baby Sea Lion* was issued in 1998 and has black eyes and a black nose. There are no known variations to date. The suggested retail is $49.50.

CRV: $49.50

Baby Shark

7644 000 007/269 236
Designer: Anton Hirzinger
Size: 4-7/8"/120mm
Trademark: Swan

The *Baby Shark* was issued in 2001 with a retail of $160. There are no known variations.

CRV: $160

Baby Snails On Vine Leaf

7550 NR 000 009/268 196
Designer: Edith Mair
Size: 1-3/4"/45mm
Trademark: Swan

The *Baby Snails on Vine* Leaf were issued in 2001 and has a suggested retail of $49.50. There are no known variations. The snails sit on a frosted leaf and have crystal antennae.

CRV: $49.50

Baby Tortoises (Set Of Two)

7632 000 002/220 960
Designer: Edith Mair
Size: 1"/25mm
Trademark: Swan

The *Baby Tortoises* were issued in 1998 as a set of two, and as companion pieces to the Tortoise issued one year earlier in the 2" size. The suggested retail is $46.50.

CRV: $46.50

Bald Eagle

7670 000 002/248 003
Designer: Adi Stocker
Size: 5"/125mm
Trademark: Swan

The *Bald Eagle* was issued in 2000. The eagle is perched and getting ready to take flight. The suggested retail is $280.

CRV: $280

Ballerina

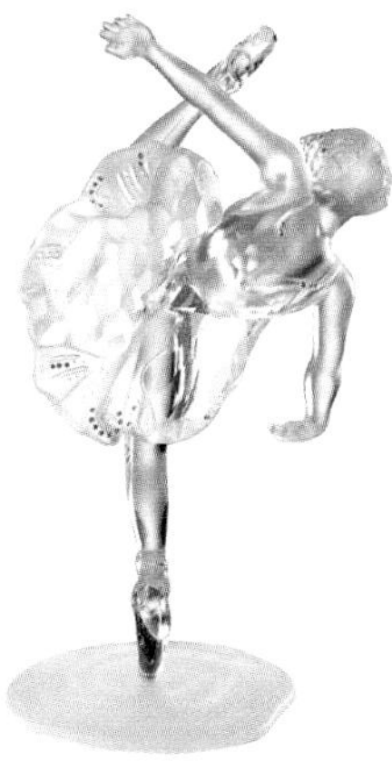

7550 000 005/236 715
Designer: Martin Zendron
Size: 5"/125mm
Trademark: Swan

The *Ballerina* was issued in 1999. This piece is elaborately embellished with many rose-colored stones on the dancer's hair and tutu. The suggested retail price is $330.

CRV: $330

Ballerina, Young

7550 000 004/254 960
Designer: Edith Mair
Size: 3"/75mm
Trademark: Swan

The *Young Ballerina* was introduced one year after the larger Ballerina as a companion piece. The suggested retail is $160. There are no known variations.

CRV: $160

Beagle, Playing

7619 NR 000 004/172 296
Designer: Adi Stocker
Size: 1-3/4"/44mm
Trademark: Swan

The *Playing Beagle* was issued in 1993 and has black eyes and nose with frosted tail. There are no known variations. The suggested retail is $49.50.

CRV: $49.50

Beagle Puppy

7619 000 001/158 418
Designer: Adi Stocker
Size: 1-3/4"/44mm
Trademark: Swan

The *Beagle Puppy* was issued in 1990. The *Beagle Puppy* has black eyes and nose with a frosted tail. There are no known variations. The U.S. retail is $49.50.

CRV: $49.50

Bear, Giant

7637 NR 112/7637 112 000
Designer: Max Schreck
Size: 4-7/16"/112mm
Trademark: SC or Swan

The *Giant Bear* was issued only in the U.S. in 1983. Being a U.S.-only release has fueled some international demand among collectors. Notable variations of this piece exist relating to the tilt of the head and placement of the eyes. It was retired on July 1, 1988 at the then-suggested retail of $190. Currently, this is one of the most popular animals with collectors.

CRV: $3000

Bear, King

7637 NR 92/7637 092 000
Designer: Max Schreck
Size: 3-5/8"/92mm
Trademark: SC

The *King Bear* was only distributed in North America and was issued in 1983. This limited distribution has caused increased demand by international collectors and has driven up the value of this piece significantly. Variations exist regarding the tilt of the head and placement of the bear's eyes. It retired December 1, 1987 at the then-suggested retail of $100.

CRV: $2000

Bear, Koala

7673 040 000/014 366
Designer: Adi Stocker
Size: 1-3/4"/44mm
Trademark: SC or Swan

The *Koala Bear* was issued in 1987 with the U.S. design facing right. After 1993, the *Koala Bear* was made facing left throughout the worldwide market. The right-facing koala was discontinued from production in 1993.

CRV: $125
Suggested Retail for Current Koala: $75

Koala, Mini

7673 NR 030/119 472
Designer: Adi Stocker
Size: 1-1/8"/29mm
Trademark: Swan

The *Mini Koala* was introduced in the U.S. in 1989 with a left-facing variation. This *Mini Koala* was discontinued in 1993 when worldwide production of the right-facing *Mini Koala* continued. The left-facing koala has a CRV of **$850**.

The right-facing *Mini Koala* was retired in December 2000 at a suggested retail of $45. The CRV for the right-facing *Mini Koala* is **$75**.

Bear, Kris

7367 000 001/174 957
Designer: Martin Zendron
Size: 1-3/4"/45mm
Trademark: Swan

The *Kris Bear* was first issued in 1993 and was notable as the first piece issued with ribbon around the bear's neck. It was retired in December 2001 at a suggested retail of $75. There are no known variations.

CRV: $75

Bear, Kris With Honey Pot

7637 000 003/213 068
Designer: Martin Zendron
Size: 1-1/2"/38mm
Trademark: Swan

The *Kris Bear with Honey Pot* was issued in 1997. This piece is popular with collectors of bumblebees, since a bee (gold) sits on the frosted honey pot. There are no known variations. The suggested retail is $85.

CRV: $85

Bear, Kris Clock

7481 000 001/212 687
Designer: Martin Zendron
Size: 2-1/2"/63mm
Trademark: Swan

The *Kris Bear Clock* was issued in 1997 and features a Seiko movement clock. It was retired in December 2000. There are no known variations. The suggested retail at retirement was $210.

CRV: $210

Bear, Kris Celebration

7637 000 005/238 168
Designer: Martin Zendron
Size: 1-1/2"/38mm
Trademark: Swan

The *Celebration Kris Bear* was issued in 1999 as a festive bear that can be given for many of life's celebrations. The suggested retail is $85. There are no known variations.

CRV: $85

Bear, Kris On Skates

7637 000 002/193 011
Designer: Martin Zendron
Size: 2"/50mm
Trademark: Swan

The *Kris Bear on Skates* was issued in 1995. There are no known variations. Note the ribbon around the bear's neck that represents a scarf. The suggested retail is $85.

CRV: $85

Bear, Kris With Skis

7637 000 004/234 710
Designer: Martin Zendron
Size: 2"/50mm
Trademark: Swan

The *Kris Bear with Skis* was issued in 1999. It can be found without the crystal base attached, since it was first produced without the base. The suggested retail is $85.

Variation without base CRV: $225
Variation with base CRV: $85

Bear, Kris Picture Frame

7506 000 002/214 805
Designer: Martin Zendron
Size: 5-1/2"/138mm
Trademark: Swan

The *Kris Bear Picture Frame* was issued in 1997 with the crystal *Kris Bear* appearing on the right front of the frame. There are no known variations. It was retired December 2000. The suggested retail at retirement was $95.

CRV: $110

Bear, Large

7637 075 000/010 009
Designer: Max Schreck
Size: 2-3/4"/70mm
Trademark: SC or Swan

The *Large Bear* was issued in 1981 and has been found to have some notable variations. The most dramatic variation relates to the distance between the bear's paws. Variations also exist regarding the placement of the eyes and the head tilt. The current suggested retail is $99.

CRV: $99

Bear, Mini (Current)

7644 044 000/012 262
Designer: Max Schreck
Size: 1-3/4"/44mm
Trademark: SC or Swan

The *Mini Bear* was issued in 1985 and has been found to have three distinct variations. One style has round stones for feet. Two others have oval-shaped stones for feet. Differences also exist due to the head tilt and the closeness of the bear's paws. The suggested retail is $55.

CRV: $55

(Known variations have a premium of 20-50%)

Bear, Mini (Retired)

7670 NR 32/7670 032 000
Designer: Max Schreck
Size: 1-1/4"/32mm
Trademark: SC or Swan

The *Mini Bear* was introduced only in the U.S. during 1985 in this style and number. This bear has a fatter look and teardrop-shaped arms and feet. The suggested retail when it was retired in December 1988 was $25.

CRV: $300

Bear, Baby Panda

7611 000 002/181 081
Designer: Adi Stocker
Size: 7/8"/22mm
Trademark: Swan

The *Baby Panda Bear* was issued in 1994 and was notable when released for the use of solid black crystal stones for the feet, ears, eyes, and nose. The suggested retail is $27.50.

CRV: $27.50

Bear, Mother Panda

7611 000 001/181 080
Designer: Adi Stocker
Size: 2"/51mm
Trademark: Swan

The *Mother Panda Bear* was issued in 1994 and was notable when released for the use of solid black crystal stones for the feet, ears, eyes, and nose. The suggested retail is $125.

CRV: $125

Bear, Polar

7649 NR 85/7649 085 000
Designer: Adi Stocker
Size: 3-1/2"/89mm
Trademark: SC or Swan

The *Polar Bear* was issued in 1986 and has been noted to have two styles of facets on the bear's back. One style is hexagonal, and the other has square facets of the bear's back. The suggested retail at retirement was $210.

CRV: $225

Bear, Small

7637 NR 54/7637 054 000
Designer: Max Schreck
Size: 2"/50mm
Trademark: SC or Swan

The *Small Bear* was issued in 1982. It has been found with three variations regarding the position of the head, arms, and feet. The suggested retail at retirement in December 1995 was $85.

CRV: $110

Beaver, Lying Baby Beaver

7616 NR 000 003/7616 000 003
Designer: Adi Stocker
Size: 1-1/2"/38mm
Trademark: Swan

The *Lying Baby Beaver* was introduced in 1992, and is notable for its large frosted front teeth. There are no notable variations to date. The suggested retail at retirement in December 1995 was $49.50.

CRV: $100

Beaver, Mother

7616 NR 000 001/7616 000 001
Designer: Adi Stocker
Size: 3"/76mm
Trademark: Swan

The *Mother Beaver* was introduced in 1992. There are no known variations. The suggested retail was $125 when it was retired in December 1996.

CRV: $130

Beaver, Sitting Baby

7616 NR 000 002/7616 000 002
Designer: Adi Stocker
Size: 1-3/4"/44mm
Trademark: Swan

The *Sitting Baby Beaver* was introduced in 1992 and features large frosted front teeth. There are no known variations. The suggested retail was $49.50 at retirement in December 1999.

CRV: $100

Bee On Lily, Gold

7553 NR 100/7553 100 000
Designer: Team
Size: 4"/102mm
Trademark: SC or Swan

The *Gold Bee on Lily* was only issued in the U.S. and Canada in 1985. Variations exist on the style of "feet" on which the piece rests. It was retired in December 1988 at a suggested retail of $230.

CRV: $2000

Bee On Lily, Rhodium

7553 NR 200/7553 200 000
Designer: Team
Size: 4"/102mm
Trademark: SC

The *Rhodium Bee on Lily* was issued only in the U.S. in 1985. Feet variations are noted of smoothness or facets. The suggested retail at was $200 at retirement in December 1986.

CRV: $5750

Beetle Bottle Opener, Gold

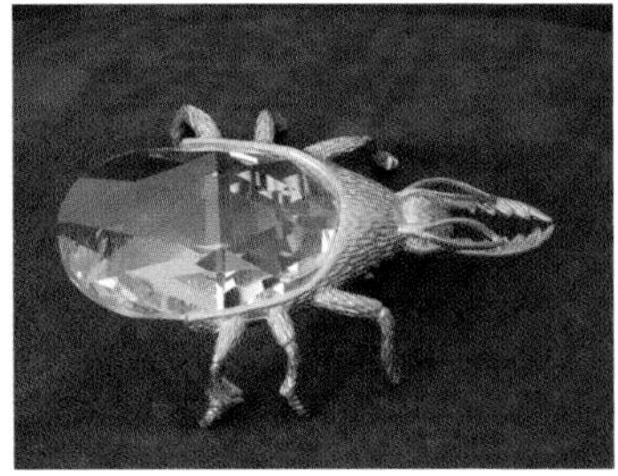

7505 NR 76/7505 076 001
Designer: Team
Size: 4-3/8"/110mm
Trademark: SC

The *Gold Beetle Bottle Opener* was introduced in 1978 in very limited quantities. Two different styles of stones were used for the beetle's body. The variation that is more rounded at the front commands a premium. The suggested retail was $80 at retirement in December 1983.

CRV: $1400-$1800

Beetle Bottle Opener, Rhodium

7505 NR 76/7505 076 002
Designer: Team
Size: 4-3/8"/110mm
Trademark: SC

The *Rhodium Beetle Bottle Opener* was introduced in 1978 in very limited quantities. Two different styles of stones were used for the beetle's body. The variation with the rounded stone at the front commands a premium. The suggested retail was $80 at retirement in December 1983.

CRV: $1400-$1600

Bell, Table, Large

7467 NR 071 000/7467 071 000
Designer: Max Schreck
Size: 5-3/4"/146mm
Trademark: SC or Swan

The *Large Table Bell* was introduced in 1981 and features three frosted flowers delicately placed near the bell's top. The suggested retail was $110 at retirement in December 1991.

CRV: $200

Bell, Table, Medium

7467 NR 05400/7467 054 000
Designer: Max Schreck
Size: 4-1/2"/114mm
Trademark: SC or Swan

The *Medium Table Bell* was issued in 1987. There are no known significant variations. The suggested retail was $95 at retirement in December 1997.

CRV: $125

Bell, Table, Small

7467 NR 039 000/7467 039 000
Designer: Max Schreck
Size: 4-1/2"/114mm
Trademark: SC or Swan

The *Small Table Bell* was issued in 1987. There are no known significant variations. The suggested retail was $65 at retirement in December 1997.

CRV: $75

Bell, Solaris

7467 000 001/235 526
Designer: Anton Hirzinger
Size: 4-3/4"/120mm
Trademark: Swan

The *Solaris Bell* was issued in 1999. Various colored crystals adorn this bell. It became part of the Crystal Home Accessories line by Swarovski in 2003. There are no known variations. The suggested retail is $185.

CRV: $185

Bird Bath

7460 108 000/010 029
Designer: Max Schreck
Size: 3-1/2"/89mm
Trademark: SC or Swan

The *Bird Bath* was issued in 1980. It features two frosted birds resting on the edge of the bowl. The purchase of this piece now includes a package of many colored stones. The suggested retail is $215. No variations are known to exist.

CRV: $215

Birds' Nest

7470 NR 50/7470 050 000
Designer: Team
Size: 2"/50mm
Trademark: SC or Swan

The *Birds' Nest* was introduced in 1987. It features a mother bird with three baby birds. The suggested retail was $125 at retirement in December 1996. There are no known variations.

CRV: $195

Birthday Cake

003-0169678/169 678
Designer: Gabriele Stamey
Size: 2"/50mm
Trademark: SCS Swan

The *Birthday Cake* was issued in 1992 to celebrate the Swarovski Collectors Society's fifth anniversary. It became a closed edition in 1993. There are no known variations. The issue price was $85.

CRV: $300

Blowfish, Large

7644 NR 41/7644 041 000
Designer: Team
Size: 3"/76mm
Trademark: SC or Swan

The *Large Blowfish* was issued in 1984. The blowfish has frosted eyes, nose, tail, and fins. There are no known variations. The suggested retail was $75 at retirement in December 1991.

CRV: $200

Blowfish, Mini

7644 020 000/013 960
Designer: Team
Size: 1-1/4"/32mm
Trademark: SC and Swan

The *Mini Blowfish* was issued in 1987 and has frosted eyes, fins, and nose. The suggested retail is $29.50, and there are no known variations.

CRV: $29.50

Blowfish, Small

7644 030 000/012 724
Designer: Team
Size: 2"/50mm
Trademark: SC or Swan

The *Small Blowfish* was issued in 1987. There are no known variations. The suggested retail is $55.

CRV: $55

Blush Brush

SCBB000001
Designer: Team
Size: 3 1/4"/85mm
Trademark: SC

The *Blush Brush* was produced in very limited quantities. It is believed to be a prototype production since no item number was ever assigned to this piece. It was made for European distribution and features a crystal ball with bristles and the SC trademark stamped on the crystal ball's metal head. The original U.S. equivalent retail was approximately $30. This is an extremely rare Silver Crystal item.

CRV: $1500

Box, Coin, SCS Member

7400/090/001
Designer: Team
Size: 1-7/8"/45mm
Trademark: SCS Swan

The *SCS Member Coin Box* was only made available to SCS Members visiting the Swarovski Company gift shop in Wattens, Austria. Two variations exist. One example does not have a lid hinge and the other comes with a hinged lid. Various commemorative coins have been produced at the rate of four styles per year from 1990 to date in copper, gold plate, silver, and gold. Limited availability.

No Hinge CRV: $1200
Hinged CRV: $500

Buffalo, The

624598
Designer: Martin Zendron
Size: 3-1/2"/88mm
Trademark: Swan

The *Buffalo* was issued in the spring of 2003 as part of the "Symbols" theme group. No known variations. Suggested retail at time of issue was $385.

CRV: $385

Bumblebee

7615 NR 000 002/7615 000 002
Designer: Claudia Schneiderbauer
Size: 1-15/16"/49mm
Trademark: Swan

The *Bumblebee* was issued in 1992. The suggested retail was $85 at retirement in December 1997. There are no known variations.

CRV: $135

Butterfly

7639 NR 55/7639 055 000/010 002
Designer: Team
Size: 2"/50mm
Trademark: SC or Swan

The *Butterfly*, now marketed as item number 010 002, has evolved with several variations since it was first issued in 1982. The *Butterfly* was first seen with black crystal stones atop the rhodium antennae. The subsequent production evolved into a butterfly with crystal tips on the gold antennae. These first two variations bear the SC trademark. The current model can be found with greater metal content making up the nose. The suggested retail for the current *Butterfly* is $90.

Version #1–Trademark SC CRV: $300
Version #2–Trademark SC CRV: $250
Version #3–Trademark SC or Swan CRV: $90

Butterfly, Gold

7551 NR 100/7551 100 000
Designer: Team
Size: 4" /102mm
Trademark: SC or Swan

The *Gold Butterfly* was issued in 1985. It was retired in December 1988 reportedly due to the large quantity of individual stones that had to be handset for the flower's middle. It was marketed only in the U.S. and Canada. The suggested retail was $230 at its retirement. Variations exist with three styles of support crystals.

CRV: $1395

Butterfly, Mini

7667 035 000/012 774
Designer: Team
Size: 1-1/4"/32mm
Trademark: SC or Swan

The *Mini Butterfly* was issued in 1986 with the SC trademark. Older pieces will have some greater value. The Mini Butterfly rests on a concave faceted base. The current suggested retail is $46.50.

Trademark SC
CRV: $65
Trademark Swan
CRV: $65

Butterfly, Mini

7671 NR 30/7671 030 000
Designer: Team
Size: 1"/25mm
Trademark: SC or Swan

This *Mini Butterfly* was introduced only in the U.S. market in 1985. There are two notable variations. Neither variation has a base. One variation has black-tipped antennae; the other has crystal tips. The suggested retail was $35 at retirement in December 1988.

Trademark SC
–Black Tips CRV: $350
Trademark Swan
–Black Tips CRV: $300
Trademark SC
–Crystal Tips CRV: $175
Trademark Swan
–Crystal Tips CRV: $100

Butterfly, Rhodium

7551 NR 200/7551 200 000
Designer: Team
Size: 4"/102mm
Trademark: SC

The *Rhodium Butterfly* was only marketed in the U.S. and was issued in 1985. There are three variations in the support crystals' style. The *Rhodium Butterfly* was reportedly retired due to the intensive labor needed to apply the stones making up the flower's center. The suggested retail was $200 at retirement in December 1986. The short production length of time and exclusive U.S. distribution makes this a somewhat rare item to acquire.

CRV: $3750

Butterfly Fish

7644 NR 077 000/7644 077 000
Designer: Michael Stamey
Size: 3"/76mm
Trademark: Swan

The *Butterfly Fish* was issued in 1991 and sits atop a base resembling frosted ocean coral. There are no known variations. The suggested retail was $175 at retirement in December 1998.

CRV: $200

Butterfly On Leaf

7615 000 003/182 920
Designer: Claudia Schneiderbauer
Size: 2-1/2"/63mm
Trademark: Swan

The *Butterfly on Leaf* was first issued in 1994. The butterfly sits on a frosted crystal leaf. There are no known variations. The suggested retail is $90.

CRV: $90

Cactus, Flowering

7484 000 001/291 549
Designer: Michael Stamey
Size: 2-7/16"/40mm
Trademark: Swan

The *Flowering Cactus* was issued in 2002. There are no known variations. The suggested retail is $160.

CRV: $160

Cactus, Member Renewal

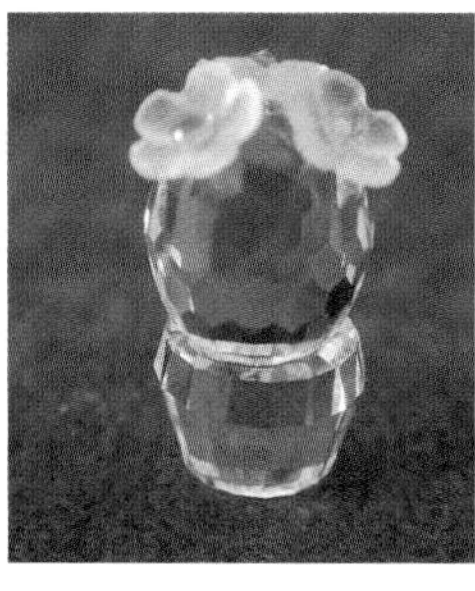

SCMR88
Designer: Michael Stamey
Size: 15/16"/24mm
Trademark: SCS.

The limited edition Swarovski Collectors Society Member *Renewal Cactus* was issued in 1988 and was only available in the North American and British markets. It is a very highly demanded piece on the secondary market, and was the first renewal gift for Society members. It was retired in 1988.

CRV: $295

Camel

7607 000 004/247 683
Designer: Heinz Tabertshofer
Size: 5"/125mm
Trademark: Swan

The *Camel* was issued in 2000, and there are no known variations. The suggested retail is $380.

CRV: $380

Candleholder 101 (Snowflake)

7600 NR 101/7600 101 000
Designer: Team
Size: 2-1/4"/57mm
Trademark: SC or Swan

The *Candleholder 101* has been nicknamed the "Snowflake" candleholder. Issued in 1976, it was retired in the U.S. during 1981 and was retired in Europe during 1990. At its retirement, it had a suggested retail of $28.

SC CRV: $190
Swan CRV: $100

Candleholder 102

7600 NR 102/7600 102 000
Designer: Hermann Koch
Size: 2-1/4"/57mm
Trademark: SC

This candleholder number 102 was issued in 1976 and was produced with both the hole for the candle and the pin style. Base variations have been produced. It was retired in December 1986 at a suggested retail of $44.

Pin Style CRV: $150
Hole Style CRV: $250

Candleholder 103 (U.S. Version)

7600 NR 103/7600 103 000
Designer: Team
Size: 1-1/4"/32mm
Trademark: SC

The U.S. version of candleholder number 103 was issued in 1986. Distributed throughout the U.S. and Canada, it was produced only for a short time. The suggested retail when it was retired in June 1988 was $55. There are no known variations.

CRV: $175

Candleholder 103 (European Version)

7600 NR 103/7600 103 000
Designer: Team
Size: 2-7/8"/73mm
Trademark: SC

The *Candleholder 103* (round ball with pin) was exclusively distributed in the European market. There are no known variations and it is becoming more difficult to obtain. It was retired in 1983 at a U.S. equivalent of approximately $45.

CRV: $850

Candleholder 104 (U.S. Version)

7600 NR 104/7600 104 000
Designer: Team
Size: 2-1/8"/54mm
Trademark: SC

The candleholder number 104 was issued exclusively in the U.S. and Canada in 1986. The candleholder is pyramid shaped and has a hole for the candle. There are no known variations. It was retired in June 1988 at a suggested retail of $150.

CRV: $300

Candleholder 104 (European Version)

7600 NR 104/7600 104 000
Designer: Team
Size: 4-3/8"/111mm
Trademark: SC or Swan

The candleholder number 104 was distributed exclusively in the European market and is a pin-style candleholder. There are no known variations. It was retired in December 1989 at a U.S. equivalent of $60.

CRV: $475

Candleholder 106

7600 NR 106/7600 106 000
Designer: Team
Size: 8-1/4"/210mm
Trademark: SC

The candleholder number 106 was issued in 1981 as a triple candleholder. Two styles were produced; one with holes for candles and one with pins. It was retired in December 1985 with a suggested retail of $100.

Holes CRV: $750
Pin CRV: $600

Candleholder 107

7600 NR 107/7600 107 000
Designer: Team
Size: 7-1/2"/190mm
Trademark: SC

The candleholder number 107 was issued in 1976 in two styles. One style has holes for the candles, and the other has metal pins. It was retired in December 1985 with a suggested retail of $120.

Hole Style CRV: $800
Pin Style CRV: $450

Candleholder 108 (European)

7600 NR 108/7600 108 000
Designer: Team
Size: 6"/150mm
Trademark: SC

Candleholder number 108 was issued in the European market in 1976. The only style produced was the pin-type candleholder. It was retired in December 1987 at a U.S. equivalent retail of approximately $45. There are no known variations.

CRV: $750

Candleholder 109

7600 NR 109/7600 109 000
Designer: Team
Size: 2-7/8"/73mm
Trademark: SC

Candleholder number 109 was issued in 1976 in both the hole and pin styles. It holds one single taper candle. It was retired in December 1985 at a suggested retail of $40.

Hole Style CRV: $250
Pin Style CRV: $195

Candleholder 110

7600 NR 110/7600 110 000
Designer: Team
Size: 3-1/8"/80mm
Trademark: SC

The candleholder number 110 was introduced during 1976 in both the hole and pin styles. It holds one single taper candle. It was retired in December 1985 at a suggested retail of $100.

Hole Style CRV: $300
Pin Style CRV: $195

Candleholder 111

7600 NR 111/7600 111 000
Designer: Team
Size: 6"/150mm
Trademark: SC

Candleholder number 111 was issued in 1976 in both the hole and pin styles. It holds one single taper candle. It was retired in December 1985 at a suggested retail of $100. There are no known variations.

Hole Style CRV: $900
Pin Style CRV: $750

Candleholder 112

7600 NR 112/7600 112 000
Designer: Team
Size: 6-1/2"/165mm
Trademark: SC

Candleholder number 112 was issued in 1976 in both the hole and pin styles. It holds two taper candles. It was retired in December 1985 at a suggested retail of $80. It has been produced in a topaz color in limited quantities. This rare color variation sells for $3000 or more on the secondary market.

Hole Style CRV: $750
Pin Style CRV: $325

Candleholder 113 (European)

7600 NR 113/7600 113 000
Designer: Team
Size: 3-1/2"/88mm
Trademark: SC

Candleholder number 113 was issued exclusively in the European market in 1976. It holds one taper candle, and was only produced in the pin style. It was retired in December 1981 at a U.S. retail equivalent of approximately $35. U.S. collectors find it difficult to obtain this candleholder.

CRV: $1350

Candleholder 114

7600 NR 114/7600 114 000
Designer: Team
Size: 2-3/4"/70mm
Trademark: SC

Candleholder number 114 was issued in 1981 in both the hole and pin styles. It holds one taper candle. It was retired in December 1985 at a suggested retail of $40.

Hole Style CRV: $500
Pin Style CRV: $400

Candleholder 115

7600 NR 115/7600 115 000
Designer: Team
Size: 8-1/2"/215mm
Trademark: SC

Candleholder number 115 was issued in 1976 and holds three taper candles. It was produced in both the hole and pin styles. It was retired in December 1986 at a suggested retail of $150. There are no known variations in color.

Hole Style CRV: $900
Pin Style CRV: $800

Candleholder 116

7600 NR 116/7600 116 000
Designer: Team
Size: 13"/330mm
Trademark: SC

Candleholder 116 was issued in 1981 in both the hole and pin styles. It holds five taper candles. It was retired in December 1985 at a suggested retail of $350.

Hole Style CRV: $3500
Pin Style CRV: $2750

Candleholder 117

7600 NR 117/7600 117 000

No example has yet been found with this number. There may be limited quantities of this item number still to be discovered. Keep searching! This would be an extremely rare find.

Candleholder 118 (European)

7600 NR 118/7600 118 000
Designer: Team
Size: 6-1/2"/165mm
Trademark: SC

Candleholder number 118 was issued only in the European market. It was likely released between 1976 and 1978, and only produced in the pin style. It holds two taper candles. This is an extremely rare item to locate.

Pin Style CRV: $3500

Candleholder 119 (European)

7600 NR 119/7600 119 000
Designer: Team
Size: 3-1/2"/90mm
Trademark: SC or Swan

Candleholder number 119 was exclusively issued in the European market during 1977 in only the pin style. It holds one single taper candle. It was retired in December 1989 at a U.S. retail equivalent of approximately $48.

CRV: $400

Candleholder 120 (U.S. Version)

7600 NR 120/7600 120 000
Designer: Team
Size: 4"/102mm
Trademark: SC

Candleholder number 120 was issued exclusively in the U.S. in 1986. It holds one taper candle in the hole-style design. It was retired in December 1987 at a suggested retail of $65. There are no known variations.

Hole Style CRV: $525

Candleholder 120 (European)

7600 NR 120/7600 120 000
Designer: Team
Size: 2-1/4"/55mm
Trademark: SC

Candleholder number 120 was issued in 1984 in Europe with the pin-style design. It holds one taper candle. It was retired in December 1987 at a U.S.-equivalent retail of approximately $65.

CRV: $550

Candleholder 121

7600 NR 121/7600 121 000
Designer: Team
Size: 5-1/4"/135mm
Trademark: SC

Candleholder number 121 was issued in 1983 and can be found in three style variations. All versions are the hole style, and each holds one taper candle. The faceted base has three different styles of cuts: diamond-shaped, honeycomb-shaped, and triangular-shaped. It was retired in December 1986 at a suggested retail of $150. All three variations sell for nearly the same price.

CRV: $500

Candleholder 122

7600 NR 122/7600 122 000
Designer: Team
Size: 3-5/8"/92mm
Trademark: SC

Candleholder number 122 was issued in 1986 exclusively in the U.S. market. It was only produced in the hole style. It was retired in December 1987 at a

suggested retail of $100. There are no known variations.

CRV: $600

Candleholder 123, Water Lily, Medium

7600 NR 123/010 001
Designer: Max Schreck
Size: 3-3/4"/95mm
Trademark: SC or Swan

Candleholder number 123 was issued in 1982, and holds one taper candle with the hole style. Some components have been deleted in the current production style. The older SC version holds increased value for collectors. The suggested retail is $260.

SC CRV: $300
Swan CRV: $260

Candleholder 124, Water Lily, Small

7600 NR 124/011 867
Designer: Max Schreck
Size: 3"/76mm
Trademark: SC or Swan

Candleholder number 124 was issued in 1985 and holds one taper candle with the hole style. Some original components have been deleted in the current production style. The older SC version holds increased value for collectors. The suggested retail is $175.

SC CRV: $250
Swan CRV: $175

Candleholder 125, Water Lily, Large

7600 NR 125/119 747
Designer: Max Schreck
Size: 4-1/4"/108mm
Trademark: SC or Swan

Candleholder number 125 was issued in 1985 and was marketed in the U.S. exclusively. This U.S.-style *Large Water Lily* was discontinued in 1989 when worldwide production was centralized. The current worldwide version is still being produced and marketed at a suggested retail of $375. The current model measures 5-1/4" and 135mm.

SC CRV: $600
Swan CRV: $375

Candleholder 126

7600 NR 126/7600 126 000
Designer: Team
Size: 4-3/16"/106mm
Trademark: SC

Candleholder number 126 was issued in 1986 exclusively for the U.S. and Canada. It was produced only in the hole style. *Candleholder 126* holds one taper candle. It was retired in December 1987 at a suggested retail of $110. No known variations.

CRV: $750

Candleholder 127

7600 NR 127/7600 127 000
Designer: Team
Size: 3"/76mm
Trademark: SC

Candleholder number 127 was introduced in 1985 exclusively in the U.S. and Canada. It was designed to hold one taper candle with the hole style. Some variation has been noted regarding the shape of the top piece. It was retired in December 1987 at a suggested retail of $85.

CRV: $375

Candleholder 128

7600 NR 128/7600 128 000
Designer: Team
Size: 4-1/2"/115mm
Trademark: SC

Candleholder number 128 was issued in 1985 with the hole style. It was marketed exclusively in the U.S. and Canada. This candleholder holds one taper candle, and can have a top crystal piece variation, which can be more rounded in shape. It was retired in December 1987 at a suggested retail of $110.

CRV: $425

Candleholder 129

7600 NR 129/7600 129 000
Designer: Team
Size: 5-1/4"/135mm
Trademark: SC

Candleholder number 129 was issued in 1985 with the hole style. It was marketed exclusively in the U.S. and Canada. This candleholder holds one taper candle and can be found with a top crystal piece variation which can be flat rather than rounded. It was retired in December 1987 at a suggested retail of $130.

CRV: $495

Candleholder 130

7600 NR 130/7600 130 000
Designer: Team
Size: 11-7/8"/300mm
Trademark: SC

Candleholder number 130 was issued in 1981 with both the hole and pin styles. This candleholder holds four taper candles. There are no known variations. It was retired in December 1985 at a suggested retail of $300.

Hole Style CRV: $3500
Pin Style CRV: $2500

Candleholder 131

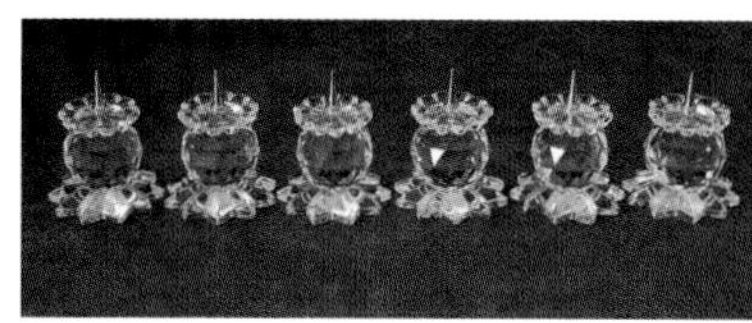

7600 NR 131/7600 131 000
Designer: Team
Size: 15/16"/24mm
Trademark: SC or Swan

Candleholder number 131 was released both as a set of six and individually. It was only produced in the pin style. It was retired in December of 1981 in the U.S. Base style variations exist. The suggested retail at its retirement was $48 for the set of six.

SC (Set Of Six) CRV: $400
SC (Individual) CRV: $50
Swan (Set Of Six) CRV: $250
Swan (Individual) CRV: $40

Candleholder 132

7600 NR 132/7600 132 000
Designer: Team
Size: 1-3/16"/30mm
Trademark: SC or Swan

Candleholder number 132 was issued during 1981 in the hole style, and was only produced in this style. It holds one small-sized candle, and was sold as a set of four. It was retired in December 1989 at a suggested retail of $80.

SC CRV: $225
Swan CRV: $175

Candleholder 133

7600 NR 133/7600 133 000
Designer: Team
Size: 1-9/16"/40mm
Trademark: SC or Swan

Candleholder number 133 was issued in 1981, and retailed as a set of two. It is only available in the hole style and holds one taper candle. It was sold exclusively in the U.S. and was retired in December 1990 at a suggested retail of $60.

SC CRV: $200
Swan CRV: $175

Candleholder 134

7600 NR 134/7600 134 000
Designer: Team
Size: 2"/50mm
Trademark: SC or Swan

Candleholder number 134 was issued in 1981 and was sold as a single item. It holds one taper candle, and bears the SC or the Swan trademarks. It was retired in December 1990 at a suggested retail of $60.

SC CRV: $150
Swan CRV: $125

Candleholder 135

7600 NR 135/7600 135 000
Designer: Team
Size: 2-3/8"/60mm
Trademark: SC or Swan

Candleholder number 135 was issued in 1981 in the hole style and holds one taper candle. There are no known variations. It was retired in December 1988 at a suggested retail of $85.

SC CRV: $175
Swan CRV: $125

Candleholder 136

7600 NR 136/7600 136 000
Designer: Max Schreck
Size: 4-3/8"/110mm
Trademark: SC

Candleholder number 136 was issued in 1986 in the hole style only. It holds one taper candle with gold pineapple leaves forming the candle receptacle. It is available in both gold and rhodium finishes. It was retired in December 1986 at a suggested retail of $150.

Rhodium (European-only release-retired December 1987)
CRV: $750
Gold CRV: $595

Candleholder 137

7600 NR 137/7600 137 000
Designer: Team
Size: 7-1/2"/190mm
Trademark: SC or Swan

Candleholder number 137 was issued in 1983 with the hole-style candle receptacle decorated with frosted crystal flowers. It was retired in December 1990 at a suggested retail of $190.

SC CRV: $400
Swan CRV: $350

Candleholder 138

7600 NR 138/7600 138 000
Designer: Team
Size: 7-3/4"/195mm
Trademark: SC

Candleholder number 138 was issued during 1986 exclusively in the U.S. market. It holds one taper candle with the hole style. There are no major variations to note. It was retired in December 1986 at a suggested retail of $160.

CRV: $1250

Candleholder 139

7600 NR 139/7600 139 000
Designer: Team
Size: 7-3/4"/195mm
Trademark: SC

Candleholder number 139 was issued in 1986 exclusively in the U.S. market. It holds one taper candle with the hole style. No major variations have been noted. It is difficult to find for collectors outside the U.S. It was retired in December 1986 at a suggested retail of $140.

CRV: $1400

Candleholder 140

7600 NR 140/7600 140 000
Designer: Team
Size: 6-1/2"/158mm
Trademark: SC

Candleholder number 140 was issued in 1986 exclusively for the U.S. market. It holds one taper candle with the hole style. There are no major variations that have been reported. It was retired in December 1986 at a suggested retail of $120. It is difficult to find for collectors outside the U.S.

CRV: $1400

Candleholder 141

7600 NR 141/7600 141 000
Designer: Max Schreck
Size: 7-3/4"/195mm
Trademark: SC or Swan

Candleholder number 141 was issued in the European market in 1986. It holds one taper candle with the hole style. There are no known major variations. It was retired in December 1991 at a suggested U.S. retail of approximately $130.

SC CRV: $950
Swan CRV: $750

Candleholder 142

7600 NR 142/7600 142 000
Designer: Max Schreck
Size: 4-1/4"/100mm
Trademark: SC or Swan

Candleholder number 142 was issued in 1986 exclusively for the European market in the hole style, and holds one taper candle. There are no known variations. It was retired in December 1990 at a U.S. retail of approximately $110.

SC CRV: $425
Swan CRV: $375

Candleholder 143

7600 NR 143/7600 143 000
Designer: Team
Size: 4-1/2"/115mm
Trademark: SC or Swan

Candleholder number 143 was issued in 1987, and has the hole-style candle receptacle. Variations have been noted with or without facets on the spike ends. It was retired in December 1996 at a suggested retail of $375.

SC CRV: $450
Swan CRV: $400

Candleholder 143001, Star, Medium

7600 143 001/119 430
Designer: Team
Size: 3-5/8"/93mm
Trademark: Swan

Candleholder number 143 was issued in 1989. Holds in one taper candle in the hole style. The suggested retail is $260. There are no known variations.

CRV: $260

Candleholder 144070

7600 NR 144 070/7600 144 070
Designer: Adi Stocker
Size: 2-5/8"/67mm
Trademark: Swan

Candleholder number 144070 was issued in 1990 and holds one taper candle in the hole style. There are no known variations. The suggested retail when it was retired in December 1992 was $175.

CRV: $195

Candleholder 144080

7600 NR 144 080/7600 144 080
Designer: Adi Stocker
Size: 3-3/8"/86mm
Trademark: Swan

Candleholder number 144080 was issued during 1990 in the hole style, and holds one taper candle. There are no known variations. The suggested retail was $175 when it was retired in December 1992.

CRV: $275

Candleholder 144090

7600 NR 144 090/7600 144 090
Designer: Adi Stocker
Size: 4-1/8"/105mm
Trademark: SC or Swan

Candleholder number 144090 was issued in 1988 in the hole style and holds one taper candle. There are no known variations. The suggested retail was $225 when it was retired in December 1992.

SC CRV: $350
Swan CRV: $300

Candleholder 145

7600 NR 145/7600 145 000
Designer: Team
Size: 5-1/8"/130mm
Trademark: Swan

Candleholder number 145 was issued in 1994 only in the Hong Kong market, and the functional use is an incense holder. It was reportedly only produced in a limited edition of 1000 pieces. There are no known variations. This candleholder is difficult to obtain for worldwide collectors.

CRV: $4000-$5000

Candleholder 146

7600 146 000/207 012
Designer: Gabriele Stamey
Size: 6"/150mm
Trademark: Swan

Candleholder number 146 was issued in 1996 in the hole style and holds one taper candle.

There are no known varieties. It was retired in December 2001. The suggested retail at its retirement was $260.

CRV: $275

Candleholder 147

7600 147 000/236 719
Designer: Adi Stocker
Size: 5-1/2"/138mm
Trademark: Swan

Candleholder number 147 was issued in 1999. It was produced in the hole-style with an opening large enough to accommodate various sized candles. There are no known variations. It was retired in December 2001 at a suggested retail of $350. Note the short production time making this a limited production item.

CRV: $375

Candleholder 148

7600 NR 148 000/236 716
Designer: Martin Zendron
Size: 5-1/2"/140mm
Trademark: Swan

Candleholder number 148 was issued in 1999 in the hole style and holds one taper candle. It was marketed with a complimentary bag of decorative crystals. There are no known variations. The suggested retail is $185.

CRV: $185

Cardholders, Large

7403 NR 030/7403 030 000
Designer: Kurt Mignon
Size: 1-9/16"/41mm
Trademark: SC or Swan

The large cardholders were issued during 1978 in ten colors, and with both gold and rhodium finishes. These cardholders were issued as a set of six in the European market, and as a set of four in the U.S. market. The gold finish brings a slight premium of about $100 to $125 each. The cardholders were retired in December 1989 with the U.S. set retailing for $80.

SC (set of four) CRV: $400
Swan (set of four) CRV: $350

Cardholders, Small

7403 NR 020/7403 020 000
Designer: Kurt Mignon
Size: 1-3/16"/30mm
Trademark: SC or Swan

The small cardholders were issued in 1978 in a variety of colors (ten) and with both the gold and rhodium finishes. The cardholders were issued as a set of six in the European market and as a set of four in the U.S. market. The gold finish brings a slight premium at approximately $65 to $75 each. The small cardholders were retired in December 1989 with the U.S. set of four retailing for $40.

SC (set of four) CRV: $225
Swan (set of four) CRV: $200

COLORS FOUND ON CARDHOLDERS

Bermuda Blue	Seal
Crystal Cal	Tabac
Helio	Vitrail Light
Inn Green	Vitrail Medium
Sahara	Volcano

TWO METAL FINISHES
Gold
Rhodium

Carriage, Train (Wagon)

7471 000 003/015 150
Designer: Gabriele Stamey
Size: 1-5/8"/41mm
Trademark: SC or Swan

The *Train Carriage* (Wagon in the U.S.) was issued in 1988 as part of the train set. There are variations noted in the window placement on the car's side. It was retired in December 2003 at a suggested retail of $125.

SC CRV: $175
Swan CRV: $150

Cat, Large

7634 NR 70/7634 070 000
Designer: Max Schreck
Size: 2-7/8"/73mm
Trademark: SC or Swan

The *Large Cat* was issued in 1977 and featured a braided-metal tail. Variations have been noted in the tail style. Some tails were produced that are floppy, while others are stiff. It was retired in December 1991 at a suggested retail of $55.

SC CRV: $125-$175
Swan CRV: $125-$150

Cat, Medium

7634 NR 52/7634 052 000
Designer: Max Schreck
Size: 2"/50mm
Trademark: SC

The *Medium Cat* was issued in 1983 exclusively in the U.S. and Canada. Known variations exist in the metal tail style. It is in demand by collectors worldwide. It was retired in December 1987 at a suggested retail of $35.

CRV: $575

Cat, Mini

7659 031 000/010 011
Designer: Max Schreck
Size: 1-1/4"/32mm
Trademark: SC or Swan

The *Mini Cat* was introduced in 1982 in Europe and then in 2000 in the U.S. The cat's head on the European style faces to the side more than the U.S. version. It was discontinued in the U.S. in December 1991, and then reissued in 2000. The current suggested retail is $27.50.

SC CRV: $50
Swan CRV: $27.50

Cat, Replica

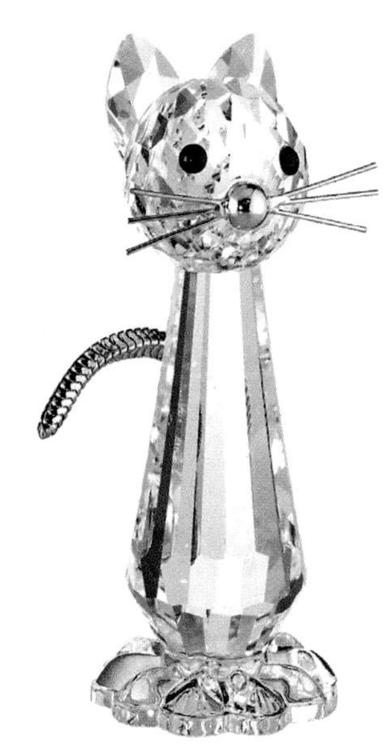

7606 000 003/183 274
Designer: Team
Size: 2"/50mm
Trademark: Swan

The *Replica Cat* was issued in 1994 and resembles the *Medium Cat*. There are no known variations. The current suggested retail is $42.50.

CRV: $42.50

Cat, Sitting

7634 046 000/160 799
Designer: Michael Stamey
Size: 1-3/4"/44mm
Trademark: Swan

The *Sitting Cat* was issued in 1991. The *Sitting Cat* represents the more sculpted look that has evolved with the Swarovski Silver Crystal pieces. The suggested retail is $90. There are no known variations.

CRV: $90

Cat, The

7685 000 002/289 478
Designer: Adi Stocker
Size: 4-3/4"/112mm
Trademark: Swan

The Cat was introduced in 2002 with a unique green-colored crystal collar. The suggested retail is $265. *The Cat* has a very elongated sleek, sculpted appearance.

CRV: $265

Cat, Tomcat

7634 NR 028 000/7634 028 000
Designer: Anton Hirzinger
Size: 2-1/8"/55mm
Trademark: Swan

The new-style *Cigarette Holder* is entirely made of crystal and holds the cigarette as a small glass would. It is utilized as a cigarette storage piece. There are no known variations. It was issued in 1981 and retired in December 1990 at a suggested retail of $95.

SC CRV: $195
Swan CRV: $175

Cigarette Holder, Gold

7503 NR 50/7503 050 000
Designer: Team
Size: 5-1/2"/140mm
Trademark: SC

The gold *Cigarette Holder* looks more like a gold metal canister. It features a gold band of metal with crystal stones on the top and bottom. It was issued in 1977 and retired in December 1983 at a suggested retail of $130.

CRV: $2500

Cigarette Holder, Brushed Rhodium

7503 NR 50/7503 050 000
Designer: Team
Size: 5-1/2"/140mm
Trademark: SC

The brushed rhodium *Cigarette Holder* was issued in 1977. It is recognized by its brushed metal finish and crystal stones on the top and bottom. This style is more difficult to obtain than the polished version. It was retired in December 1983 at a suggested retail of $130.

CRV: $2500

Cigarette Holder, Polished Rhodium

7503 NR 50/7503 050 000
Designer: Team
Size: 5-1/2"/140mm
Trademark: SC

The polished rhodium *Cigarette Holder* was issued in 1977. It is recognized by its polished or shiny finish and crystal stone on the top and bottom. This style is somewhat easier to find than the brushed version. It was retired in December 1983 at a suggested retail of $130.

CRV: $2250

Cigarette Lighter

7462 NR 062/7462 062 000
Designer: Max Schreck
Size: 3-1/2"/90mm
Trademark: SC or Swan

The *Cigarette Lighter* was issued in 1981. It features a crystal body with a metal/rhodium top. Two variations exist; one is more beveled on the rhodium component. It was retired in December 1990 at a suggested retail of $160.

SC CRV: $500
Swan CRV: $350

Cigarette Lighter, Gold Polished

7500 NR 50/7500 050 000
Designer: Team
Size: 3-5/8"/92mm
Trademark: SC

The gold polished *Cigarette Lighter* was issued in 1977. It is recognized by its polished gold metal body with crystal stones decorating the top and bottom. It was retired in December 1983 at a suggested retail price of $160.

CRV: $2750

Cigarette Lighter, Rhodium Brushed

7500 NR 50/7500 050 000
Designer: Team
Size: 3-5/7"/92mm
Trademark: SC

The brushed rhodium *Cigarette Lighter* was issued in 1977. It is recognized by its brushed metal body with Swarovski Silver Crystal stones at the top and bottom. It was retired in December 1983 at a suggested retail of $160.

CRV: $2500

Cigarette Lighter, Rhodium, Polished

7500 NR 50/7500 050 000
Designer: Team
Size: 3-5/8"/92mm
Trademark: SC

The polished rhodium *Cigarette Lighter* was issued in 1977 and is recognized by its polished metal body with Swarovski Silver Crystal stones on the top and bottom. It was retired in December 1983 at a suggested retail of $160. This style is the more common of the metal lighters.

CRV: $1750

Cinderella

7550 000 008/255 108
Designer: Martin Zendron
Size: 4-1/4"/106mm
Trademark: Swan

Cinderella was issued in 2001 as a part of the "Fairy Tales" group. Note that Cinderella's shoe is a separate piece and is intended to display just away from the base. The suggested retail is $330.

CRV: $330

City Gates

7474 NR 000 023/7474 000 023
Designer: Gabriele Stamey
Size: 1-1/2"/38mm
Trademark: Swan

The *City Gates* were issued in 1991 and were produced for the "Crystal City" grouping. It was retired in December 1994 at a suggested retail of $95.

CRV: $125

City Tower

7474 NR 000 022/7471 000 022
Designer: Gabriele Stamey
Size: 1-3/4"/45mm
Trademark: Swan

The *City Tower* was issued in 1991 and was produced for the "Crystal City" grouping. It was retired in December 1994 at a suggested retail of $42.50.

CRV: $95

Clock, Athena

9280 NR 102
Designer: Team
Size: 2-1/4"/58mm
Trademark: Swarovski

The *Athena Clock* was introduced in 1987 and is found in both gold and rhodium finishes. Other known variations include the clock with alarm function, date display, or moon dial. It was retired in December 1992 at a suggested retail of $300.

CRV: $400

Clock, Belle Epoque

9280 NR 104
Designer: Team
Size: 4-3/8"/110mm wide
Trademark: Swarovski

The *Belle Epoque Clock* was introduced in 1987 and is found in both gold and rhodium finishes. Other known variations include the clock with alarm function, date display, or moon dial. It was retired in December 1992 at a suggested retail of $585.

CRV: $900

Clock, Colosseum

9280 NR 105
Designer: Team
Size: 4-1/8"/105mm tall
Trademark: Swarovski

The *Colosseum Clock* was issued only in the European market in 1987. It can be found with either the gold or rhodium finish. Additional variations include an alarm, date display, or moon dial. It was retired in December 1992 at an approximate U.S. dollar equivalent of $500.

CRV: $950

Clock, Kris Bear

7481 000 001/212 687
Designer: Martin Zendron
Size: 2-1/2"/63mm
Trademark: Swan

The *Kris Bear Clock* was introduced in 1997 and was the first Swarovski clock to incorporate a figural design such as the Kris Bear. There are no known variations. It was retired in December 2002 at a suggested retail of $210.

CRV: $250

Clock, El Dorado

9280 NR 106
Designer: Team
Size: 2-7/8"/73mm
Trademark: Swarovski

The *El Dorado Clock* was issued solely in the European market in 1987. It can be found in either the gold or rhodium finish. Additional variations include an alarm, date display, and moon dial. It was retired in December 1992 at an approximate U.S. dollar equivalent of $500.

CRV: $900

Clock, Napoleon

9280 NR 101
Designer: Team
Size: 2-1/4"/57mm
Trademark: Swarovski

The *Napoleon Clock* was issued in 1987 and can be found in both the gold and rhodium finish. Additional variations include an alarm, date display, and moon dial. It was retired in December 1992 at a suggested retail of $380.

CRV: $500

Clock, Polar Star

9280 NR 103
Designer: Team
Size: 3"/76mm
Trademark: Swarovski

The *Polar Star Clock* was issued in 1987 and is found in both the gold and rhodium finish. Additional variations include an alarm, date display, and moon dial. It was retired in December 1992 at a suggested retail of $520.

CRV: $675

Clock, Solaris

7481 000 002/221 626
Designer: Adi Stocker
Size: 5"/125mm
Trademark: Swan

The *Solaris Clock* was issued in 1998 and has multicolored stones surrounding the clock face. There are no known variations. The suggested retail is $375.

CRV: $375

Clover, Four Leaf

7483 000 001/212 101
Designer: Anton Hirzinger
Size: 2-1/2"/63mm
Trademark: Swan

The *Four Leaf Clover* was introduced in 1997. There are no known variations. The current suggested retail is $49.50.

CRV: $49.50

Cobra

7603 000 003/243 979
Designer: Heinz Tabertshofer
Size: 2-5/8"/68mm
Trademark: Swan

The *Cobra* was issued in 2000 and is unique with a silver metal fang. There are no known variations. The suggested retail is $145.

CRV: $145

Cockatoo

7621 000 007/261 635
Designer: Heinz Tabertshofer
Size: 3-1/8"/78mm
Trademark: Swan

The *Cockatoo* was issued in 2001 and features a bright yellow crest. There are no known variations. The suggested retail is $145.

CRV: $145

Cockerel

7674 000 001/247 759
Designer: Michael Stamey
Size: 2"/50mm
Trademark: Swan

The *Cockerel* (also known as the *Rooster*) was issued in 2000. It is very colorful with red- and yellow-colored crystal trim. The suggested retail is $75. There are no known variations.

CRV: $75

Coin Box

7400/090/001
Designer: Team
Size: 1-7/8"/45mm
Trademark: Swan

The *Coin Box* was only available to SCS members who visited the Swarovski Company Shop in Wattens, Austria. It can be found with a lid that lifts off, which is more difficult to obtain. The hinged version is somewhat easier to find. It was issued in 1990 in the no-hinge style for one year. The hinged style was discontinued in 1995.

Swan (No Hinge) CRV: $1500
Swan (Hinged) CRV: $450

Columbine

DO1X001/7400 200 000/242 032
Designer: Gabriele Stamey
Size: 6-3/4"/169mm
Trademark: Swan

Columbine was issued in 2000 as the second addition in the "Masquerade" series. This SCS Member redemption piece was produced only for one year and sold for a suggested retail of $350.

CRV: $400

Columbine Plaque

9003142557822
Designer: Team
Size: 2-1/4"/57mm
Trademark: Swan ERA.

The *Columbine Plaque* was issued in 2000 at a suggested retail of $35. It is used as a crystal title plaque for the *Columbine* limited edition figurine.

CRV: $75

Conch

7624 000 002/191 691
Designer: Michael Stamey
Size: 1-3/8"/35mm
Trademark: Swan

The *Conch* was issued in 1995 as part of the "Maritime Trio" grouping. There are no known variations. It was retired in December 2003 at a suggested retail of $29.50.

CRV: $40

Crab, Mini

7624 000 004/206 481
Designer: Michael Stamey
Size: 1-3/4"/38mm
Trademark: Swan

The *Mini Crab* was issued in 1996 as part of the "Maritime Trio" group. There are no known variations. The suggested retail is $65.

CRV: $65

Cross Of Light, The

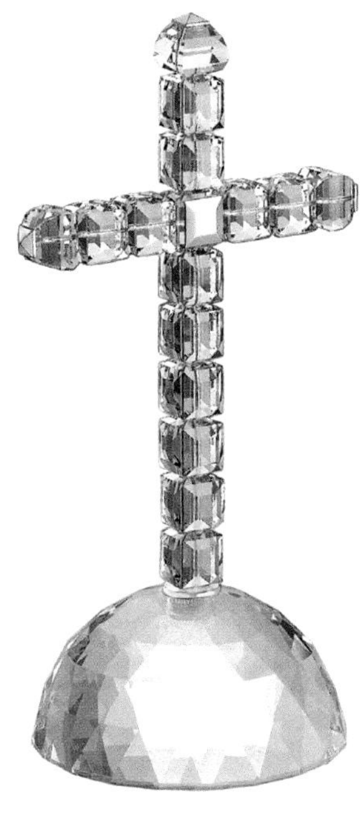

7512 000 001/285 865
Designer: Stefano Ricci
Size: 7"/175mm
Trademark: Swan

The *Cross of Light* was issued in 2001. There are no known variations. The suggested retail for this piece is $385. A larger rendition made specifically for "Touring the World" is not for sale at retail.

CRV: $385

Cruet Set (Salt & Pepper/Rhodium)

7502 NR 030–031–032/7502 030 031 032
Designer: Team
Size: 3-1/8"/80mm
Trademark: SC

The *Cruet Set* was issued in the late 1970s and features a rhodium stand to hold salt & pepper shakers. The shakers have wine bands of rhodium with crystal stones at the top and bottom. They resemble the *Cigarette Holder* number 7503 NR 50. It was retired in December 1983 at an approximate U.S. retail of $100. The *Cruet Set* is very hard to locate on the secondary market.

CRV: $2750

Crystal Planet (Millennium Edition)

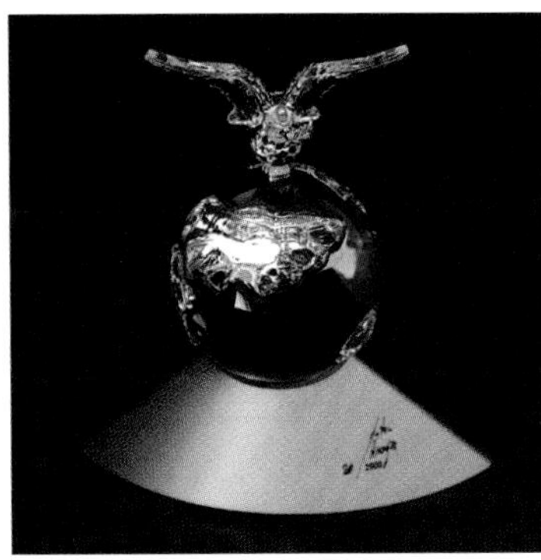

7607 000 004/238 985
Designer: Anton Hirzinger
Size: 5"/125mm
Trademark: Swan

The *Crystal Planet* was issued in 2000 as a celebratory symbol for the beginning of the new century. It features a sapphire blue globe with a clear dove sitting on top. It was produced as a one-year limited edition and then was retired in December 2000 at a suggested retail of $275.

CRV: $300

Dachshund

7641 NR 75/7641 075 000
Designer: Max Schreck
Size: 2-15/16"/74mm
Trademark: SC or Swan

The *Dachshund* was issued in 1984 and can be found in three variations: floppy braided metal tail, flexible metal braided tail, and spring-coil metal tail. The floppy style commands the highest premium. It was retired in December 1991 at a suggested retail of $70.

SC/Swan (Floppy) CRV: $500
SC/Swan (Flexible) CRV: $200
SC/Swan (Spring-coil) CRV: $175

Dachshund, Mini

7672 NR 42/7672 042 000
Designers: Max Schreck (Metal Style)
Adi Stocker (Frosted Style)
Sizes: 1-1/4"/32mm (Metal Style)
2"/50mm (Frosted Style)
Trademark: SC or Swan

The *Mini Dachshund* was issued in 1985 with a braided floppy metal tail. A second version was produced with a frosted tail. The metal-tail version was retired in December 1988 with the frosted-tail version following in December 1995. The original suggested retail were $35 for the metal style, and $49.50 for the frosted style.

SC (Metal) CRV: $200
SC (Frosted) CRV: $180
Swan (Metal) CRV: $150
Swan (Frosted) CRV: $150

Dalmatian Puppy, Sitting

628909
Designer: Edith Mair
Size: 2-1/8"/54mm
Trademark: Swan

The *Sitting Dalmatian Puppy* was issued in 2004 as part of the "Pet's Corner" grouping. Suggested retail at the time of issue was $115. No known variations.

CRV: $115

Dalmatian Puppy, Standing

628947
Designer: Edith Mair
Size: 2-1/4"/57mm
Trademark: Swan

The *Dalmatian Puppy* Standing was issued in 2004 as part of the "Pet's Corner" grouping. Suggested retail at the time of issue was $175. No known variations.

CRV: $115

Dalmatian, Mother

628948
Designer: Edith Mair
Size: 2-3/4"/70mm
Trademark: Swan

The *Mother Dalmatian* was issued in 2004 at an issue price of $165. This piece features black spots applied by laser jet process with ink. Part of the "Pet's Corner" grouping. No known variations.

CRV: $165

Dino

7550 000 010/268 204
Designer: Edith Mair
Size: 3-1/4"/87mm
Trademark: Swan

Dino was issued in 2002 as a part of the "Fairy Tales" grouping. There are no known variations. The current suggested retail is $130.

CRV: $130

Doe

7608 000 003/247 963
Designer: Martin Zendron
Sizes: 3-3/4"/94mm
Trademark: Swan

The *Doe* was issued in 2000 as a part of the "Woodland Friends" grouping. The current suggested retail is $215. There are no known variations.

Swan CRV: $215

Dog, Standing

7635 NR 70/7635 070 000
Designer: Max Schreck
Size: 2-3/4"/70mm
Trademark: SC or Swan

The *Standing Dog* was issued in 1979 and is commonly referred to as "Pluto." It was retired in December 1990 at a suggested retail of $50. There are no known variations.

SC CRV: $150
Swan CRV: $125

Dog, The

7685 000 001/289 202
Designer: Anton Herzinger
Sizes: 4-1/2"/113mm
Trademark: Swan

The *Dog* was issued in 2002 at a suggested retail of $300. There are no known variations.

CRV: $300

Doll

626247
Designer: Gabriele Stamey
Size: 1-5/8"/41mm
Trademark: Swan

The *Doll* was issued in the fall of 2003 as an addition to the "When We Were Young" theme group. Also issued as a companion piece to *Puppet*. Suggested retail at time of issue was $130.

CRV: $130

Dolphin

7644 000 001/190 365
Designer: Michael Stamey
Size: 3-7/8"/98mm
Trademark: Swan

The *Dolphin* was issued in 1995. There are no known variations. It is very similar in design to the 1990 Dolphin SCS Membership Redemption Annual. The current suggested retail is $215.

Swan CRV: $215

Dolphin Brooch (Scs Member)

003-8901707
Designer: Team
Sizes: 2-3/8"/60mm
Trademark: Swan/SCS.

The *Dolphin Brooch* was issued in 1991 to members of the Swarovski Collectors Society. It was retired in December 1992 at a retail of $75. It is considered a limited edition.

CRV: $150

Dolphin, Maxi

7644 000 004/221 628
Designer: Michael Stamey
Size: 8"/400mm
Trademark: Swan

The *Maxi Dolphin* was issued in 1998. There are no known variations. The current suggested retail is $895.

Swan CRV: $895

Dolphins, Member

DO1X901/153 850
Designer: Michael Stamey
Sizes: 4-3/4"/120mm
Trademark: Swan/SCS.

Dolphins were issued to members of the Swarovski Collectors Society in 1990. This piece was the first in the "Mother and Child Series." It was retired in December 1990 at the issue price of $225. It is also known as the *1990 Annual Edition*.

CRV: $1250

Donald Duck

14013010
Designer: Arribas Brothers
Size: 2-1/8"/44mm
Trademark: Swan

Donald Duck was issued in 2001 by The Arribas Brothers Shops at the Disney Theme Park Stores. It was issued as a limited edition of 10,000 pieces. The current retail price is $295. There are no known variations.

CRV: $295

Dove

7605 000 001/191 696
Designer: Edith Mair
Sizes: 1-3/4"/48mm
Trademark: Swan

The *Dove* was issued in 1995 with frosted crystal feet. There are no known variations. The current suggested retail is $60.

CRV: $60

Dragon

7550 000 005/238 202
Designer: Gabriele Stamey
Size: 5-3/4"/144mm
Trademark: Swan

The *Dragon* was issued in 1999 and was offered with a mahogany wooden stand and crystal ball. The *Dragon*, wooden stand, and the crystal ball make it a three-piece set. The current suggested retail is $330.

CRV: $330

Dragon

DO1X971/208 398
Designer: Gabriele Stamey
Size: 5-1/2"/137mm
Trademark: Swan/Swarovski.

The *Dragon* was issued in 1997 as the annual limited edition for members of the Swarovski Collectors Society. It was second in the "Fabulous Creatures" series. It is notable with red eyes. Early pieces have the initials GS97 etched into the design. It is also known as the *1997 Annual Edition*. The issue price was $325 and it was retired in December 1997.

CRV: $750

Dragon, Zodiac

625 191
Designer: Anton Hirzinger
Size: 1-3/8"/34mm
Trademark: Swan

The *Zodiac Dragon* was issued in 2004 as part of the "Chinese Zodiacs" theme group. No known variations. Suggested retail at time of issue was $65.

CRV: $65

Dragonfly

7615 000 004/190 264
Designer: Claudia Schneiderbauer
Size: 2-5/8"/65mm
Trademark: Swan

The *Dragonfly* was issued in 1995 and sits above a crystal frosted leaf. The current suggested retail is $85. There are no known variations.

CRV: $85

Drake, Mini

7660 040 000/010 007
Designer: Max Schreck
Size: 1-5/8"/41mm
Trademark: SC or Swan

The *Mini Drake* was issued in 1983. With over twenty years of production to date, this piece to date has no known variations. The current suggested retail with the Swan trademark is $46.50.

SC CRV: $60
Swan CRV: $46.50

Duck, Giant Mallard

7647 250 000/014 438
Designer: Michael Stamey
Size: 9-5/8"/250mm
Trademark: SC or Swan

The *Giant Mallard* was issued in 1989. It is often called the *Giant Duck*. There is some confusion as to the introduction date, since some pieces were produced in 1987. Two known variations exist, with only the earliest variations bearing the SC trademark. The current suggested retail is $4600.

SC CRV: $6000
Swan CRV: $4600

Duck, Large

7653 NR 75/7653 075 000
Designer: Max Schreck
Size: 3"/76mm
Trademark: SC

The *Large Duck* was issued in 1983, and was sold originally only in Canada and the U.S. It was retired in December 1987 at a suggested retail of $44. There are no known variations. This is very popular with worldwide collectors; thus it is a very strong secondary-market seller.

SC CRV: $695

Duck, Mallard

7647 NR 80/7647 080 000
Designer: Max Schreck
Size: 3-1/2"/90mm
Trademark: SC or Swan

The *Mallard* was issued in 1986. One variation has been noted with protective crystal pieces on the mallard's bottom to protect it from sitting directly on the surface. It was retired in December 1984 at a suggested retail of $135.

SC CRV: $200
Swan CRV: $185

Duck, Medium

7653 NR 55/7653 055 000
Designer: Max Schreck
Size: 2-1/8"/57mm
Trademark: SC or Swan

The *Medium Duck* was issued in 1983 and features a clear crystal bill. It was issued exclusively in Canada and the U.S. It was retired in June 1988, at a suggested retail of $40. There are no known variations and it is very desirable to worldwide collectors.

SC CRV: $250
Swan CRV: $225

Duck, Mini

7653 NR 45/7653 045 000
Designer: Max Schreck
Size: 1-7/8"/45mm
Trademark: SC or Swan

The *Mini Duck* was issued in 1980 and is notable with a silver bill. It was retired in December 1988 at a suggested retail of $25. There are no known variations.

SC CRV: $110
Swan CRV: $80

Duck, Mini Standing

7665 032 000/012 728
Designer: Adi Stocker
Size: 1-1/4"/32mm
Trademark: SC or Swan

The *Mini Standing Duck* was issued in 1986. There are no known variations. The current suggested retail is $42.50.

SC CRV: $60
Swan CRV: $42.50

Duck, Mini Swimming

7665 037 000/012 531
Designer: Adi Stocker
Size: 1-3/8"/35mm
Trademark: SC or Swan

The *Mini Swimming Duck* was issued in 1986. There are no known variations. It was retired in December 2001 with a suggested retail of $37.50.

SC CRV: $60
Swan CRV: $45

Dumbo

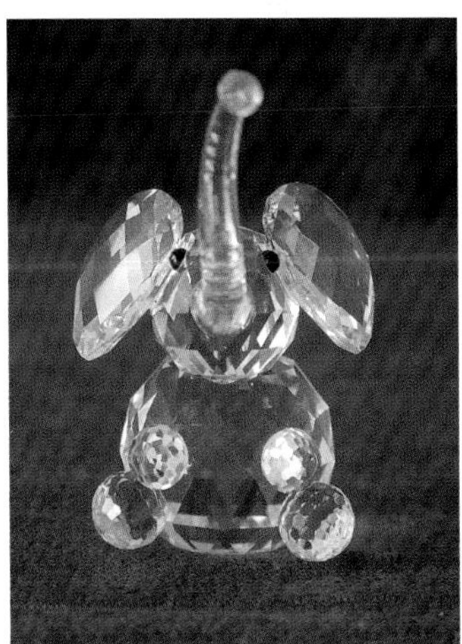

7640 NR 35
Designer: Adi Stocker
Sizes: 2-7/16"/62mm
Trademark: SC

The *Dumbo* by Adi Stocker was issued beginning in 1987 as a special production for the Arribas Brothers Shops in the Disney Theme Parks. Over the years, this very limited production item has been found with several variations in ear and tusk styles. Some pieces have been noted without any trademark.

SC CRV: $4000-$5000

Dumbo

SDW008/A516
Designer: Arribas Stores
Size: 3-3/4"/94mm
Trademark: © Disney/Swan

Dumbo was issued as an exclusive edition in 2002 by the Arribas Stores at the Disney theme parks. Each of the 10,000 pieces sold for a suggested retail of $350. Notable as a hanging piece to simulate Dumbo's flying.

CRV: $375

Dumbo, 1990

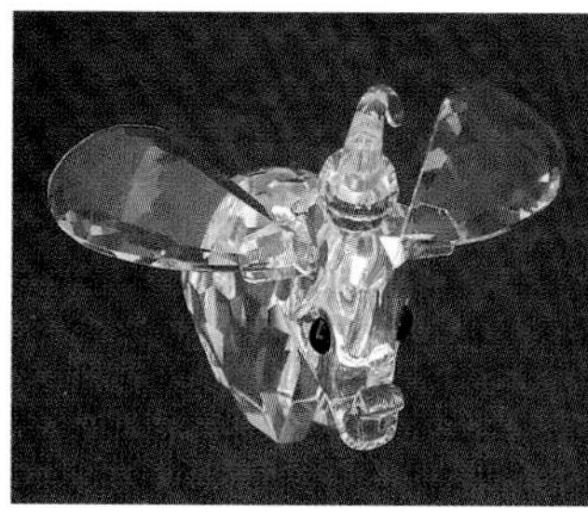

7640 NR 100
Designer: Team
Size: 2-5/8"/67mm
Trademark: Swan

The *1990 Dumbo* was issued in 1990 for the Swarovski Gala held at Walt Disney World, Florida, U.S.A. It was produced as a limited edition of 3000 pieces with a suggested retail of $125. The edition quickly sold out and has steadily risen in secondary market value.

The *1990 Dumbo* has black eyes, flying ears and a clear crystal top hat.

Swan CRV: $1200

Dumbo, 1993

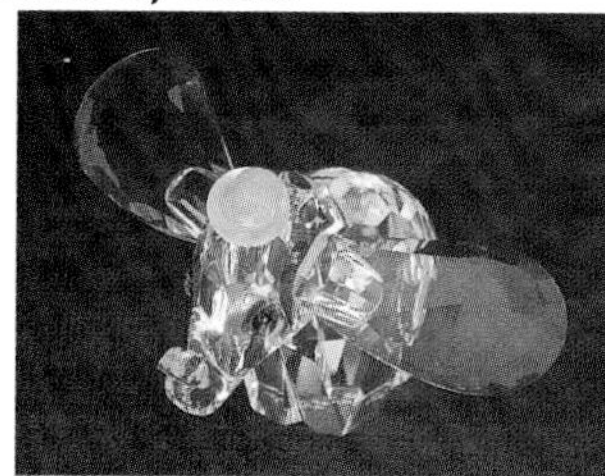

7640 NR 100 001
Designer: Team
Size: 2-3/16"/56mm
Trademark: Swan

Dumbo 1993 was introduced in Arribas stores at Disney Theme Parks in 1993 at a suggested retail of $195. Notable with blue eyes and a frosted hat. The limited edition is popular with Disney collectors and Swarovski collectors.

CRV: $500

Eagle

7607 000 001/184 872
Designer: Adi Stocker
Size: 9"/225mm
Trademark: Swan

The *Eagle* is a numbered limited edition of 10,000 pieces issued in 1995. It is only available by lottery allocation to 2900 U.S. Swarovski Collectors Society members. The *Eagle* was produced to commemorate the 100th Anniversary of the Swarovski Company. The *Eagle* is posed ready to take flight and features a bill and talons of solid sterling silver with rhodium plating. The issue price was $1750.

CRV: $7500

Eagle, The

624599
Designer: Edith Mair
Size: 5-7/8"/147mm
Trademark: Swan

The *Eagle* was issued in the spring of 2003 as the second addition to the "Symbols" theme group. This *Eagle* is decidedly contemporary in style. Suggested retail at time of issue was $300. No known variations.

CRV: $300

Elephant, Baby

7640 000 001/191 371
Designer: Martin Zendron
Size: 2-1/2"/64mm
Trademark: Swan

The *Baby Elephant* was issued in 1995 as part of the "African Wildlife" grouping. Note the position of the trunk in the upright position, which is a symbol of hope and good fortune in many cultures. The current suggested retail is $160.

CRV: $160

Elephant Brooch

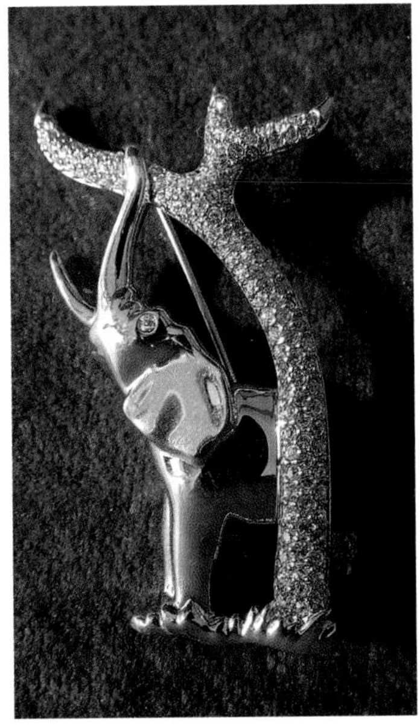

003-8902448
Designer: Team
Size: 2"/64mm
Trademark: Swan

The *Elephant Brooch* was a limited edition offering to members of the Swarovski Collectors Society in 1993/1994. It was retired in December 1994 at a suggested retail of $85.

CRV: $100

Elephant, Club Member Annual

DO1X931/169 970
Designer: Martin Zendron
Size: 4-3/8"/112mm
Trademark: Swan/SCS.

The *Elephant* was issued in 1993 as the limited edition for members of the Swarovski Collectors Society. It was issued with an optional black wooden stand and was the first piece in the "Inspiration Africa" series. It was retired in December 1993 at the issue price of $325.

CRV: $1500

Elephant, Large

7640 NR 55/7640 055 000
Designer: Max Schreck
Size: 2-1/2"/64mm
Trademark: SC or Swan

The *Large Elephant* was issued in 1982 and features a floppy metal tail. Some variations in the body size or height have been verified. It was retired in December 1989 at a suggested retail of $90.

SC CRV: $300

Swan CRV: $250

Elephant, Large

7640 NR 60/7640 060 000
Designer: Adi Stocker
Size: 2"/50mm
Trademark: SC or Swan

The *Large Elephant* was issued in 1988 and was part of the "African Wildlife" grouping. The elephant's tail is frosted crystal. It was retired in December 1995 at a suggested retail of $95.

SC CRV: $150

Swan CRV: $125

Elephant, Small

7640 040 000/151 489
Designer: Adi Stocker
Size: 1-1/4"/32mm
Trademark: Swan

The *Small Elephant* was issued in 1989 as part of the "African Wildlife" grouping. It is all made of clear crystal, except for the frosted tail. The current suggested retail is $65.

CRV: $65

Falcon Head, Large

7645 NR 100/7645 100 000
Designer: Max Schreck
Size: 4"/102mm
Trademark: SC or Swan

The *Large Falcon Head* was issued in 1984. One variation exists on the latter-produced pieces, where the bird's neck is flatter than the earlier examples. It was retired in December 1991 at a suggested retail of $825.

SC CRV: $3250
Swan CRV: $2800

Falcon Head, Small

7645 NR 45/7645 045 000
Designer: Max Schreck
Size: 1-3/4"/45mm
Trademark: SC or Swan

The *Small Falcon Head* was issued in 1986. One variation exists with one model having a wider, flatter neck on the front side. It was retired in December 1991 at a suggested retail of $85.

SC CRV: $200
Swan CRV: $185

Fawn

7608 000 002/235 045
Designer: Martin Zendron
Size: 2-1/2"/62mm
Trademark: Swan

The *Fawn* was issued in 1999 to complement the "Woodland Friends" grouping. The current suggested retail is $125.

CRV: $125

Field Mouse

7631 025 000/162 886
Designer: Adi Stocker
Size: 1"/25mm
Trademark: Swan

The *Field Mouse* was introduced in 1991. There are no known variations. The *Field Mouse* has frosted feet and tail. It was retired in December 2002 at a suggested retail of $55.

CRV: $60

Field Mice (Set Of Three)

7631 015 000/181 513
Designer: Adi Stocker
Size: 3/4"/19mm
Trademark: Swan

The *(Set of Three) Field Mice* was issued in 1994. Usually sold as a set of three, these mice have frosted tails. There are no known variations. The current suggested retail is $46.50.

CRV: $46.50

Fish, Mini Telescope

7644 000 010/631103
Designer: Michael Stamey
Size: 1-1/4"/31mm
Trademark: Swan

The *Mini Telescope Fish* was issued in 2004 as part of the "South Sea" theme group. Notable with large protruding eyes in Sahara color. Suggested retail at time of issue was $65.

CRV: $65

Flacon, Napoleon

7482 000 003/265 518
Designer: Anton Hirzinger
Size: 3"/75mm
Trademark: Swan

The *Napoleon Flacon* was issued in 2000. There are no known variations, and it is part of the "Exquisite Accents" grouping. The current suggested retail is $185.

Swan CRV: $185

Flacon, Oriental

7482 000 001/217 826
Designer: Martin Zendron
Size: 4-1/4"/106mm
Trademark: Swan

The *Oriental Flacon* was issued in 1997. There are no known variations, and it is part of the "Exquisite Accents" grouping. It was retired in December 2002 at a suggested retail of $185.

CRV: $200

Flacon, Rose

7482 000 002/236 693
Designer: Martin Zendron
Size: 2-5/8"/68mm
Trademark: Swan

The *Napoleon Flacon* was issued in 1999. There are no known variations, and it is part of the "Exquisite Accents" grouping. It was retired in December 2002 from the Silver Crystal line at the suggested retail of $185.

CRV: $200

Flamingo

7670 000 003/289 733
Designer: Gabriele Stamey
Size: 5-1/2"/70mm
Trademark: Swan

The *Flamingo* was issued in 2002. It has pink highlights on the wing tips. There are no known variations. The current suggested retail is $265.

CRV: $265

Flower Arrangement, Maxi

7478 000 004/252 976
Designer: Michael Stamey
Size: 6-1/2"/150mm
Trademark: Swan

The *Maxi Flower Arrangement* was issued in 2000. The flowers' centers display yellow crystal stones. This is one of the most delicate and complex of pieces with many parts to assemble. The current suggested retail is $540.

CRV: $540

Foals

627637
Designer: Martin Zendron
Size: 3-3/4"/95mm
Trademark: Swan

The *Foals* were issued in the fall of 2003 as part of the "Horses On Parade" theme group. Suggested retail at time of issue was $330. No known variations.

CRV: $330

Fox, Large

7629 NR 70/7629 070 000
Designer: Adi Stocker
Size: 2-3/4"/70mm
Trademark: SC or Swan

The *Large Fox* was issued in 1987. The first pieces produced until 1988 were made with a plain frosted nose. Pieces after 1988 had a black tip at the end of the fox's nose. It was retired in December 1999 at a suggested retail of $75.

SC (Plain Nose) CRV: $150
Swan (Plain Nose) CRV: $125
SC (Black-tipped Nose) CRV: $90
Swan (Black-tipped Nose) CRV: $80

Fox, Mini Running

7677 NR 055/7677 055 000
Designer: Adi Stocker
Size: 1-3/4"/45mm
Trademark: SC or Swan

The *Mini Running Fox* was issued in 1988. This piece has a frosted tail and nose. Some head and tail placement variations exist. It was retired in December 1996 at a suggested retail of $45.

SC CRV: $80
Swan CRV: $70

Fox, Mini Sitting

7677 045 000/014 955
Designer: Adi Stocker
Size: 2-1/4"/57mm
Trademark: SC or Swan

The *Mini Sitting Fox* was issued in 1988, and has a frosted tail and nose. Some head and tail placement variations exist. It was retired in December 2002 at a suggested retail of $45.

SC CRV: $75
Swan CRV: $50

Frog

7642 000 001/183 113
Designer: Gabriele Stamey
Size: 1-1/4"/32mm
Trademark: Swan

The *Frog* was issued in 1994 with blackish-green eyes as part of the "Beauties of the Lake" grouping. The current suggested retail is $49.50.

CRV: $49.50

Frog, Prince (Clear Eyes/Black Eyes)

7642 NR 48/7642 048 000
Designer: Max Schreck
Size: 2"/50mm
Trademark: SC or Swan

The *Prince Frog* was first issued in 1984 with clear eyes. The design changed to black eyes in 1985. It was retired in December 1991 at a suggested retail of $47.50.

SC (Clear Eyes) CRV: $400
SC (Black Eyes) CRV: $175
Swan (Black Eyes) CRV: $160

German Shepherd

7619 000 007/235 484
Designer: Heinz Tabertshofer
Size: 2-3/4"/70mm
Trademark: Swan

The *German Shepherd* was issued in 1999. This design is Heinz Tabertshofer's first entry into the Silver Crystal line. The current suggested retail is $145. There are no known variations.

CRV: $145

Geometric Paperweight

7432 NR 57002/7432 057 002
Designer: Team
Size: 2"/50mm
Trademark: SC or Swan

The *Geometric Paperweight* was issued in 1986. There are no known variations. It was retired in December 1990 at a suggested retail of $85.

SC CRV: $250
Swan CRV: $225

Goat, Zodiac

7693 000 003/275 438
Designer: Anton Hirzinger
Size: 1-5/8"/41mm
Trademark: Swan

The *Zodiac Goat* was issued in 2001. There are no known variations. The current suggested retail is $60.

CRV: $60

Goldfish, Miniature

7644 000 002/202 103
Designer: Michael Stamey
Size: 1-3/4"/44mm
Trademark: Swan

The *Miniature Goldfish* was issued in 1996. This goldfish is very small with green eyes. There are no known variations. It was retired in December 2000 at a suggested retail of $45.

CRV: $60

Goose, Mother

7613 NR 000 001/7613 000 001
Designer: Adi Stocker
Size: 2-1/2"/64mm
Trademark: Swan

The *Mother Goose* was issued in 1993 as part of the "Barnyard Friends" grouping. It has a coordinating frosted beak and feet design element. It was retired in December 1999 at a suggested retail of $75. There are no known variations.

CRV: $95

Gorilla, Young

7618 000 002/273 394
Designer: Adi Stocker
Size: 2-1/2"/64mm
Trademark: Swan

The *Young Gorilla* was issued in 2001, and is adorned with a bunch of bananas. The current suggested retail is $145.

CRV: $145

Gosling, Dick

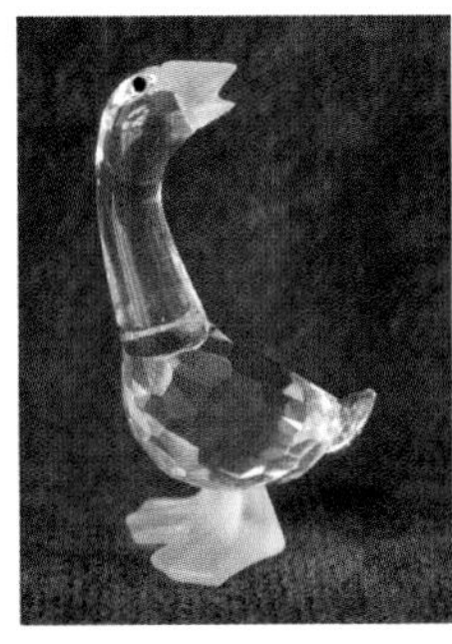

7613 NR 000 004/7613 000 004
Designer: Adi Stocker
Size: 1-3/4"/45mm
Trademark: Swan

The *Dick Gosling* piece was issued in 1993 as part of the "Barnyard Friends" grouping. It has a coordinating frosted beak and feet design element. It was retired in December 1999 with a suggested retail of $37.50.

CRV: $75

Gosling, Harry

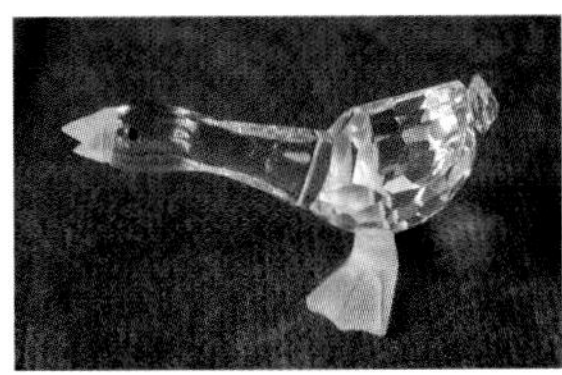

7613 NR 000 003/7613 000 003
Designer: Adi Stocker
Size: 1-3/4"/45mm
Trademark: Swan

The *Harry Gosling* piece was issued in 1993. As part of the "Barnyard Friends" grouping, it has a coordinating frosted beak and feet design element. It was retired in December 1999 at a suggested retail of $37.50. Head and feet placement variations exist.

CRV: $75

Gosling, Tom

7613 NR 000 002/7613 000 002
Designer: Adi Stocker
Size: 1-5/8"/41mm
Trademark: Swan

The *Tom Gosling* piece was issued in 1993. As part of the "Barnyard Friends" grouping, it has a coordinating frosted beak and feet design element. It was retired in December 1999 at a suggested retail of $37.50. There are no known variations.

CRV: $75

Grand Piano & Stool

7477 000 006/174 506
Designer: Martin Zendron
Size: 2-9/16"/67mm
Trademark: Swan

The *Grand Piano with Stool* was issued in 1993. There are no known variations. The current suggested retail is $280. The trademark is located on the sounding board's front.

CRV: $280

Grapes, Gold Or Rhodium

7509 150 070/011 864
Designer: Team
Size: 6-3/8"/162mm
Trademark: SC or Swan

The *Grapes* were issued in 1985 both in the European and American markets. Several variations of the *Grapes* have been produced, with many being offered only in the European market. Some variations have gold leaves, while other have rhodium leaves. The current suggested retail on the U.S. and Canada production piece is $375 U.S. The European designs were discontinued in 1989.

SC; Gold; U.S. CRV: $475
Swan; Gold; U.S. CRV: $375
SC; Gold; Euro CRV: $850
SC; Rhodium; Euro CRV: $900-$1500
Swan; Rhodium; Euro CRV: $900-$1500

Grapes, Large, Gold Or Rhodium

7550 NR 030 015/7550 030 015
Designer: Team
Size: 5-1/2"/140mm
Trademark: SC

The *Large Grapes* were issued in 1983. This style was created for, and marketed only in, the Canadian and U.S. markets. Several metal surface variations exist of the leaves and stem. It was retired in December 1988 at a suggested retail of $270. There is a very limited (rare in quantity) number of the gold leaves and rhodium stem variation.

SC (Gold Leaves/Rhodium Stem) CRV: $3500
SC (Gold Leaves & Stem) CRV: $2500
SC (Rhodium Leaves & Stem) CRV: $3000

Grapes, Medium, Gold Or Rhodium

7550 NR 02029/7550 020 029
Designer: Team
Size: 5"/127mm
Trademark: SC

The *Medium Grapes* were issued in 1983. The medium-size grapes were created for, and marketed only in, the Canadian and U.S. markets. Several metal surface variations exist regarding the leaves and stems. It was retired in 1995 at a suggested retail of $375.

SC (Gold Leaves & Stem) CRV: $450
Swan (Gold Leaves & Stem) CRV: $425
SC (Rhodium Leaves & Stem) CRV: $2000
SC (Gold Leaves/Rhodium Stem) CRV: $1600

Grapes, Small, Gold Or Rhodium

7550 NR 020 015/7550 020 015
Designer: Team
Size: 4"/102mm
Trademark: SC or Swan

The *Small Grapes* were issued in 1983. The *Small Grapes* were created for and marketed only in Canada and the U.S. markets. Several metal surface variations exist regarding the leaves and the stem. It was retired in December 1995 at a suggested retail of $260. The Rhodium versions were discontinued in 1985.

SC (Gold Leaves & Stem) CRV: $395
Swan (Gold Leaves & Stem) CRV: $325
SC (Rhodium Leaves & Stem) CRV: $2500
SC (Rhodium Stem & Gold Leaves) CRV: $2750

Grizzly

7637 000 006/243 880
Designer: Heinz Tabertshofer
Size 3-1/2"/82mm
Trademark: Swan

The *Grizzly* was issued in 2000 as part of the "Woodland Friends" grouping. There are no known variations. The current suggested retail is $330.

CRV: $330

Grizzly Cub

7637 000 007/261 925
Designer: Heinz Tabertshofer
Size: 2-1/4"/55mm
Trademark: Swan

The *Grizzly Cub* was issued in 2001 as part of the "Woodland Friends" grouping. A unique design feature is the silver-metal fish in the cub's mouth. The current suggested retail is $99.

CRV: $99

Harlequin

7400 200 100/254 044
Designer: Anton Hirzinger
Size: 5-1/8"/129mm
Trademark: Swan

The *Harlequin* was issued in 2001 as the annual limited edition redemption piece for members of the Swarovski Collectors Society. *Harlequin* is the third piece in the "Masquerade" series. The etched 01AH stands for the year the piece was designed, plus the artist's initials. It was retired in December 2001 at the issue price of $350.

CRV: $400

Harlequin Plaque

276 870
Designer: Anton Hirzinger
Size: 2-1/4"/63mm
Trademark: Swan Era

The *Harlequin Plaque* was issued in 2001 to complement the *Harlequin* annual limited edition. It is used as a title plaque. It was retired in December 2001 at a suggested retail of $35.

CRV: $75

Harp

7477 NR 000 003/7477 000 003
Designer: Martin Zendron
Size: 4"/102mm
Trademark: Swan

The *Harp* was issued in 1992, and then retired in December 1998 at a suggested retail of $210. There are no known variations.

CRV: $250

Heart, Renewal 1996

9003141991306
Designer: Team
Size: 1-7/16"/37mm
Trademark: Swan

This limited edition heart was issued in 1996 and was given free to Swarovski Collectors Society members as a renewal gift. The *1996 Renewal Heart* is clear. It was retired in December 1996.

CRV: $125

Heart, Renewal 1997

9003141991307
Designer: Team
Size: 1-7/16"/37mm
Trademark: Swan

This limited edition heart was issued in 1997, and was given free to Swarovski Collectors Society members as a renewal gift. The *1997 Renewal Heart* is blue in color. It was retired in December 1997.

CRV: $110

Heart, Renewal 1998

9003141991308
Designer: Team
Size: 1-7/16"/37mm
Trademark: Swan

This limited edition heart was issued in 1998 and was given free to Swarovski Collectors Society members as a renewal gift. The *1998 Renewal Heart* is red in color. It was retired in December 1998.

CRV: $80

Hedgehog, King

7630 NR 60/7630 060 000
Designer: Max Schreck
Size: 2-3/4"/70mm
Trademark: SC

The *King Hedgehog* was exclusively sold in the Canadian and U.S. markets when it was issued in 1982. Features include silver whiskers, and black crystal eyes and nose. It was retired in December 1987 at a suggested retail of $100. This piece is of special interest to worldwide collectors.

CRV: $1200

Hedgehog, Large

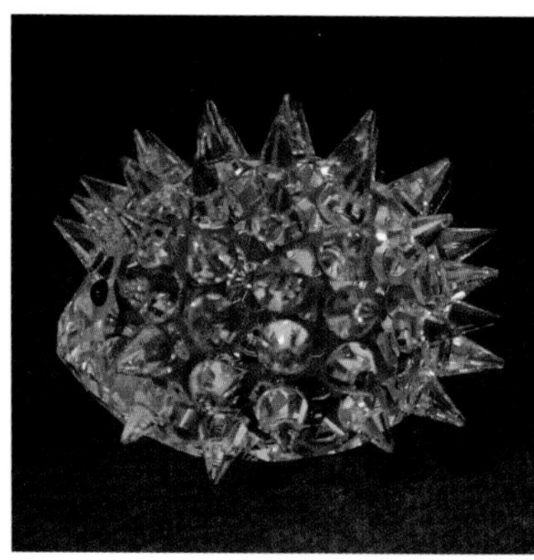

7630 NR 50/7630 050 000
Designer: Max Schreck
Size: 2-1/2"/64mm
Trademark: SC

The *Large Hedgehog* number 50 was issued in 1976 in the European market. This hedgehog has silver whiskers and black crystal eyes and nose. It was retired in December 1987 at a suggested retail of $65.

CRV: $275

Hedgehog, Large

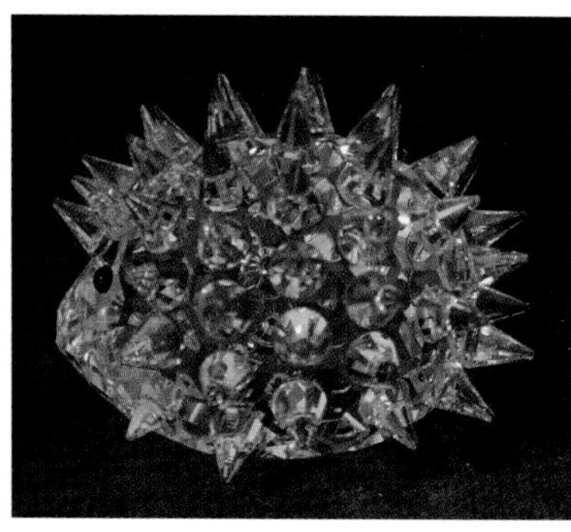

7630 NR 70/7630 070 000
Designer: Max Schreck
Size: 2-3/4"/70mm
Trademark: SC or Swan

The *Large Hedgehog* number 70 was issued in 1985, and does not have whiskers. It was retired in December 1996 at a suggested retail of $140. Known variations include one style with a higher quill density.

SC CRV: $500
Swan CRV: $200

Hedgehog, Medium

7630 NR 40/7630 040 000
Designer: Max Schreck
Size: 2-1/8"/54mm
Trademark: SC

The *Medium Hedgehog* was issued in 1976. This hedgehog has silver metal whiskers and is recognized by its elliptical egg-shaped body. It was retired in December 1987 at a suggested retail of $50. The "not so rare" version has a rounded body shape.

SC (egg shaped) CRV: $2000
SC (round shaped) CRV: $200

Hedgehog, Medium

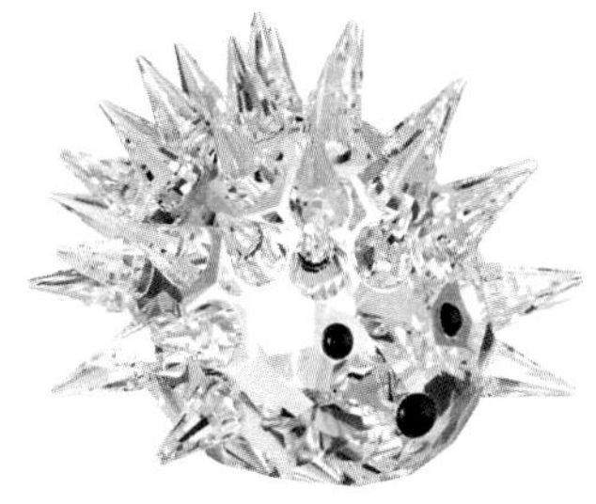

7630 045 000/013 265
Designer: Max Schreck
Size: 2-1/8"/54mm
Trademark: SC or Swan

The *Medium Hedgehog* number 045 was issued in 1985, and is still currently in production. It does not have whiskers. The current suggested retail is $90.

SC CRV: $125
Swan CRV: $90

Hedgehog, Replica

7606 000 002/183 273
Designer: Team
Size: 1"/25mm
Trademark: Swan

The *Replica Hedgehog* was produced as a replica of the *Small Hedgehog* number 7630 NR 30. The *Replica Hedgehog* was issued in 1994 and has silver whiskers and black crystal eyes and nose. At 25mm it is smaller than the 30mm *Small Hedgehog*. The current suggested retail is $42.50.

CRV: $42.50

Hedgehog, Small

7630 NR 30/7630 030 000
Designer: Max Schreck
Size: 1-9/16"/40mm (length)/30mm (width)
Trademark: SC

The *Small Hedgehog* was issued in 1982, and has silver whiskers. This hedgehog was sold exclusively in the Canadian and U.S. markets. It is very desirable to worldwide collectors. It was retired in December 1987 at the suggested retail of $40.

CRV: $500

Hedgehog, Small

7669 035 000/013 989
Designer: Max Schreck
Size: 1-1/2"/38mm
Trademark: SC or Swan

The *Small Hedgehog* was issued worldwide in 1987 when the Canadian and U.S. version was retired. This style has no whiskers. The current suggested retail is $60.

SC CRV: $100
Swan CRV: $60

Hen

7674 000 002/608721
Designer: Michael Stamey
Size: 1-3/4"/44 mm
Trademark: Swan

The *Hen* was issued in 2003. No known variations. Price at time of issue was $75.

MSRP: $75

Hen, Mini

7675 030 000/014 492
Designer: Gabriele Stamey
Size: 1-3/8"/35mm
Trademark: SC or Swan

The *Mini Hen* was issued in 1987, and has a frosted comb and black crystal eyes. It was retired in December 2001 at a suggested retail of $45.

SC CRV: $75
Swan CRV: $60

Heron, Silver

7670 000 001/221 627
Designer: Adi Stocker
Size: 6"/150mm
Trademark: Swan

The *Silver Heron* was issued in 1998. Stately in its presence, it features a golden-brown beak and black crest feathers. The current suggested retail is $280.

CRV: $280

Hippo

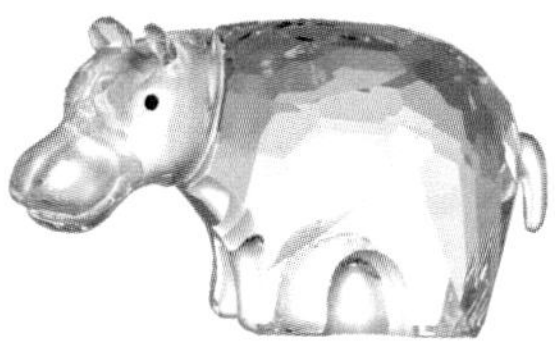

7610 000 005/622940
Designer: Anton Hirzinger
Size: 1-1/8"/29mm
Trademark: Swan

The *Hippo* was issued in 2003. There are no known variations. Price at the time of issue was $65.

MSRP: $65

Hippopotamus, Large

7626 NR 65/7626 065 000
Designer: Adi Stocker
Size: 2-5/8"/67mm
Trademark: SC or Swan

The *Large Hippopotamus* was issued in 1988, and has a frosted tail and black crystal eyes. There are no known variations. It was retired in December 1992 at a suggested retail of $95.

SC CRV: $195
Swan CRV: $175

Hippopotamus, Small

7626 NR055 000/7626 055 000
Designer: Adi Stocker
Size: 2-1/4"/57mm
Trademark: Swan

The *Small Hippopotamus* was issued in 1989 and has a frosted tail and black crystal eyes. There are no known variations. It was retired in December 1995 at a suggested retail of $75.

CRV: $150

Holy Family Arch (For Nativity)

7475 NR 000 010/7475 000 010
Designer: Team
Size: 3-5/8"/92mm
Trademark: Swan

The *Holy Family Arch* was sold as a separate piece in the European market. It was retired in December 1993 at an approximate U.S. equivalent retail of $50. It was to be displayed with the *Holy Family* set as a backdrop.

CRV: $200

Holy Family (Set Of Three)

7475 NR 100 000/7475 100 000
Size: 1-5/8"/38mm
Trademark: Swan

The *Holy Family* as a set of three was sold in the European market and is part of the "Nativity" grouping. It was retired in December 1993 at a U.S. retail equivalent of $175.

CRV: $225

Holy Family With Arch

7475 NR 000 001/7475 001 000
Designer: Team
Size: 3-5/8"/92mm
Trademark: Swan

The *Holy Family with Arch* was sold complete with four pieces everywhere except Europe. It was retired in December 1993 at a suggested retail of $250. There are no known variations.

CRV: $350

Horse, Arabian Stallion

7612 000 002/221 609
Designer: Martin Zendron
Size: 4-1/4"/106mm
Trademark: Swan

The *Arabian Stallion* was issued in 1998. Great care and detail in design made this fragile piece become possible, as horse legs on figurines are extremely fragile. The current suggested retail is $265.

CRV: $265

Horse, Rocking

7479 000 001/183 270
Designer: Gabriele Stamey
Size: 2-3/4"/70mm
Trademark: Swan

The *Rocking Horse* was issued in 1994 as part of the "When We Were Young" grouping. The current suggested retail is $125.

CRV: $125

Horse, White Stallion

7612 000 001/174 958
Designer: Martin Zendron
Size: 4-1/4"/108mm
Trademark: Swan

The *White Stallion* was issued in 1993, and is shown in a rearing position. It is part of the "Horses on Parade" grouping. The current suggested retail is $265.

CRV: $265

Horse, Zodiac

7693 000 005/289 908
Designer: Anton Hirzinger
Size: 1-5/8"/41mm
Trademark: Swan

The *Zodiac Horse* was issued in 1992 as part of the "Chinese Zodiacs" grouping. There are no known variations. The current suggested retail is $65.

CRV: $65

Houses, I & II

7474 NR 100 000/7474 100 000
Designer: Gabriele Stamey
Size: 1-1/4" & 7/8"/32mm & 22mm
Trademark: Swan

The *Houses I & II* were designed as part of the "Silver Crystal City" grouping and were issued in 1990. They were retired in December 1994 at a suggested retail of $75.

CRV: $125

Houses III & IV

7474 NR 200 000/7474 200 000
Designer: Gabriele Stamey
Size: 1-1/4" & 7/8"/32mm & 22mm
Trademark: Swan

The *Houses III & IV* were designed as part of the "Silver Crystal City" grouping and were issued in 1990. They were retired in December 1994 at a suggested retail of $75.

CRV: $125

Hummingbird

7615 000 001/166 184
Designer: Claudia Schneiderbauer
Size: 2-3/8"/60mm
Trademark: Swan

The *Hummingbird* was issued in 1992 and is a very popular subject. There are no known variations. The current suggested retail is $215.

CRV: $215

Hummingbird, Gold

7552 NR 100/7552 100 000
Designer: Team
Size: 4"/ 102mm
Trademark: SC or Swan

The gold *Hummingbird* was issued exclusively in Canada and the U.S. in 1985. This piece proved to be very labor intensive with all the tiny stones hand-applied in the flower's center. This is a very high demand piece with collectors worldwide. It was retired in December 1988 at a suggested retail of $230.

SC CRV: $1500
Swan CRV: $1250

Hummingbird, Rhodium

7552 NR 200/7552 200 000
Designer: Team
Size: 4"/102mm
Trademark: SC

The rhodium *Hummingbird* was issued exclusively in the U.S. market in 1985, and had a short production time. The hand application of all the tiny stones at the flower's center proved to be very labor intensive. There is extremely high demand for this item with collectors worldwide. It was retired in December 1986 at a suggested retail of $200. The rhodium *Hummingbird* is one of the top three sought-after Swarovski Silver Crystal items by collectors.

CRV: $6500

Ibex

7618 000 001/275 439
Designer: Heinz Tabertshofer
Size: 4-1/8"/108mm
Trademark: Swan

The *Ibex* was issued in 2001 and belongs to the "Endangered Species" grouping. There are no known variations. The current suggested retail is $215.

CRV: $215

Isadora

7400 200 200/279 648
Designer: Adi Stocker
Size: 7-7/8"/172mm
Trademark: Swan

Isadora was issued in 2002 as the annual edition for members of the Swarovski Collectors Society. Produced as first in the "Magic of Dance" series, it serves as a tribute piece to famous dancer Isadora Duncan. Etched into the piece is 02AS, representing the design year and the designer's initials. This limited edition piece was retired in December 2002 at the issue/redemption price of $370.

CRV: $450

Isadora Plaque

602 383
Designer: Team
Size: 2-1/2"/62mm
Trademark: Dated 2002

The *Isadora Display Plaque* was produced to provide a title plaque for the limited edition *Isadora Annual Edition*. It was originally sold at a $35 suggested retail.

CRV: $50

Jester

7550 000 011/275 555
Designer: Edith Mair
Size: 7"/175mm
Trademark: Swan

The *Jester* was issued in 2002, and is a complementary piece to the "Fairy Tales" grouping. The current retail is $215.

CRV: $215

Jewel Box, Blue Flower

7464 000 001/207 886
Designer: Gabriele Stamey
Size: 3-1/4"/85mm
Trademark: Swan

The *Blue Flower Jewel Box* was issued in 1996. The removable lid is adorned with a brilliant blue stone. It was retired in December 2000 at a suggested retail of $210. There are no known variations.

CRV: $225

Jewel Box, Sweet Heart

7480 000 002/219 966
Designer: Edith Mair
Size: 2-3/8"/62mm
Trademark: Swan

The *Sweet Heart Jewel Box* was issued in 1998. It is adorned with a blue-colored bow on the removable lid. It was retired in December 2001 at a suggested retail of $140.

CRV: $175

Jubilee Vase Of Roses

7400 200 204/283 394
Designer: Gabriele Stamey
Size: 2-3/4"/70mm
Trademark: Swan

The *Jubilee Vase of Roses* was issued in 2002 to celebrate the fifteenth anniversary of the Swarovski Collectors Society. The vase holds fifteen red roses with silver metal stems in a crystal vase, each of the flowers representing one year of the SCS. It was retired in December 2002 at a suggested retail of $140. This exclusive edition was originally only sold to members of the Swarovski Collectors Society.

CRV: $150

Kangaroo, Mother/Joey

7609 000 001/181 756
Designer: Gabriele Stamey
Size: 2-1/16"/52mm
Trademark: Swan

The *Mother Kangaroo* with Baby Joey was issued in 1994 as part of the "Endangered Species" grouping. There are known variations. The current suggested retail is $99.

CRV: $99

Key Chain, 1989 Renewal Item

SCMR89
Designer: Team
Size: 3/4"/20mm
Trademark: Swan

The *1989 Member Renewal Key Chain* was a gift to renewing members of the Swarovski Collectors Society. It features a blue swan with an SCS inside the crystal ball on the end of the key chain and was limited to SCS members.

CRV: $110

Kingfisher

7621 NR 000 001/7621 000 001
Designer: Michael Stamey
Size: 2-1/8"/54mm
Trademark: Swan

The *Kingfisher* was issued in 1990 as part of the "Up In The Trees" grouping. It was retired after a short production run in December 1992. The suggested retail at retirement was $85. It is somewhat difficult to locate due to the short time in production.

CRV: $185

Kingfishers, Malachite

7621 000 010/623323
Designer: Adi Stocker
Size: 3-13/16"/97mm
Trademark: Swan

The *Malachite Kingfishers* were issued in 2003, and reside on a base reminiscent of *The Lovebirds'* base. Price at time of issue was $160. No known variations.

MSRP: $160

Kitten

7634 NR 028 000/7634 028 000
Designer: Michael Stamey
Size: 1-1/4"/32mm
Trademark: Swan

The *Kitten* was issued in 1991. There are no known variations. It features a crystal tail. It was retired in December 1995 with a suggested retail of $49.50.

CRV: $110

Kitten, Lying

631857
Designer: Hainz Tabertshofer
Size: 15/16"/23mm
Trademark: Swan

The *Lying Kitten* was issued in 2004 as part of the "Pet's Corner" grouping. Suggested retail at time of issue was $90. No known variations.

CRV: $90

Kitten, Standing

631856
Designer: Heinz Tabertshofer
Size: 15/16"/23mm
Trademark: Swan

The *Standing Kitten* was issued in 2004 as part of the "Pet's Corner" grouping. Suggested retail at time of issue was $90. No known variations.

CRV: $90

Kiwi

7617 NR 043 000/7617 043 000
Designer: Michael Stamey
Size: 1-3/4"/45mm
Trademark: Swan

The *Kiwi* was issued in 1991 as part of the "Endangered Species" grouping. It was retired in December 1996 at a suggested retail of $45. The recent demand for this item has caused movement upward in the price of the Kiwi.

CRV: $130

Kristallwelten Wall

9990 NR 000 006
Designer: Team
Size: 4-3/4"/119mm
Trademark: Swan Era

This special limited edition Swarovski Silver Crystal showpiece is only sold at the gift shop at Kristallwelten in Wattens, Austria. First available in 1997. In demand on secondary market due to limited availability.

CRV: $400

Kudu

DO1X941/175 703
Designer: Michael Stamey
Size: 3-7/8"/98mm
Trademark: Swan/SCS

The *Kudu* was issued in 1994 as the limited annual edition for members of the Swarovski Collectors Society. A black wooden stand was offered at a suggested retail of $29.50. Oftentimes these stands were given to collectors as a gift with purchase. The stand currently has a replacement value of $90. The *Kudu* was retired in December 1994 at the issue price of $295.

CRV: $575

Ladybug

7604 000 001/190 858
Designer: Edith Mair
Size: 1"/25mm
Trademark: Swan

The *Ladybug* was issued in 1995 and has a black crystal head and black crystals to represent the spots on the body. The current suggested retail is $29.50.

CRV: $29.50

Ladybug Picture Frame

7506 000 003/211 739
Designer: Edith Mair
Size: 5-1/2"/138mm
Trademark: Swan

The *Ladybug Picture Frame* was issued in 1997 as a part of the "Exquisite Accents" grouping. It was retired in December 2000 at a suggested retail of $55. There are no known variations.

CRV: $70

Leopard

7610 000 002/217 093
Designer: Michael Stamey
Size: 5-1/2"/167mm
Trademark: Swan

The *Leopard* was issued in 1997. There are no known variations. The current suggested retail is $265.

CRV: $265

Lion

7610 000 004/269 377
Designer: Martin Zendron
Size: 4-3/4"/120mm
Trademark: Swan

The *Lion* was issued in 2001 and is noteworthy for the newer sculpted design and clear crystal body. The current suggested retail is $330.

CRV: $330

Lion Cub

760 300 001/210 460
Designer: Adi Stocker
Size: 2-1/2"/62mm
Trademark: Swan

The *Lion Cub* was issued in 1997 as part of the "African Wildlife" grouping. No known variations.

CRV: $125

Lion, The

DO1X951/185 410
Designer: Adi Stocker
Size: 5"/127mm
Trademark: Swan (SCS)

The *Lion* was issued in 1995 as the limited annual edition for members of the Swarovski Collectors Society. A black wooden stand was sold at a suggested retail of $29.50. Many retailers gave this stand as a gift with purchase. The stand currently has a replacement value of $70. The *Lion* was retired in December 1995 at the suggested retail of $325. There are no known variations.

CRV: $600

Lion Fish

7644 000 008/604 011
Designer: Martin Zendron
Size: 2-5/8"/91mm
Trademark: Swan

The *Lion Fish* was issued in 2002 as a new introduction to the "South Sea" grouping. There are no known variations. This is a very fragile design. The current suggested retail is $145.

CRV: $145

Little Red Riding Hood

7550 000 001/191 695
Designer: Edith Mair
Size: 3-1/2"/86mm
Trademark: Swan

Little Red Riding Hood was issued in 1996. The girl's basket is a separate piece that she holds. There are no known variations. The current suggested retail is $190.

CRV: $190

Locomotive

7471 000 001/015 145
Designer: Gabriele Stamey
Size: 2-1/2"/64mm
Trademark: SC or Swan

The *Locomotive* was issued in 1988 as a component to the train set. There are no known variations. It was retired in December 2003 at a suggested retail of $155. The train was originally sold as a set, but was later offered as individual pieces.

SC CRV: $200
Swan CRV: $170

Lovebirds, Annual Edition

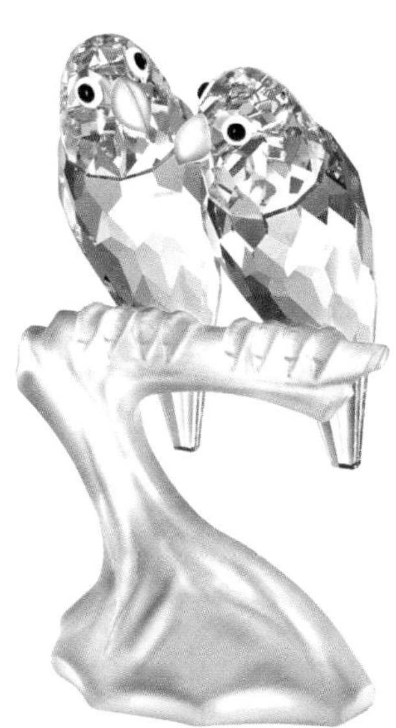

DO1X861/013 560
Designer: Max Schreck
Size: 4-1/16"/103mm
Trademark: SCS

The *Lovebirds* was the very first annual edition issued to members of the Swarovski Collectors Society in 1987. It was only available in Canada, the U.S., and Great Britain during that first year of issue. There is a very high demand for this piece by collectors worldwide. There are no known variations. The suggested retail at the time of issue was $150.

CRV: $4000-$5000

Luggage Tag, Member Renewal

SCMR93
Designer: Team
Size: 3-1/2"/89mm
Trademark: Swan/SCS

The black leather *Luggage Tag* was given to Swarovski Collectors Society club members renewing their membership for the year during 1993. It is adorned with a Swarovski crystal. It was retired in December 1993.

CRV: $50

Lute

7477 NR 000 004/7477 000 004
Designer: Martin Zendron
Size: 3-3/8"/85mm
Trademark: Swan

The *Lute* was issued in 1992 and was sold with an accompanying rhodium stand. There are no known variations. It was retired in December 1997 at a suggested retail of $140.

CRV: $160

Madame Penguin

7661 NR 000 002/7661 000 002
Designer: Adi Stocker
Size: 1-1/2"/38mm
Trademark: Swan

The *Madame Penguin* was issued in 1996, and was sold with a plastic base that is shaped like the continent of Antarctica. There are no known variations. It was retired in December 1999 at a suggested retail of $85.

CRV: $110

Maginfier, Chain Style, Gold

7800 NR 026/7800 026 001
Designer: Team
Size: 3-3/4"/92mm
Trademark: SC

The *Magnifier with Gold Chain* was introduced in the late 1970s. Many pieces are found without the SC trademark. It was retired in 1984 at an approximate U.S. retail of $70. It is a difficult secondary market find.

CRV: $1500

Magnifier, Chain Style, Rhodium

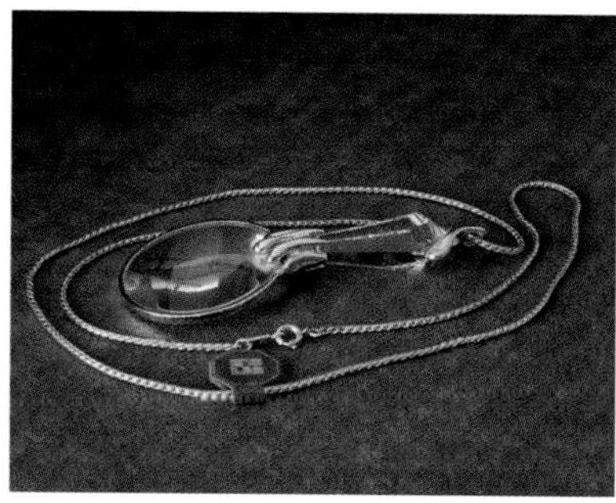

7800 NR 026/7800 026 002
Designer: Team
Size: 3-3/4"/92mm
Trademark: SC

The *Magnifier with Rhodium Chain* was introduced in the late 1970s. Many pieces have been found without the SC trademark. It was retired in 1984 at an approximate U.S. retail of $70. It is a difficult secondary market find.

CRV: $1500

Magnifier, Table, Gold

7510 NR 01/7510 001 001
Designer: Team
Size: 3-5/8"/92mm
Trademark: SC

The gold *Table Magnifier* was issued in 1978, and many have been found without the SC trademark stamped into the metal. It was retired in December 1983 at a suggested retail of $70. It is a difficult secondary market find.

CRV: $1350

Magnifier, Table, Rhodium

7510 NR 01/7510 001 002
Designer: Team
Size: 3-5/8"/92mm
Trademark: SC

The rhodium *Table Magnifier* was issued in 1978, and many have been found without the SC trademark stamped into the metal. It was retired in December 1983 at the suggested retail of $70. It is a difficult secondary market find.

CRV: $1250

Mallard:
(See Duck, Mallard)

Marguerite, 1999 Renewal

9003140086126
Designer: Team
Size: 2"/50mm
Trademark: Swan

The *1999 Renewal Marguerite* is a limited edition renewal gift that was presented to Swarovski Collectors Society members renewing their Society membership in 1999. It was retired in December 1999. The flower is yellow.

CRV: $60-$75

Marguerite, 2000 Renewal

9003140086127
Designer: Team
Size: 2"/50mm
Trademark: Swan

The *2000 Renewal Marguerite* is a limited edition renewal gift that was presented to Swarovski Collectors Society members renewing their Society membership in 2000. It was retired in December 2001. The flower is red.

CRV: $50-$60

Marguerite, 2001 Renewal

227 537
Designer: Team
Size: 2"/50mm
Trademark: Swan

The *2001 Renewal Marguerite* is a limited edition renewal gift that was presented to Swarovski Collectors Society members renewing their society membership in 2001. It was retired in December 2001. The flower is green.

CRV: $60-$75

Maritime Trio

7624 100 000/191 697
Designer: Michael Stamey
Sizes: Conch: 1-3/8"/35mm
Shell: 1-1/4"/32mm
Starfish: 1-3/4"/45mm
Trademark: Swan

The *Maritime Trio* was introduced in 1995 as a three-piece set: the *Conch, Shell,* and *Starfish*. There are no known variations. It was retired in December 2003 at a suggested retail of $104.

CRV: $125

Marmot

7608 000 005/289 305
Designer: Heinz Tabertshofer
Size: 2-1/2"/62mm
Trademark. Swan

The *Marmot* was issued in 2002. Marmot is another name for the U.S. groundhog, and is comparable in size to the raccoon. The current suggested retail is $75. There are no known variations.

CRV: $75

Minnie Mouse

14012002
Designer: Arribas Brothers
Size: 2-3/8"/63mm
Trademark: © Disney

Minnie Mouse was specially produced for sale at the Arribas Brothers Stores at Disney Theme Parks and was issued in 1999. It was a limited edition of 10,000 pieces. The suggested retail was $295.

CRV: $325

Mickey Mouse

14012000
Designer: Arribas Brothers
Size: 2-1/4"/56mm
Trademark: © Disney

Mickey Mouse was specially produced for sale at the Arribas Brothers Stores at Disney Theme Parks and was issued in 1997. It was a limited edition of 10,000 pieces. It was retired in 1997 at the issue price of $295.

CRV: $500

Monkey, Zodiac

7693 000 004/289 901
Designer: Anton Hirzinger
Size 1-1/2"/37mm
Trademark: Swan

The *Zodiac Monkey* was issued in 2002 as part of the "Chinese Zodiacs" grouping. There are no known variations. The current suggested retail is $60.

CRV: $60

Mouse, King

7631 NR 60/7631 060 000
Designer: Max Schreck
Size: 3-3/4"/95mm
Trademark: SC

The *King Mouse* was issued in 1982 exclusively in the U.S. and Canada. There are no known variations. It is easily recognized by its big ears measuring 2" in length. It was retired in December 1987 at a suggested retail of $100.

CRV: $2500

Mouse, Large

7631 NR 50/7631 050 000
Designer: Max Schreck
Size: 2-7/8"/73mm
Trademark: SC

The *Large Mouse* was issued in 1982 exclusively in the U.S. and Canada markets. Two variations exist, one with a closer eye placement than the other. Both styles have a spring-coil tail. It is very much in demand on the secondary market worldwide. It was retired in December 1987 at a suggested retail of $70.

CRV: $1200

Mouse, Medium

7631 NR 40/7631 040 000
Designer: Max Schreck
Size: 2-1/2"/65mm
Trademark: SC or Swan

The *Medium Mouse* was issued in 1976. There are five distinct variations. At the time of issue, 1,000 limited edition pieces with a leather tail were produced for Swarovski employees (**CRV: $2750**). Other variations have a floppy braided metal tail, a spring-coil tail, a flexible braided tail, and varying cuts on the ear stones. It was retired in December 1995 at a suggested retail of $60.

SC CRV: $200
Swan CRV: $125
SC (flexible braided tail) CRV: $950

Mouse, Mini

7655 NR 23/7655 023 000
Designer: Max Schreck
Size: 13/16"/21mm
Trademark: SC or Swan

The *Mini Mouse* was issued in 1979 and features a spring-coil tail. It does not have a base. The *Mini Mouse* was retired in December 1988 at a suggested retail of $25.

SC CRV: $85
Swan CRV: $75

Mouse, Replica

7606 000 001/183 272
Designer: Team
Size: 1-1/4"/31mm
Trademark: Swan

The *Replica Mouse* was initially issued in 1994 as part of a "Starter Set" of three animals. It features a foil-coated leather tail with metal whiskers. It was retired as a three-piece set in December 2003, but sold individually at a current suggested retail of $42.50.

Swan CRV: $42.50

Mouse, Small

7631 NR 30/7631 030 000
Designer: Max Schreck
Size: 1-11/16"/43mm
Trademark: SC or Swan

The *Small Mouse* was issued in 1976 and can be found in three variations with distinctly different values. The rarest variation features a leather, foil-coated tail (**SC CRV: $3250**). The other two feature a flexible braided tail, and the other a spring-coil tail. It was retired in December 1991 at a suggested retail of $42.50.

SC (Flexible braided tail) CRV: $395
SC (Spring coil tail) CRV: $150
Swan (Spring coil tail) CRV: $125

Mushrooms

7472 NR 030/7472 030 000
Designer: Adi Stocker
Size: 1-1/4"/30mm
Trademark: Swan

The *Mushrooms* were issued in 1989 as part of the "Woodland Friends" grouping. It was retired in December 1998 at a suggested retail of $45.

CRV: $75

Necklace, Swan, Member

7855/001 (Necklace)
Designer: Team
Size: 5/8"/16mm
Trademark: Swan/SCS

The *Swan Necklace* was issued to Swarovski Collectors Society members as a gift, and was used by some retailers as a gift with purchase at special events. It was retired in 1995 in the gift form, but is still sold as a Swarovski jewelry item.

CRV: $85-$100

Night Owl

7636 000 002/206 138
Designer: Anton Hirzinger
Size: 1-15/16"/48mm
Trademark: Swan

The *Night Owl* was issued in 1996. There are no known variations. It was retired in December 2001 at a suggested retail of $85.

CRV: $100

Nutcracker

7475 000 604/236 714
Designer: Anton Hirzinger
Size: 3-1/4"/82mm
Trademark: Swan

The *Nutcracker* was issued in 1999 and was produced for a relatively short time. It was retired in December 2003 at a suggested retail of $155. There are no known variations.

CRV: $175

Octron Penholder

7457 NR 41/7457 041 000
Designer: Team
Size: 1-5/8"/41mm
Trademark: SC

The *Octron Penholder* was issued in the late 1970s as a functional desk item. Some pieces have been found with etched designs. There are no known size variations. It was retired in December 1981 at a suggested retail of $100.

SC CRV: $4500

Open Shell With Pearl

7624 055 000/014 389
Designer: Michael Stamey
Size: 2-1/2"/64mm
Trademark: SC or Swan

The *Open Shell with Pearl* was issued in 1988 and is unique with a faux pearl inside the open shell. The current suggested retail is $175. There are no known variations.

SC CRV: $200
Swan CRV: $175

Orca

7644 000 009/622939
Designer: Michael Stamey
Size: 4"/100mm
Trademark: Swan

The *Orca* was issued in 2003. No known variations. The price at issue was $300.

CRV: $300

Orchid, Pink

7478 000 003/200 287
Designer: Michael Stamey
Size: 3"/75mm
Trademark: Swan

The *Orchid in Pink* was issued in 1996. A few pieces were produced with two distinctly lighter shades until the company decided to go with the darkest of the three shades of pink. It was issued with a small pillow upon which to display the delicate crystal orchid. The current suggested retail is $145.

Swan/Light Pink CRV: $300
Swan/Medium Pink CRV: $250
Swan/Darkest Pink CRV: $145

Orchid, Yellow

7478 000 002/200 280
Designer: Michael Stamey
Size: 3"/75mm
Trademark: Swan

The *Orchid in the Yellow* coloration was issued in 1996. The first pieces produced were too pale, so the color was made more intense, or darker, in color. It was retired in December 2000 at a suggested retail of $140.

Swan/Light Yellow CRV: $300
Swan/Darker Yellow CRV: $225

Ornament, Christmas 1981

1981 Annual Christmas Ornament
Designer: Team
Size: 1-15/16"/49mm
Trademark: SC

The *1981 Annual Limited Edition Christmas Ornament* was issued with a chain to allow the piece to also be worn as a holiday necklace. The SC trademark is visible on the metal hanger. It was only issued in the U.S. market, and is in very high demand by worldwide collectors. The issue price was approximately $10-$12, and it was limited to 1981 production only.

CRV: $450

Ornament, Christmas 1984

1984 Annual Christmas Ornament
Designer: Team
Size: 2-1/2"/64mm
Trademark: SC Era

The *1984 Annual Limited Edition Christmas Ornament* was produced for one year only as a tree ornament. It is extremely rare and in demand among worldwide collectors. The issue price was approximately $10-$12 in the U.S.

CRV: $600

Ornaments, Christmas 1986

1986 Annual Christmas Ornament
Designer: Team
Size: Varied
Trademark: SC Era

The *1986 Annual Christmas Ornaments* were issued in eleven different sizes and shapes. Sold only in the U.S., they can be identified by the year 1986 clearly etched on each ornament. The suggested retail at the year of issue was $12.50.

CRV: $400

Ornament, Christmas 1987

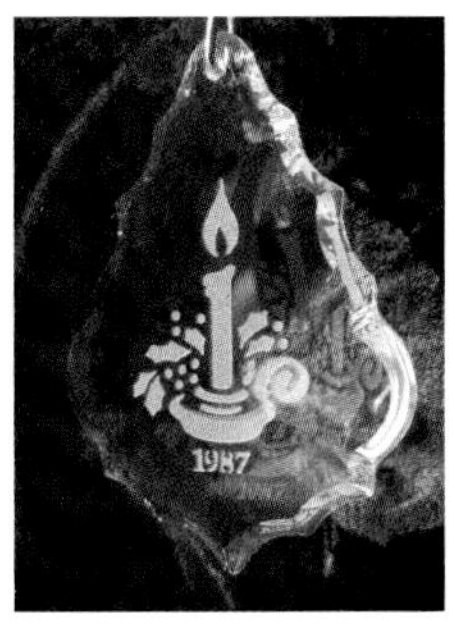

1987 Annual Christmas Ornament
Designer: Team
Size: 2-1/2"/64mm
Trademark: SC Era

The *1987 Annual Christmas Ornament* was issued in the U.S. market only, making it very much in demand by worldwide collectors. The box says "Giftware Suite." The suggested retail at the year of issue was approximately $12.50, and was a limited edition one-time production.

CRV: $400

Ornament, Christmas 1988

1988 Annual Christmas Ornament
Designer: Team
Size: 1-15/16"/49mm
Trademark: Swan Era

The *1988 Annual Christmas Ornament* was issued in the U.S. exclusively. The box says "Giftware Suite," and it has the word "Peace" and the 1988 date etched on the front. This limited annual edition sold for $12.50 in its year of issue.

CRV: $125

Ornament, Christmas 1989

1989 Annual Christmas Ornament
Designer: Team
Size: 2-3/4"/70mm
Trademark: Swan Era

The *1989 Annual Christmas Ornament* was issued in the U.S. market only. This ornament is in demand by worldwide collectors. The box says "Giftware Suites." The suggested retail was approximately $15 during its year of issue.

CRV: $400

Ornament, Christmas 1990

1990 Annual Christmas Ornament
Designer: Team
Size: 1-1/4"/30mm
Trademark: Swan Era

The *1990 Annual Christmas Ornament* was issued in the U.S. market only. "Merry Christmas 1990" is etched onto the front surface, and it features a metal holly sprig as the decorative hanger. The suggested retail was approximately $15 during its year of issue. Limited annual edition.

CRV: $325

Ornament, Christmas 1991

1991 Annual Christmas Ornament
Designer: Team
Size: 2-1/2"/65mm
Trademark: Swan Era

The *1991 Annual Christmas Ornament* was issued in the U.S. and European markets. The year "1991" is etched onto the front of both versions. The European version features a gold-plated hanger, whereas the U.S. version is silver colored. The suggested retail in the U.S. was approximately $25 during the year of issue.

U.S. CRV: $500
European CRV: $475

Ornament, Christmas 1992

1992 Annual Christmas Ornament
Designer: Team
Size: 2-1/2"/65mm
Trademark: Swan Era

The *1992 Annual Christmas Ornament* was issued at a U.S. suggested retail of $35. The year "1992" is etched on the ornament's front. There are no known variations. Like all the annual ornaments until 1995, there is no visible trademark.

CRV: $225

Ornament, Christmas 1993

1993 Annual Christmas Ornament
9445 NR 930 001
Designer: Team
Size: 3"/75mm
Trademark: Swan Era

The *1993 Annual Christmas Ornament* was issued with a metal tag near the hanger with the year engraved on it. Retailers reported a rather quick sellout of this ornament. The suggested retail during the year of issue was $37.50. This ornament has strong demand on the secondary market.

CRV: $450

Ornament, Christmas 1994

1994 Annual Christmas Ornament
9445 NR 940 001
Designer: Team
Size: 2"/50mm
Trademark: Swan Era

The *1994 Annual Christmas Ornament* was issued with a metal tag near the hanger with the year engraved on it. The suggested retail during the year of issue was $37.50. There are no known variations.

CRV: $250

Ornament, Christmas 1995

1995 Annual Christmas Ornament
9445 NR 950 001
Designer: Team
Size: 3-1/8"/80mm
Trademark: Swan

The *1995 Annual Christmas Ornament* was the first year that the swan logo appeared on the crystal itself. It has a metal tag with the year "1995" engraved on it. The suggested retail during the year of issue was $40.

CRV: $200

Ornament, Christmas 1996

1996 Annual Christmas Ornament
9445 NR 960 001
Designer: Martin Zendron
Size: 2-1/8"/54mm
Trademark: Swan

The *1996 Annual Christmas Ornament* was the first annual ornament with a designer designation by Swarovski. It has a metal tag with "1996" engraved on it. The suggested retail during the year of issue was $45.

CRV: $100

Ornament, Christmas 1997

1997 Annual Christmas Ornament
9445 NR 970 001
Designer: Martin Zendron
Size: 3-1/2"/87mm
Trademark: Swan

The *1997 Annual Christmas Ornament* was issued at a suggested retail of $45. It has a metal tag attached near the hanger with "1997" engraved on it. There are no known variations.

CRV: $100

Ornament, Christmas 1998

1998 Annual Christmas Ornament
9445 NR 980 001
Designer: Martin Zendron
Size: 3"/75mm
Trademark: Swan

The *1998 Annual Christmas Ornament* was issued at a suggested retail of $49.50. It has a metal tag attached near the hanger with "1998" engraved on it. There are no known variations.

CRV: $95

Ornament, Christmas 1999

1999 Annual Christmas Ornament
9445 NR 990 001
Designer: Martin Zendron
Size: 3"/75mm
Trademark: Swan

The *1999 Annual Christmas Ornament* was issued at a suggested retail of $55. It has a metal tag attached near the hanger with "1999" engraved on it. There are no known variations. Increasing demand saw this ornament quickly sell out.

CRV: $150

Ornament, Christmas 2000

2000 Annual Christmas Ornament
9445 NR 200 001
Designer: Martin Zendron
Size: 3"/75mm
Trademark: Swan

The *2000 Annual Christmas Ornament* was issued at a suggested retail of $55. It has a metal tag attached near the hanger with "2000" engraved on it. There are no known variations.

CRV: $175

Ornament, Christmas 2001

2001 Annual Christmas Ornament
9445 NR 200 101/267 942
Size: 3"/75mm
Trademark: Swan

The *2001 Annual Christmas Ornament* was issued at a suggested retail of $55. It has a metal tag attached near the hanger with "2001" engraved on it. There are no known variations.

CRV: $100

Ornament, Christmas 2002

2002 Annual Christmas Ornament
9445 NR 200 201/288 802
Designer: Team
Size: 3"/75mm
Trademark: Swan

The *2002 Annual Christmas Ornament* was issued at a suggested retail of $55. It has a metal tag attached near the hanger with "2002" engraved on it. There are no known variations.

CRV: $100

Ornament, Christmas 2003

2003 Annual Christmas Ornament
9445 NR 200 301/622 498
Designer: Team
Size: 2-3/4"/70mm
Trademark: Swan

The *2003 Annual Christmas Ornament* was issued at a suggested retail of $60. It has a metal tag attached near the hanger with "2003" engraved on it. There are no known variations.

CRV: $75

Ornament, Christmas 2004

9445 NR 200 401/631 562
Designer: Edith Mair
Size: 2-7/8"/73mm
Trademark: Swan

The *2004 Annual Ornament* features eleven star-spikes with a large central piece. Annual date is on the rhodium hanger. Issue price was $60.

CRV: $60

Ornament, Little Snowflake

663 147
Designer: Edith Mair
Size: 1-7/8"/48mm
Trademark: Swan

The *Little Snowflake Ornament* is the second of the series of smaller-sized ornaments issued in 2004. These ornaments are not limited to one year of production like the annual ornament. The *Little Snowflake Ornament* features six star-spikes attached to a small central piece.

CRV: $35

Ornament, Little Star

9455 NR 200 302/629 306
Designer: Edith Mair
Size: 1-7/8"/48mm
Trademark: Swan

The *Little Star Ornament* was the first in the series of smaller-sized ornaments and will be produced on a current continuous basis. Originally issued in 2003 at a suggested retail price of $25. The Swan logo is etched directly into the crystal.

CRV: $27.50

Owl

7621 NR 000 003/7621 000 003
Designer: Michael Stamey
Size: 2-1/16"/52mm
Trademark: Swan

The *Owl* was issued in 1989 as part of the "Up In The Trees" grouping. There are no known variations. It was retired in December 1992 at a suggested retail of $85.

CRV: $275

Owl, Giant

7636 165 000/010 125
Designer: Max Schreck
Size: 6-1/2"/165mm
Trademark: SC or Swan

The *Giant Owl* was issued in 1983. There are no known variations. The current suggested retail is $2055.

SC CRV: $3000
Swan CRV: $2055

Owl, Large

7636 060 000/010 022
Designer: Max Schreck
Size: 2-5/8"/69mm
Trademark: SC or Swan

The *Large Owl* was issued in 1979. There are no known variations. The current suggested retail is $130.

SC CRV: $175
Swan CRV: $130

Owl, Mini

7654 038 000/010 014
Designer: Max Schreck
Size: 1-3/8"/35mm
Trademark: SC or Swan

The *Mini Owl* was issued in 1979. Variations have been seen in different colors for the eyes: some have blue stones for the eyes while the normal eye color is green. The current suggested retail is $29.50.

SC CRV: $50
Swan CRV: $29.50

Owl, Small

7636 NR 46/7646 046 000
Designer: Max Schreck
Size: 1-15/16"/49mm
Trademark: SC or Swan

The *Small Owl* was issued in 1979. There are no known variations. It was retired in December 1995 at a suggested retail of $85.

SC CRV: $125
Swan CRV: $100

Owlet

7636 000 001/188 386
Designer: Anton Hirzinger
Size: 1-1/2"/38mm
Trademark: Swan

The *Owlet* was issued in 1995. There are no known variations. It was retired in December 2000 at a suggested retail of $45.

CRV: $70

Ox, Zodiac

7693 000 002/275 437
Designer: Anton Hirzinger
Size: 2-1/2"/63mm
Trademark: Swan

The *Zodiac Ox* was issued in 2001. There are no known variations. The current suggested retail is $65.

CRV: $65

Paperweight, Atomic, Bermuda Blue

7454 NR 060 088/7454 060 088
Designer: Max Schreck
Size: 2-3/4"/70mm high
Trademark: SC

The *Bermuda Blue Atomic Paperweight* was not distributed in the U.S. when issued in 1976. The facets on the paperweight are hexagonally shaped. Oftentimes these paperweights are found with no visible trademark. The equivalent U.S. price at retirement was approximately $80. It was retired on July 1, 1985.

CRV: $1500

Paperweight, Atomic, Crystal Cal

7454 NR 060 095/7454 060 095
Designer: Max Schreck
Size: 2-3/4"/70mm
Trademark: SC

The *Crystal Cal Atomic Paperweight* was introduced in 1976 worldwide. The facets on the paperweight are hexagonally shaped. Oftentimes these paperweights are found with no visible trademark. The suggested retail price in the U.S. was $80. The piece was retired on July 1, 1985.

CRV: $1400

Paperweight, Atomic, Helio

7454 NR 060/7454 060 000
Designer: Max Schreck
Size: 2-3/4"/70mm
Trademark: SC

The *Helio Atomic Paperweight* was not distributed in the U.S. when issued in 1976. The facets on the paperweight are hexagonally shaped. Oftentimes these paperweights are found with no visible trademark. The equivalent U.S. price at retirement was approximately $80. It was retired July 1, 1985.

CRV: $2750

Paperweight, Atomic, Inn Green

7454 NR 06090/7454 060 090
Designer: Max Schreck
Size: 2-3/4"/70mm
Trademark: SC

The *Inn Green Atomic Paperweight* was not distributed in the U.S. when issued in 1976. The facets on the paperweight are hexagonally shaped. Oftentimes these paperweights are found with no visible trademark. The equivalent U.S. price at retirement was approximately $80. It was retired July 1, 1985.

CRV: $2400

Paperweight, Atomic, Sahara

7454 NR 060/7454 060 000
Designer: Max Schreck
Size: 2-3/4"/70mm
Trademark: SC

The *Sahara Paperweight* is known to be the rarest color to locate. The Sahara color was not distributed in the U.S. when issued in 1976. Often these paperweights are found with no visible trademark. The equivalent U.S. price at retirement was approximately $80. It was retired July 1, 1985.

CRV: $3500

Paperweight, Atomic, Seal

7454 NR 060/7454 060 000
Designer: Max Schreck
Size: 2-3/4"/70mm
Trademark: SC

The *Seal Atomic Paperweight* was not distributed in the U.S. when issued in 1976. The facets on the paperweight are hexagonally shaped. Oftentimes these paperweights are found with no visible trademark. The equivalent U.S. price at retirement was approximately $80. It was retired July 1, 1985.

CRV: $2500

Paperweight, Atomic, (Tabac)

7454 NR 060/7454 060 000
Designer: Max Schreck
Size: 2-3/4"/70mm
Trademark: SC

The *Tabac Atomic Paperweight* was not distributed in the U.S. when issued in 1976. The facets are hexagonally shaped. Oftentimes these paperweights are found with no visible trademarks. The equivalent U.S. price at retirement was approximately $80. It was retired July 1, 1985.

CRV: $2500

Paperweight, Atomic, Vitrail Light

7454 NR 060/7454 060 000
Designer: Max Schreck
Size: 2-3/4"/70mm
Trademark: SC

The *Vitrail Light Atomic Paperweight* was not distributed in the U.S. when issued in 1976. The facets on the paperweight are hexagonally shaped. Oftentimes these paperweights are found with no visible trademark. The equivalent U.S. price at retirement was $80. It was retired July 1, 1985.

CRV: $3000

Paperweight, Atomic, Vitrail Medium

7454 NR 060 087/7454 060 087
Designer: Max Schreck
Size: 2-3/4"/70mm
Trademark: SC

The *Vitrail Medium Atomic Paperweight* was distributed in the U.S. when issued in 1976. The facets on the paperweight are hexagonally shaped. Oftentimes these paperweights are found with no visible trademark. The suggested retail in the U.S. was $80 when it was retired July 1, 1985.

CRV: $1500

Paperweight, Atomic, Volcano

7454 NR 060/7454 060 000
Designer: Max Schreck
Size: 2-3/4"/70mm
Trademark: SC

The *Volcano Atomic Paperweight* was not distributed in the U.S. when issued in 1976. The facets on the paperweight are hexagonally shaped. Oftentimes these paperweights are found with no visible trademark. The equivalent U.S. price at retirement was approximately $80. It was retired July 1, 1985.

CRV: $2500

Paperweight, Barrel, Bermuda Blue

7453 NR 060 088/7453 060 088
Designer: Max Schreck
Size: 2-5/8"/67mm
Trademark: SC

The *Bermuda Blue Barrel Paperweight* was not distributed in the U.S. The facets are rectangular in shape. It was issued in 1976. Oftentimes these paperweights are found with no visible trademark. The U.S. equivalent retail when it was retired in 1987 was approximately $140.

CRV: $775

Paperweight, Barrel, Crystal Cal

7453 NR 60095/7453 060 095
Designer: Max Schreck
Size: 2-5/8"/67mm
Trademark: SC

The *Crystal Cal Barrel Paperweight* was issued in 1976 and was sold in the U.S. The facets are rectangular in shape. Oftentimes these paperweights have no visible trademark. The suggested retail was $140 when the paperweight was retired December 1988.

CRV: $625

Paperweight, Barrel, Helio

7453 NR 060/7453 060 000
Designer: Max Schreck
Size: 2-5/8"/67mm
Trademark: SC

The *Helio Barrel Paperweight* was issued in 1976 and was not distributed in the U.S. The facets are rectangular in shape. Oftentimes these paperweights have no visible trademark. The equivalent U.S. price at retirement was approximately $140. It was retired in December 1987.

CRV: $1500

Paperweight, Barrel, Inn Green

7453 NR 060 090/7453 060 090
Designer: Max Schreck
Size: 2-5/8"/67mm
Trademark: SC

The *Inn Green Barrel Paperweight* was issued in 1976 and was not sold in the U.S. The facets on these paperweights are rectangular in shape. Oftentimes they have no visible trademark. The equivalent U.S. price at retirement was approximately $140. It was retired in December 1987.

CRV: $1500

Paperweight, Barrel, Sahara

7453 NR 060/7453 060 000
Designer: Max Schreck
Size: 2-5/8"/67mm
Trademark: SC

The *Sahara Barrel Paperweight* was issued in 1976 and was not distributed in the U.S. The facets are rectangular in shape.

Oftentimes these paperweights have no visible trademark. The equivalent U.S. price at retirement was approximately $140. It was retired in December 1987.

CRV: $1750

Paperweight, Barrel, Seal

7453 NR 060/7453 060 000
Designer: Max Schreck
Size: 2-5/8"/67mm
Trademark: SC

The *Seal Barrel Paperweight* was issued in 1976 and was not distributed in the U.S. The facets are rectangular in shape. Oftentimes these paperweights have no visible trademark. The equivalent U.S. price at retirement was approximately $140. It was retired in December 1987.

CRV: $1750

Paperweight, Barrel, Tabac

7453 NR 060/7453 060 000
Designer: Max Schreck
Size: 2-5/8"/67mm
Trademark: SC

The *Tabac Barrel Paperweight* was issued in 1976 and was not distributed in the U.S. The facets are rectangular in shape. Oftentimes these paperweights have no visible trademark. The equivalent U.S. price at retirement was approximately $140. It was retired in December 1987.

CRV: $1750

Paperweight, Barrel, Vitrail Light

7453 NR 060/7453 060 000
Designer: Max Schreck
Size: 2-5/8"/67mm
Trademark: SC

The *Vitrail Light Barrel Paperweight* was issued in 1976 and was never distributed in the U.S. The facets are rectangular in shape. Oftentimes these paperweights have no visible trademark. The equivalent U.S. price at retirement was approximately $140. It was retired in December 1987.

CRV: $1750

Paperweight, Barrel, Vitrail Medium

7453 NR 060 087/7453 060 087
Designer: Max Schreck
Size: 2-5/8"/67mm
Trademark: SC

The *Vitrail Medium Barrel Paperweight* was issued in 1976 and was distributed in the U.S. The facets are rectangular in shape. Oftentimes these paperweights have no visible trademark. The U.S. price at retirement was $140. It was retired in December 1988.

CRV: $575

Paperweight, Barrel, Volcano

7453 NR 060/7453 060 000
Designer: Max Schreck
Size: 2-5/8"/67mm
Trademark: SC

The *Volcano Barrel Paperweight* was issued in 1976 and was not distributed in the U.S. The facets are rectangular in shape. Oftentimes these paperweights have no visible trademark. The equivalent U.S. price at retirement was $140. It was retired in December 1987.

CRV: $1750

Paperweight, Carousel, Bermuda Blue

7451 NR 060 088/7451 060 088
Designer: Max Schreck
Size: 2-3/4"/70mm
Trademark: SC

The *Bermuda Blue Carousel Paperweight* was introduced in 1976. There are no known variations, but was produced in ten different colors. It was retired in 1983 at a suggested retail of $80. Oftentimes these paperweights are found with no visible trademark.

CRV: $1750

Paperweight, Carousel, Crystal Cal

7451 NR 060 095/7451 060 095
Designer: Max Schreck
Size: 2-3/4"/70mm
Trademark: SC

The *Crystal Cal Carousel Paperweight* was introduced in 1976. There are no known variations, but was produced in ten different colors. It was retired in 1983 at a suggested retail of $80. Oftentimes these paperweights are found with no visible trademark.

CRV: $1500

Paperweight, Carousel, Helio

7451 NR 060/7451 060 000
Designer: Max Schreck
Size: 2-3/4"/70mm
Trademark: SC

The *Helio Carousel Paperweight* was introduced in 1976. There are no known variations, but was produced in ten different colors. It was retired in 1983 at a suggested retail of $80. Oftentimes these paperweights are found with no visible trademark.

CRV: $3500

Paperweight, Carousel, Inn Green

7451 NR 060 090/7451 060 090
Designer: Max Schreck
Size: 2-3/4"/70mm
Trademark: SC

The *Inn Green Carousel Paperweight* was introduced in 1976. There are no known variations, but was produced in ten different colors. It was retired in 1983 at a suggested retail of $80. Oftentimes these paperweights are found with no visible trademark.

CRV: $3500

Paperweight, Carousel, Sahara

7451 NR 060/7451 060 000
Designer: Max Schreck
Size: 2-3/4"/70mm
Trademark: SC

The *Sahara Carousel Paperweight* was introduced in 1976. There are no known variations, but it was produced in ten different colors. It was retired in 1983 at a suggested retail of $80. Oftentimes these paperweights are found with no visible trademark.

CRV: $2750

Paperweight, Carousel, Seal

7451 NR 060/7451 060 000
Designer: Max Schreck
Size: 2-3/4"/70mm
Trademark: SC

The *Seal Carousel Paperweight* was introduced in 1976. There are no known variations, but was produced in ten different colors. It was retired in 1983 at a suggested retail of $80. Oftentimes these paperweights are found with no visible trademark.

CRV: $2750

Paperweight, Carousel, Tabac

7451 NR 060/7451 060 000
Designer: Max Schreck
Size: 2-3/4"/70mm
Trademark: SC

The *Tabac Carousel Paperweight* was introduced in 1976. There are no known variations, but it was produced in ten different colors. It was retired in 1983 at a suggested retail of $80. Oftentimes these paperweights are found with no visible trademark.

CRV: $3750

Paperweight, Carousel, Vitrail Light

7451 NR 060/7451 060 000
Designer: Max Schreck
Size: 2-3/4"/70mm
Trademark: SC

The *Vitrail Light Carousel Paperweight* was introduced in 1976. There are no known variations, but it was produced in ten different colors. It was retired in 1983 at a suggested retail of $80. Oftentimes these paperweights are found with no visible trademark.

CRV: $2500

Paperweight, Carousel, Vitrail Medium

7451 NR 060 087/7451 060 087
Designer: Max Schreck
Size: 2-3/4"/70mm
Trademark: SC

The *Vitrail Medium Carousel Paperweight* was introduced in 1976. There are no known variations, but it was produced in ten different colors. It was retired in 1983 at a suggested retail of $80. Oftentimes these paperweights are found with no visible trademark.

CRV: $1400

Paperweight, Carousel, Volcano

7451 NR 060/7451 060 000
Designer: Max Schreck
Size: 2-3/4"/70mm
Trademark: SC

The *Volcano Carousel Paperweight* was introduced in 1976. There are no known variations, but it was produced in ten different colors. It was retired in 1983 at a suggested retail of $80. Oftentimes these paperweights are found with no visible trademark.

CRV: $2600

Paperweight, Chaton

7433 000 001/238 167
Designer: Team
Size: 3"/75mm
Trademark: Swan

The *Chaton Paperweight* was issued in 1999 and was sold with a decorative pillow. The current suggested retail is $185.

CRV: $185

Paperweight, Chaton, Giant

7433 180 000/158 924
Designer: Max Schreck
Size: 7-1/8"/180mm
Trademark: Swan

The *Giant Chaton* was issued in 1990. The *Chaton* resembles a brilliant-cut, round diamond. The suggested retail is $4500.

CRV: $4500

Paperweight, Chaton, Large

7433 NR 80/7433 080 000
Designer: Max Schreck
Size: 3-3/16"/80mm
Trademark: SC or Swan

The *Large Chaton* was issued in 1986 and resembles a brilliant-cut, round diamond. It was retired in December 1998 at a suggested retail of $260.

CRV: $275

Paperweight, Chaton, Small

7433 NR 50/7433 050 000
Designer: Max Schreck
Size: 2"/50mm
Trademark: SC or Swan

The *Small Chaton Paperweight* was issued in 1986 and is a good replica of a brilliant-cut diamond. It was retired in 1998 at a suggested retail of $65.

SC CRV: $125
Swan CRV: $100

Paperweight, Chaton, Small, Dealer Gift

(No Number Assigned)
Designer: Team
Size: 1-1/8"/30mm
Trademark: Swan

Swarovski Corporate gave this small-sized *Chaton* to retailers at some special events. On the chaton's surface, the letters "SCS" and Roman numeral "X" are etched. It was issued in 1997.

CRV: $200

Paperweight, Columbine

7400 200 060
Designer: Team
Size: 2-3/8"/60mm
Trademark: D. Swarovski

The *Columbine Paperweight* was issued in 2000 at special store promotional events in Canada and the U.S. It features an etching of the Columbine face with the year 2000. It was retired at the end of the year 2000 at a suggested retail of $60. There are two size variations, 38mm and 60mm.

40mm CRV: $175
60mm CRV: $125

Paperweight, Cone, Bermuda Blue *(Known As Rio In Europe)*

7452 NR 060 088/7452 060 088
Designer: Max Schreck
Size: 3-1/8"/80mm
Trademark: SC or Swan

The *Bermuda Blue Cone Paperweight* was never distributed in the U.S. The Cone Paperweight was issued in 1976

and retired in 1992. The U.S. approximate retail value when it was retired in 1992 was $175.

SC CRV: $1200

Swan CRV: $900

Paperweight, Cone, Crystal Cal

7452 NR 060 095/7452 060 095
Designer: Max Schreck
Size: 3-1/8"/80mm
Trademark: SC or Swan

The *Crystal Cal Cone Paperweight* was issued in 1976. A special coating on the bottom, which is covered by a protective covering, produces the color of the paperweight. It was retired in December 1992 at a suggested retail of $175.

SC CRV: $400

Swan CRV: $350

Paperweight, Cone, Helio

7452 NR 060/7452 060 000
Designer: Max Schreck
Size: 3-1/8"/80mm
Trademark: SC or Swan

The *Helio Cone Paperweight* was issued in 1976. A special coating on the bottom, which is covered by a protective covering, produces the color of the paperweight. It was retired in 1990 at an approximate U.S. retail of $175. It was never sold initially in the U.S.

SC CRV: $1500

Swan SRV: $1250

Paperweight, Cone, Inn Green

7452 NR 060 090/7452 060 090
Designer: Max Schreck
Size: 3-1/8"/80mm
Trademark: SC or Swan

The *Inn Green Cone Paperweight* was issued in 1976. A special coating on the bottom, which is covered by a protective covering, produces the color of the paperweight. It was retired in 1990 at an approximate U.S. retail of $175. It was never sold initially in the U.S.

SC CRV: $1750

Swan CRV: $1500

Paperweight, Cone, Sahara

7452 NR 060/7452 060 000
Designer: Max Schreck
Size: 3-1/8"/80mm
Trademark: SC or Swan

The *Sahara Cone Paperweight* was issued in 1976. A special coating on the bottom, which is covered by a protective covering, produces the color of the paperweight. It was retired in 1990 at an approximate U.S. retail of $175. It was never sold initially in the U.S.

SC CRV: $1750

Swan SRV: $1500

Paperweight, Cone, Seal

7452 NR 060/7452 060 000
Designer: Max Schreck
Size: 3-1/8"/80mm
Trademark: SC or Swan

The *Seal Cone Paperweight* was issued in 1976. The color is produced by a special coating on the bottom, which is covered with a protective covering. It was retired in 1998 at an approximate U.S. retail of $175. It was never sold initially in the U.S.

SC CRV: $3000

Swan CRV: $2750

Paperweight, Cone, Tabac

7452 NR 060/7452 060 000
Designer: Max Schreck
Size: 3-1/8"/80mm
Trademark: SC or Swan

The *Tabac Cone Paperweight* was issued in 1976. The color is produced by a special coating on the bottom, which is covered with a protective covering. It was retired in 1998 at an approximate U.S. retail of $175. It was never sold initially in the U.S.

SC CRV: $2250

Swan CRV: $2000

Paperweight, Cone, Vitrail Light

7452 NR 060/7452 060 000
Designer: Max Schreck
Size: 3-1/8"/80mm
Trademark: SC or Swan

The *Vitrail Light Cone Paperweight* was issued in 1976. A special coating on the bottom, which is covered by a protective covering, produces the color of the paperweight. It was retired in 1990 at an approximated U.S. retail of $175. It was never initially sold in the U.S.

SC CRV: $3000

Swan CRV: $2750

Paperweight, Cone, Vitrail Medium

7452 NR 087/7452 060 087
Designer: Max Schreck
Size: 3-1/8"/80mm
Trademark: SC or Swan

The *Vitrail Medium Cone Paperweight* was issued in 1976. It was issued in the U.S. at a retail of $175. A special coating on the bottom, which is covered by a protective covering, produces the color of the paperweight. It was retired in December 1992.

SC CRV: $400
Swan SRV: $350

Paperweight, Cone, Volcano

7452 NR 060/7452 060 000
Designer: Max Schreck
Size: 3-1/8"/80mm
Trademark: SC or Swan

The *Volcano Cone Paperweight* was issued in 1976. It was never sold initially in the U.S. A special coating on the bottom, which is covered by a protective covering, produces the color of the paperweight. It was retired in 1990 at an approximate U.S. retail of $175.

SC CRV: $1200
Swan CRV: $1000

Paperweight, Dealer/Round

(No Number Assigned)/SCDPWNR1
Designer: Team
Size: 2"/50mm
Trademark: SCS

This paperweight was issued as the original Collectors Society *Ball Paperweight* for retailers. Decoration includes the "SCS" and "Edelweiss" flower in blue. It was issued in 1987 to dealers and retired in 1988.

CRV: $500

Paperweight, Dealer/Round

(No Number Assigned)/SCDPWNR2
Designer: Team
Size: 2"/50mm
Trademark: Swan SCS

This paperweight was issued to retailers as display material to promote the Swarovski Collectors Society. It was issued in 1989 and retired in 1991.

CRV: $400

Paperweight, Dealer/Round

(No Number Assigned)/SCDPWNR3
Designer: Team
Size: 2"/50mm
Trademark: Swan SCS

This paperweight was issued in 1992 to retailers as display material to promote the Swarovski Collectors Society. It was retired in 1995.

CRV: $300

Paperweight, Egg

7458 NR 063 069/7458 063 069
Designer: Max Schreck
Size: 2-5/8"/67mm
Trademark: SC or Swan

The *Egg Paperweight* was issued in 1979. It is different from the original *Egg Paperweight* with a more rounded small end and no flat area for a base. It was retired in 1992 at a suggested retail of $95. The egg symbolizes new life, and is a popular subject for many cultures.

SC CRV: $300
Swan CRV: $250

Paperweight, Egg, Bermuda Blue

7458 NR 063 088/7458 063 088
Designer: Max Schreck
Size: 2-3/4"/70mm
Trademark: SC

The *Bermuda Blue Egg Paperweight* was issued in the late 1970s and features a flattened bottom, which allows for the color application. This paperweight design has a more pointed small end of the egg. It was retired in December 1982 at an approximate U.S. retail of $50.

CRV: $3750

Paperweight, Egg, Crystal Cal

7458 NR 063 095/7458 063 095
Designer: Max Schreck
Size: 2-3/4"/70mm
Trademark: SC

The *Crystal Cal Egg Paperweight* was issued in the late 1970s and features a flattened bottom, which allows for the color application. This paperweight design has a more pointed small end of the egg. It was retired in December 1982 at an approximate U.S. retail of $50.

CRV: $3750

Paperweight, Egg, Vitrail Medium

7458 NR 063 087/7458 063 087
Designer: Max Schreck
Size: 2-3/4"/70mm
Trademark: SC

The *Vitrail Medium Egg Paperweight* was issued in the late 1970s and features a flattened bottom, which allows for the color application. This paperweight design has a more pointed small end of the egg. It was retired in December 1982 at an approximate U.S. retail of $50.

CRV: $3750

Paperweight, Employee Commemorative

(No Number Assigned)
Designer: Team
Size: 2-3/8"/60mm
Trademark: Swan Era

This paperweight can be found in a variety of forms because it has been produced to commemorate Swarovski employees' tenure of service. Generally, the more years of service the piece commemorates, the more valuable it becomes. These awards are given from five to twenty-five years of service.

CRV: $300-$1750

Paperweight, Harlequin

27871440/M6306
Designer: Team
Size: 1-1/2"/38mm
Trademark: Swan

This *Harlequin Paperweight* was available at special store events outside Canada and the U.S. It is, therefore, more difficult for U.S. and Canadian collectors to obtain. It was retired in December 2001 at an approximate U.S. retail of $50.

CRV: $150-$200

Swarovski paperweights are a marriage of both form and function. Their color tones and the variety of shapes available make them a great collectible item. Their values range from just under $100 through the thousands.

Paperweight, Harlequin

27871460/M6306
Designer: Team
Size: 2-3/8"/60mm
Trademark: Swan

This *Harlequin Paperweight* was issued in 2001 at special store events in Canada and the U.S. It was retired in December 2001 at a suggested retail of $60.

CRV: $95

Paperweight, Isadora

7400 200 060/602 838/M6550
Designer: Team
Size: 2-3/8"/60mm
Trademark: Swan

The *Isadora Paperweight* number 060 was available at stores offering a Swarovski special event for customers in Canada and the U.S. The suggested retail was $60 until it was retired in December 2002.

CRV: $80

Paperweight, Isadora

7400 200 040/608 238/M6550
Designer: Team
Size: 1-1/2"/38mm
Trademark: Swan

The *Isadora Paperweight* number 040 was made for special store events, and is smaller than the 60mm size. However, this smaller size is more difficult to obtain, and commands a higher secondary market price. The approximate U.S. equivalent was $45 when it was retired in December 2002.

CRV: $150-$175

Paperweight, Member (Version 1)

(No Number Assigned)/SCMPWNR1
Designer: Team
Size: 1-9/16"/40mm
Trademark: SCS

This 40mm paperweight was issued to members joining the Swarovski Collectors Society in 1987. The design incorporates the blue "SCS" and "Edelweiss" flower. It was originally free with Society membership.

CRV: $100

Paperweight, Member (Version 2)

(No Number Assigned)/SCMPWNR2
Designer: Team
Size: 1-9/16"/40mm
Trademark: Swan SCS (Blue)

This paperweight was issued to members of the Swarovski Collectors Society in 1988. It was retired in 1991. It is notable with the blue print and the blue-colored swan.

CRV: $90

Paperweight, Member (Version 3)

(No Number Assigned)/SCMPWNR3
Designer: Team
Size: 1-9/16"/40mm
Trademark: Swan SCS (Black)

This paperweight was issued to members of the Swarovski Collectors Society in 1992. It was retired in 1995. It is notable by the black color of the swan and SCS initials.

CRV: $75

Paperweight, Octron, Bermuda Blue

7456 NR 041 088/7456 041 088
Designer: Team
Size: 1-5/8"/41mm
Trademark: SC or Swan

The *Bermuda Blue Octron Paperweight* was issued in 1987, and was not originally marketed in the U.S. It was retired in December 1991 at an approximate U.S. retail of $95.

SC CRV: $450
Swan CRV: $400

Paperweight, Octron, Clear

7456 NR 041/7456 041 000
Size: 1-5/8"/41mm
Trademark: SC or Swan

The *Clear Octron Paperweight* was issued in 1987. Any surface can be used as a base for this piece. It was retired in December 1991 at a suggested retail of $95.

SC CRV: $300
Swan CRV: $275

Paperweight, Octron, Crystal Cal

7456NR041095/7456 041 095
Designer: Team
Size: 1-5/8"/41mm
Trademark: SC or Swan

The *Crystal Cal Octron Paperweight* was issued in 1987. It was retired in December 1991 at a suggested retail of $95.

SC CRV: $225
Swan CRV: $200

Paperweight, Octron, Helio

7456 NR 041/7456 041 000
Designer: Team
Size: 1-5/8"/41mm
Trademark: SC or Swan

The *Helio Octron Paperweight* was issued in 1987, and was not originally retailed in the U.S. market. It was retired in 1990 at a comparative U.S. suggested retail of $95.

SC CRV: $750
Swan CRV: $600

Paperweight, Octron Inn Green

7456 NR 041 090/7456 041 090
Designer: Team
Size: 1-5/8"/41mm
Trademark: SC or Swan

The *Inn Green Octron Paperweight* was issued in 1987 and was not originally retailed in the U.S. market. It was retired in 1990 at a comparative U.S. suggested retail of $95.

SC CRV: $800
Swan: $700

Paperweight, Octron, Sahara

7456 NR 041/7456 041 000
Designer: Team
Size: 1-5/8"/41mm
Trademark: SC or Swan

The *Sahara Octron Paperweight* was issued in 1987 and was not originally retailed in the U.S. market. It was retired in 1990 at a comparative U.S. suggested retail of $95.

SC CRV: $1200
Swan CRV: $1000

Paperweight, Octron, Seal

7456 NR 041/7456 041 000
Designer: Team
Size: 1-5/8"/41mm
Trademark: SC or Swan

The *Seal Octron Paperweight* was issued in 1987, and was not originally retailed in the U.S. market. It was retired in 1990 at a comparative U.S.-suggested retail of $95.

SC CRV: $800
Swan CRV: $700

Paperweight, Octron, Tabac

7456 NR 041/7456 041 000
Designer: Team
Size: 1-5/8"/41mm
Trademark: SC or Swan

The *Tabac Octron Paperweight* was issued in 1987 and was not originally retailed in the U.S. market. It was retired in 1990 at a comparative U.S.-suggested retail of $95.

SC CRV: $950
Swan CRV: $800

Paperweight, Octron Vitrail Light

7456 NR 041/7456 041 000
Designer: Team
Size: 1-5/8"/41mm
Trademark: SC or Swan

The *Vitrail Light Octron Paperweight* was issued in 1987 and was not originally retailed in the U.S. market. It was retired in 1990 at a comparative U.S.-suggested retail of $95.

SC CRV: $800
Swan CRV: $725

Paperweight, Octron, Vitrail Medium

7456 NR 041 087/7456 041 087
Designer: Team
Size: 1-5/8"/41mm
Trademark: SC or Swan

The *Vitrail Medium Octron Paperweight* was issued in the U.S. in 1987. It was retired in December 1991 at a suggested retail of $95.

SC CRV: $225
Swan CRV: $175

Paperweight, Octron, Volcano

7456 NR 041/7456 041 000
Designer: Team
Size: 1-5/8"/41mm
Trademark: SC or Swan

The *Volcano Octron Paperweight* was issued in 1987 and was not originally retailed in the U.S. market. It was retired in 1990 at a comparative U.S. suggested retail of $95.

SC CRV: $800
Swan CRV: $750

Paperweight, Octron, Giant

7456 NR 090/7456 090 000
Designer: Team
Size: 3-9/16"/90mm
Trademark: SC or Swan

The *Giant Octron Paperweight* was issued in 1987 exclusively in Canada and Europe. This piece was produced by special order for awards of achievement, and is often found with an inscription of some type. The presentation pieces were sold with a decorative base. Most rare paperweights are completely plain with no base. It was retired in 1990.

SC (Inscribed) CRV: $3250
SC (Plain) CRV: $3750
Swan (Inscribed) CRV: $3000
Swan (Plain) CRV: $3500

Paperweight, One Ton

7459 NR 065/7459 065 000
Designer: Team
Size: 2-1/2"/64mm
Trademark: SC or Swan

The *One Ton Paperweight* was issued in 1987. There are no known variations. It was retired in December 1990 at a suggested retail of $85.

SC CRV: $190
Swan CRV: $170

Paperweight, Pegasus

9409 060 000/M5714
Designer: Team
Size: 2-3/8"
Trademark: D. SWAROVSKI

This paperweight was given as a gift to Swarovski Collectors at retail events during 1998 and was a limited edition for one year. It was available only in the U.S. and Canada and features an etched Pegasus and the year 1998.

CRV: $100

Paperweight, Pierrot

9409 060 000
9409 040 000
Designer: Team
Size: 1-1/2" & 2-3/8"/38mm & 60mm
Trademark: D. Swarovski

The *Pierrot Paperweight* was issued at special SCS events

during the year 1999. It depicts an etching of the *Pierrot* face and the year 1999. It was retired in 1999 with no retail price, since it was a gift item.

40mm CRV: $175
60mm CRV: $150

Paperweight, Pyramid, Large–Bermuda Blue

7450 NR 050 088/7450 050 088
Designer: Max Schreck
Size: 2-1/2"/64mm
Trademark: SC or Swan

The *Bermuda Blue Large Pyramid Paperweight* was exclusively issued in Europe and Canada only in 1976. It was retired in 1992 at a suggested retail of $195.

SC CRV: $450
Swan CRV: $400

Paperweight, Pyramid, Large–Crystal Cal

7450 NR 050 095/7450 050 095
Designer: Max Schreck
Size: 2-1/2"/64mm
Trademark: SC or Swan

The *Crystal Cal Large Pyramid Paperweight* was issued in 1976. It was retired in 1993 at a suggested retail of $195.

SC CRV: $300
Swan CRV: $250

Paperweight, Pyramid, Large–Helio

7450 NR 050 000/7450 050 000
Designer: Max Schreck
Size: 2-1/2"/64mm
Trademark: SC or Swan

The *Helio Large Pyramid Paperweight* was issued in 1976 as an exclusive European release. It was retired in 1990 at a comparative suggested U.S. retail of approximately $175. It is a difficult secondary market find.

SC CRV: $950
Swan CRV: $800

Paperweight, Pyramid, Large–Inn Green

7450 NR 050 090/7450 050 090
Designer: Max Schreck
Size: 2-1/2"/64mm
Trademark: SC or Swan

The *Inn Green Large Pyramid Paperweight* was issued in 1976 as an exclusive European release. It was retired in 1990 at a comparative suggested U.S. retail of approximately $175. It is a difficult secondary market find.

SC CRV: $1000
Swan CRV: $900

Paperweight, Pyramid, Large–Sahara

7450 NR 050 000/7450 050 000
Designer: Max Schreck
Size: 2-1/2"/64mm
Trademark: SC or Swan

The *Sahara Large Pyramid Paperweight* was issued exclusively in the European marketplace in 1976. It was retired in 1990 at a comparative suggested U.S. retail of approximately $175. It is a difficult secondary market find.

SC CRV: $800
Swan CRV: $700

Paperweight, Pyramid, Large–Seal

7450 NR 050 000/7450 050 000
Designer: Max Schreck
Size: 2-1/2"/64mm
Trademark: SC or Swan

The *Seal Large Pyramid Paperweight* was issued in 1976 as an exclusive European release. It was retired in 1990 at a comparative suggested U.S. retail of approximately $175. It is a difficult secondary market find.

SC CRV: $950
Swan CRV: $850

Paperweight, Pyramid, Large–Tabac

7450 NR 050 000/7450 050 000
Designer: Max Schreck
Size: 2-1/2"/64mm
Trademark: SC or Swan

The *Tabac Large Pyramid Paperweight* was issued in 1976 as an exclusive European release. It was retired in 1990 at a comparative suggested U.S. retail of approximately $175. It is a difficult secondary market find.

SC CRV: $1000
Swan CRV: $900

Paperweight, Pyramid, Large–Vitrail Light

7450 NR 050 000/7450 050 000
Designer: Max Schreck
Size: 2-1/2"/64mm
Trademark: SC or Swan

The *Vitrail Light Large Pyramid Paperweight* was issued in 1976 exclusively in the European market. It was retired in 1990 at a comparative suggested U.S. retail of approximately $175. It is a difficult secondary market find.

SC CRV: $950

Swan CRV: $800

Paperweight, Pyramid, Large–Vitrail Medium

7450 NR 050 000/7450 050 000
Designer: Max Schreck
Size: 2-1/2"/64mm
Trademark: SC or Swan

The *Vitrail Meduim Large Pyramid Paperweight* was issued in 1976 worldwide. It was retired in December 1993 at a suggested retail of $195. It is a difficult secondary market find.

SC CRV: $300

Swan CRV: $250

Paperweight, Pyramid, Large–Volcano

7450 NR 050 000/7450 050 000
Designer: Max Schreck
Size: 2-1/2"/64mm
Trademark: SC or Swan

The *Volcano Large Pyramid Paperweight* was issued in 1976 exclusively in the European market. It was retired in 1990 at a comparative suggested U.S. retail of approximately $175. It is a difficult secondary market find.

SC CRV: $900

Swan CRV: $800

Paperweight, Pyramid, Small–Bermuda Blue

7450 NR 040 088/7450 040 088
Designer: Max Schreck
Size: 2-1/4"/57mm
Trademark: SC or Swan

The *Bermuda Blue Small Pyramid Paperweight* issued in 1986 as an exclusive European and Canadian release. It was retired in 1992 at a comparative suggested U.S. retail of approximately $80.

SC CRV: $300

Swan CRV: $250

Paperweight, Pyramid, Small—Crystal Cal

7450 NR 040 095/7450 040 095
Designer: Max Schreck
Size: 2-1/4"/57mm
Trademark: SC or Swan

The *Crystal Cal Small Pyramid Paperweight* was issued in 1986. It was retired in December 1997 at a suggested U.S. retail of $125.

CRV: $195

Paperweight, Pyramid, Small—Helio

7450 NR 040/7450 040 000
Designer: Max Schreck
Size: 2-1/4"/57mm
Trademark: SC or Swan

The *Helio Small Pyramid Paperweight* was issued in 1986. It was originally sold exclusively in the European market. It was retired in 1990 at an approximate U.S. retail of $90.

SC CRV: $800

Swan CRV: $700

Paperweight, Pyramid, Small—Inn Green

7450 NR 040 090/7450 040 090
Designer: Max Schreck
Size: 2-1/4"/57mm
Trademark: SC or Swan

The *Inn Green Small Pyramid Paperweight* was issued in 1986. It was originally sold exclusively in the European market. It was retired in 1990 at an approximate U.S. retail of $90.

SC CRV: $1000

Swan CRV: $950

Paperweight, Pyramid, Small—Sahara

7450 NR 040/7450 040 000
Designer: Max Schreck
Size: 2-1/4"/57mm
Trademark: SC or Swan

The *Sahara Small Pyramid Paperweight* was issued in 1986. It was originally sold exclusively in the European market. It was retired in 1990 at an approximate U.S. retail of $90.

SC CRV: $1000

Swan CRV: $950

Paperweight, Pyramid, Small—Seal

7450 NR 040/7450 040 000
Designer: Max Schreck
Size: 2-1/4"/57mm
Trademark: SC or Swan

The *Seal Small Pyramid Paperweight* was issued in 1986. It was originally sold exclusively in the European market. It was retired in 1990 at an approximate U.S. retail of $90.

SC CRV: $900

Swan CRV: $800

Paperweight, Pyramid, Small—Tabac

7450 NR 040/7450 040 000
Designer: Max Schreck
Size: 2-1/4"/57mm
Trademark: SC or Swan

The *Tabac Small Pyramid Paperweight* was issued in 1986. It was originally sold exclusively in the European market. It was retired in 1990 at an approximate U.S. retail of $90.

SC CRV: $850
Swan CRV: $750

Paperweight, Pyramid, Small—Vitrail Light

7450 NR 040/7450 040 087
Designer: Max Schreck
Size: 2-1/4"/57mm
Trademark: SC or Swan

The *Vitrail Light Small Pyramid Paperweight* was issued in 1986. It was originally sold exclusively in the European market. It was retired in 1990 at an approximate U.S. retail of $90.

SC CRV: $700
Swan CRV: $600

Paperweight, Pyramid, Small—Vitrail Medium

7450 NR 040 087/7450 040 087
Designer: Max Schreck
Size: 2-1/4"/57mm
Trademark: SC or Swan

The *Vitrail Medium Small Pyramid Paperweight* was issued in 1986. It was originally sold in the U.S. It was retired in December 1997 at a suggested retail of $125.

SC CRV: $200
Swan CRV: $175

Paperweight, Pyramid, Small—Volcano

7450 NR 040/7450 040 000
Designer: Max Schreck
Size: 2-1/4"/57mm
Trademark: SC or Swan

The *Volcano Small Pyramid Paperweight* was issued in 1986. It was originally sold exclusively in the European market. It was retired in 1990 at an approximate U.S. retail of $90.

SC CRV: $900
Swan CRV: $800

Paperweight, Round, 30mm—Bermuda Blue

7404 NR 030 088/7404 030 088
Designer: Team
Size: 1-3/16"/30mm
Trademark: SC

The *Bermuda Blue 30mm Round Paperweight* was issued in the late 1970s. It was retired in December 1982 at a suggested retail of $15.

SC CRV: $250

Paperweight, Round, 30mm—Crystal Cal

7404 NR 030 095/7404 030 095
Designer: Team
Size: 1-3/16"/30mm
Trademark: SC or Swan

The *Crystal Cal 30mm Round Paperweight* was issued in the late 1970s. It was retired in 1989 at a suggested retail of $20.

SC CRV: $175
Swan CRV: $150

Paperweight, Round, 30mm—Inn Green

7404 NR 030 090/7404 030 090
Designer: Team
Size: 1-3/16"/30mm
Trademark: SC

The *Inn Green 30mm Round Paperweight* was issued in the late 1970s. It was retired in December 1982 at a suggested retail of $15.

CRV: $275

Paperweight, Round, 30mm—Sahara

7404 NR 030/7404 030 000
Designer: Team
Size: 1-3/16"/30mm
Trademark: SC

The *Sahara 30mm Round Paperweight* was issued in the late 1970s. It was retired in December 1982 at a suggested retail of $15.

CRV: $250

Paperweight, Round, 30mm—Vitrail Medium

7404 NR 030 087/7404 030 087
Designer: Team
Size: 1-3/16"/30mm
Trademark: SC or Swan

The *Vitrail Medium 30mm Round Paperweight* was issued in the late 1970s. It was retired in June 1989 at a suggested retail of $20.

SC CRV: $125
Swan CRV: $100

Paperweight, Round, 40mm—Bermuda Blue

7404 NR 040 088/7404 040 088
Designer: Team
Size: 1-9/16"/40mm
Trademark: SC

The *Bermuda Blue 40mm Round Paperweight* was issued in the late 1970s. It was retired in December 1981 at a suggested retail of $20.

CRV: $295

Paperweight, Round, 40mm—Crystal Cal

7404 NR 040 095/7404 040 095
Designer: Team
Size: 1-9/16"/40mm
Trademark: SC or Swan

The *Crystal Cal 40mm Round Paperweight* was issued in the late 1970s. It was retired in 1989 at a suggested retail of $30.

SC CRV: $150
Swan CRV: $120

Paperweight, Round, 40mm—Inn Green

7404 NR 040 090/7404 040 090
Designer: Team
Size: 1-9/16"/40mm
Trademark: SC

The *Inn Green 40mm Round Paperweight* was issued in the late 1970s. It was retired in December 1981 at a suggested retail of $20.

CRV: $325

Paperweight, Round, 40mm—Sahara

7404 NR 040/7404 040 000
Designer: Team
Size: 1-9/16"/40mm
Trademark: SC

The *Sahara 40mm Round Paperweight* was issued in the late 1970s. It was retired in December 1982 at a suggested retail of $25.

CRV: $400

Paperweight, Round, 40mm—Vitrail Medium

7404 NR 040 087/7404 040 087
Designer: Team
Size: 1-9/16"/40mm
Trademark: SC or Swan

The *Vitrail Medium 40mm Round Paperweight* was issued in the late 1970s. It was retired in December 1981 at a suggested retail of $20.

SC CRV: $175
Swan CRV: $125

Paperweight, Round, 40mm—Volcano

7404 NR 040/7404 040 000
Designer: Team
Size: 1-9/16"/40mm
Trademark: SC

The *Volcano 40mm Round Paperweight* was issued in the late 1970s. It was retired in December 1981 at a suggested retail of $20.

CRV: $350

Paperweight, Round, 50mm—Bermuda Blue

7404 NR 050 088/7404 050 088
Designer: Team
Size: 2"/50mm
Trademark: SC

The *Bermuda Blue 50mm Round Paperweight* was issued in the late 1970s. It was retired in 1982 at a suggested retail of $40.

CRV: $400

Paperweight, Round, 50mm—Crystal Cal

7404 NR 050 095/7404 050 095
Designer: Team
Size: 2"/50mm
Trademark: SC or Swan

The *Crystal Cal 50mm Round Paperweight* was issued in the late 1970s. It was retired in 1989 at a suggested retail of $55.

SC CRV: $200
Swan CRV: $175

Paperweight, Round, 50mm—Helio

7404 NR 050/7404 050 000
Designer: Team
Size: 2"/50mm
Trademark: SC or Swan

The *Helio 50mm Round Paperweight* was issued in the late 1970s. It was retired in 1982 at a suggested retail of $40.

SC CRV: $450
Swan CRV: $400

Paperweight, Round, 50mm—Inn Green

7404 NR 050 090/7404 050 090
Designer: Team
Size: 2"/50mm
Trademark: SC

The *Inn Green 50mm Round Paperweight* was issued in the late 1970s. It was retired in December 1982 at a suggested retail of $40.

SC CRV: $375

Paperweight, Round, 50mm—Sahara

7404 NR 050/7404 050 000
Designer: Team
Size: 2"/50mm
Trademark: SC or Swan

The *Sahara 50mm Round Paperweight* was issued in the late 1970s. It was retired in 1989 at a suggested retail of $55.

SC CRV: $600
Swan CRV: $500

Paperweight, Round, 50mm—Vitrail Medium

7404 NR 050 087/7404 050 087
Designer: Team
Size: 2"/50mm
Trademark: SC or Swan

The *Vitrail Medium 50mm Round Paperweight* was issued in the late 1970s. It was retired in 1989 at a suggested retail of $55.

SC CRV: $250
Swan CRV: $200

Paperweight, Round, 50mm—Volcano

7404 NR 050/7404 050 000
Designer: Team
Size: 2"/50mm
Trademark: SC or Swan

The *Volcano 50mm Round Paperweight* was issued in the late 1970s. It was retired in 1989 at a suggested retail of $55.

SC CRV: $500
Swan CRV: $400

Paperweight, Round, 60mm—Bermuda Blue

7404 NR 060 088/7404 060 088
Designer: Team
Size: 2-3/8"/60mm
Trademark: SC or Swan

The *Bermuda Blue 60mm Round Paperweight* was issued in the late 1970s. It was retired in 1989 at a suggested retail of $85.

SC CRV: $450
Swan CRV: $400

Paperweight, Round, 60mm—Crystal Cal

7404 NR 060 095/7404 060 095
Designer: Team
Size: 2-3/8"/60mm
Trademark: SC or Swan

The *Crystal Cal 60mm Round Paperweight* was issued in the late 1970s. It was retired in 1989 at a suggested retail of $85.

SC CRV: $400
Swan CRV: $350

Paperweight, Round, 60mm—Helio

7404 NR 060/7404 060 000
Designer: Team
Size: 2-3/8"/60mm
Trademark: SC or Swan

The *Helio 60mm Round Paperweight* was issued in the late 1970s. It was retired in 1989 at a suggested retail of $85.

SC CRV: $500
Swan CRV: $450

Paperweight, Round, 60mm—Inn Green

7404 NR 060 090/7404 060 090
Designer: Team
Size: 2-3/8"/60mm
Trademark: SC or Swan

The *Inn Green 60mm Round Paperweight* was issued in the late 1970s. It was retired in 1989 at a suggested retail of $85.

SC CRV: $500
Swan CRV: $450

Paperweight, Round, 60mm—Sahara

7404 NR 060/7404 060 000
Designer: Team
Size: 2-3/8"/60mm
Trademark: SC or Swan

The *Sahara 60mm Round Paperweight* was issued in the late 1970s. It was retired in 1989 at a suggested retail of $85.

SC CRV: $600
Swan CRV: $500

Paperweight, Round, 60mm—Vitrail Medium

7404 NR 060 087/7404 060 087
Designer: Team
Size: 2-3/8"/60mm
Trademark: SC or Swan

The *Vitrail Medium 60mm Round Paperweight* was issued in the late 1970s. It was retired during 1989 at a suggested retail of $85.

SC CRV: $400
Swan CRV: $350

Paperweight, Round, 60mm—Volcano

7404 NR 060/7404 060 000
Designer: Team
Size: 2-3/8"/60mm
Trademark: SC or Swan

The *Volcano 60mm Round Paperweight* was issued in the late 1970s. It was retired in 1989 at a suggested retail of $85.

SC CRV: $500
Swan CRV: $450

Paperweight, Wild Horses

2833 324/M6414
Designer: Team
Size: 2-3/8"/60mm
Trademark: Swan

The *Wild Horses Paperweight* was produced for special promotional events, and was issued in the year 2001. It also commemorates twenty-five years of Swarovski Silver Crystal with an etching of the Wild Horses and "25 years." It was retired in 2001 at the suggested retail of $60.

CRV: $85-$100

Parrot

7621 NR 000 004/7621 000 004
Designer: Michael Stamey
Size: 2-1/4"/55mm
Trademark: Swan

The *Parrot* was issued in 1989 as part of the "Up in the Trees" series. It was retired in December 1992 at a suggested retail of $85.

CRV: $225

Parrot

7621 000 009/294 047
Designer: Michael Stamey
Size: 2-1/4"/55mm
Trademark: Swan

The *Parrot* was issued in 2002 and is the second piece issued with the *Parrot* name. It is notable with its red beak. The suggested retail is $90.

CRV: $90

Partridge

7625 NR 50/7625 050 000
Designer: Adi Stocker
Size: 2-1/4"/57mm
Trademark: SC or Swan

The *Partridge* was issued in 1988. There are two variations in the *Partridge*—one style has a more defined tail than the other. It was retired in December 1990 at a suggested retail of $110.

SC CRV: $175 (both styles)
Swan CRV: $150 (both styles)

Pear

7476 NR 000 002/7476 000 002
Designer: Michael Stamey
Size: 3-1/2"/90mm
Trademark: Swan

The *Pear* was issued in 1991 as part of the "Sparkling Fruit" grouping. It was retired in December 1997 at a suggested retail of $185.

CRV: $195

Peacock

7607 000 002/218 123
Designer: Adi Stocker
Size: 7"/175mm
Trademark: Swan

The *Peacock* was distributed worldwide by lottery selection among members of the Swarovski Collectors Society. All pieces are laser-etched with the serial limited edition number. There were 10,000 pieces issued in 1998 at a suggested retail of $1800 at the time of issue. The *Peacock* was the second numbered limited edition piece issued.

CRV: $5000-$6000

Pegasus

DO1X981/7400 098 000/216 327
Designer: Adi Stocker
Size: 6"/150mm
Trademark: Swan

The *Pegasus* was issued in 1998 as the Swarovski Collectors Society annual member redemption limited edition. It was retired in December 1998 at the issue price of $350. The SCS mark is etched into the piece along with the artist's initials and date, i.e. AS98.

CRV: $375

Pelican

7679 000 001/171 899
Designer: Anton Hirzinger
Size: 1-1/8"/29mm
Trademark: Swan

The *Pelican* was issued in 1993 as a part of the "Feathered Friends" grouping. It was retired in December 2002 at a suggested retail of $37.50.

CRV: $50

Pen, Writing

Member Renewal 1992
Designer: Team
Size: 5 "/127mm
Trademark: Swan/SCS

The *Writing Pen* was issued as a Swarovski Collectors Society member renewal gift in 1992. It features a crystal top with a silver body.

CRV: $50

Penguin, Father

627068
Designer: Gabriele Stamey
Size: 5-1/8"/129mm
Trademark: Swan

The *Father Penguin* was issued in the fall of 2003 as part of the "Symbols" theme group. Suggested retail at the time of issue was $280. No known variations.

CRV: $280

Penguin, Large

7643 NR 85/7643 085 000
Designer: Max Schreck
Size: 3-3/8"/86mm
Trademark: SC or Swan

The *Large Penguin* was issued in 1984 and was made entirely of clear crystal with the exception of its black eyes. It was retired in December 1995 at the suggested retail of $95.

SC CRV: $150
Swan CRV: $125

Penguin, Madame

7661 NR 000 002/7661 000 002
Designer: Adi Stocker
Size: 1-1/2"/38mm
Trademark: Swan

The *Madame Penguin* was issued in 1996 and was sold with a plastic base that is shaped like the continent of Antarctica. There are no known variations. It was retired in December 1999 at a suggested retail of $85.

CRV: $110

Penguin, Mini

7661 033 000/010 027
Designer: Max Schreck
Size: 1-1/4"/32mm
Trademark: SC or Swan

The *Mini Penguin* was issued in 1985. It was retired in December 2001 at a suggested retail of $37.50.

SC CRV: $75
Swan CRV: $50

Penguin, Mother And Babies

627 067
Designer: Gabriele Stamey
Size: 4-5/8"/116mm
Trademark: Swan

The *Mother Penguin with Babies* was issued in the fall of 2003 as part of the "Symbols" theme group. Suggested retail at time of issue was $280. No known variations.

CRV: $280

Penguin, Sir

7661 000 001/191 448
Designer: Adi Stocker
Size: 1-1/2"/38mm
Trademark: Swan

The *Sir Penguin* was issued in 1995. *Sir Penguin* rests on a plastic Antarctica-shaped base. It was retired in December 2000 at a suggested retail of $85.

CRV: $125

Penguins, Baby (Set Of 3)

7661 000 003/209 588
Designer: Adi Stocker
Size: 15/16"/23mm
Trademark: Swan

The *Baby Penguins* were issued as a three-piece set in 1997. The plastic base upon which they sit comes with the group. The suggested retail is $75.

CRV: $75

Perfume Bottle, Lancome, Tresor, 1994

Unnumbered
Designer: Unknown
Size: 2-1/8"/55mm
Trademark: Swarovski

This limited edition *Lancome Tresor Perfume Bottle* was issued in 1994 in an edition of 5,000 pieces. Each piece is marked with the edition number. Issue price in 1994 was $250.

CRV: $500

Perfume Bottle, Lancome, Tresor, 1995

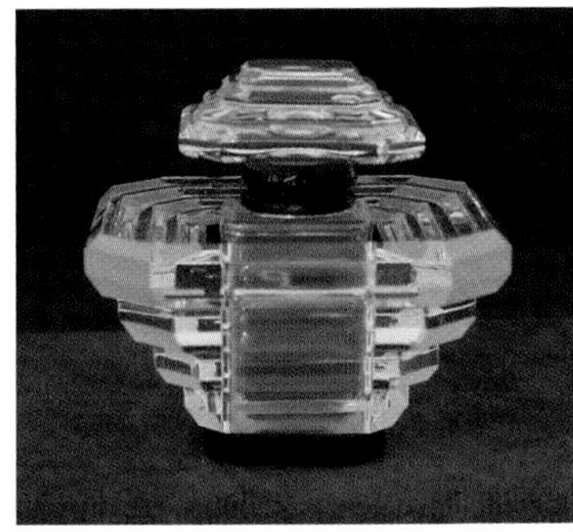

Unnumbered
Designer: Unknown
Size: 2-1/8"/55mm
Trademark: Swarovski

This limited edition *Lancome Tresor Perfume Bottle* was issued in 1995 in an edition in excess of 5,000 pieces. Each piece is etched with the name SWAROVSKI. Issue price was $275.

CRV: $350

Petrol Wagon

7471 000 004/015 151
Designer: Gabriele Stamey
Size: 1-5/8"/41mm
Trademark: Swan

The *Petrol Wagon* was issued in 1990 as part of the *Crystal Train*. It was retired in December 2002 at a suggested retail of $95. There are no known variations.

CRV: $100

Piano With Stool

7477 000 006/174 506
Designer: Martin Zendron
Size: 2-9/16"/67mm
Trademark: Swan

The *Piano with Stool* was issued in 1993. The current suggested retail is $280.

CRV: $280

Picture Frame, Butterfly

7506 000 004/211 742
Designer: Claudia Schneiderbauer
Size: 5-1/2"/138mm
Trademark: Swan

The *Butterfly Picture Frame* was issued in 1997, and was retired in December 2002 at a suggested retail of $85.

CRV: $95

Picture Frame, Blue Flower

7506 000 004/211 742
Designer: Gabriele Stamey
Size: 4"/100mm
Trademark: Swan

The *Blue Flower Picture Frame* was issued in 1996. It was retired in December 2000 at a suggested retail of $260.

CRV: $275

Picture Frame, 1994 Renewal Item

SCMR94
Designer: Team
Size: 3-3/4"/95mm
Trademark: Swan/SCS

The *Picture Frame* was the 1994 renewal gift for members of the Swarovski Collectors Society. It is made of leather (black) and folds together billfold style. It was issued one year only in 1994.

CRV: $45

Picture Frame, Oval

7505 NR 75 G/7505 075 000 G
Designer: Team
Size: 3"/76mm
Trademark: SC or Swan

The *Oval Picture Frame* was issued in 1986 exclusively in the Canadian and U.S. markets. It was retired in December 1989 at a suggested retail of $95. There are no known variations and it is in good demand by worldwide collectors.

SC CRV: $600
Swan CRV: $500

Picture Frame, Square—Gold/U.S.

7506 NR 60 G/7506 060 000 G
Designer: Team
Size: 2-5/16"/60mm
Trademark: SC or Swan

The *Gold Square Picture Frame* was issued in Canada and the U.S. in 1984. It was retired in December 1989 at a suggested retail of $120. There are no known variations.

SC CRV: $400
Swan CRV: $350

Picture Frame, Square—Gold/European

7506 NR 060 001/7506 060 001 G
Designer: Max Schreck
Size: 2-5/16"/60mm
Trademark: SC

The *Gold Square Picture Frame* was issued in Europe in 1983. It features a square crystal unattached from a gold metal easel. It was retired in 1987 at a comparative U.S. suggested retail of $100. There are no known variations.

CRV: $375

Picture Frame, Square—Rhodium/European

7506 NR 060 002 R/7506 060 002 R
Designer: Max Schreck
Size: 2-5/16"/60mm
Trademark: SC

The *Rhodium Square Picture Frame* was issued in 1983 in the European market. A crystal piece sets against a rhodium metal stand. There are no known variations.

CRV: $375

Pierrot

DO1X991/7400 099 000/230 586
Designer: Adi Stocker
Size: 8"/200mm
Trademark: Swan/Swarovski

The *Pierrot* piece was issued as the annual edition for members of the Swarovski Collectors Society. This annual edition was issued in 1999, and features an etched SCS mark, the designer's initials, and the year of issue, i.e. AS99. It was retired in December 1999 at the issue price of $350.

CRV: $400

Pig, Large

7638 NR 65/7638 065 000
Designer: Max Schreck
Size: 3"/76mm
Trademark: SC

The *Large Pig* was issued in 1982. It features a curly crystal tail. Another European variation has been noted with a flat, round crystal disk-shaped tail. It was retired in December 1987 at a suggested retail of $50.

European Style CRV: $600
U.S. Version (curly tail) CRV: $475

Pig, Medium—Crystal Tail Version

7638 050 000/010 031
Designer: Max Schreck
Size: 2"/50mm
Trademark: SC

The *Medium Pig* was issued in 1984. This early version has a crystal tail and was only made for a short time. The suggested retail when it was discontinued was $42.50.

SC/Crystal Tail CRV: $575

Pig, Medium—Metal Tail Version

7638 050 000/010 031
Designer: Max Schreck
Size: 2"/50mm
Trademark: SC or Swan

The *Medium Pig* with the metal tail was issued in 1984. It is still produced with a suggested retail of $60.

SC/Metal Tail CRV: $90
Swan/Metal Tail CRV: $60

Pig, Mini—Crystal Tail

7657 027 000/010 028
Designer: Max Schreck
Size: 1-1/32"/27mm
Trademark: SC or Swan

The *Mini Pig* with the crystal tail was issued in 1982, and was produced this way until 1993. It was discontinued by early 1994 at a suggested retail of $29.50. The U.S.-style crystal tail was the round disk style.

SC CRV: $110
Swan CRV: $90

Pig, Mini—Crystal Tail, European Version

7657 027 000/010 028
Designer: Max Schreck
Size: 1-1/32"/27mm
Trademark: SC

The *Mini Pig* with the European-style crystal tail was produced for a short time. The crystal tail looks like a small/mini chaton. The suggested retail when it was discontinued was approximately $29.50.

CRV: $250

Pig, Mini—Wire Tail, U.S. Version

7657 027 000/010 028
Designer: Max Schreck
Size: 1-1/32"/27mm
Trademark: SC

The *Mini Pig* was issued with the wire tail in the U.S. in 1982. It is now produced in all markets with the wire tail. The current suggested retail is $29.50.

CRV: $29.50

Pig, Zodiac

7693 000 006/289 914
Designer: Anton Hirzinger
Size: 1-5/8"/41mm
Trademark: Swan

The *Zodiac Pig* was issued in 2002. There are no known variations. The current suggested retail is $60.

CRV: $60

Pillbox

7506 NR 030
Designer: Team
Size: 1-3/16"/30mm
Trademark: SC

The *Pillbox* was issued in the late 1970s. This 30mm size was made in both gold and rhodium finishes. It was retired in 1983 at the suggested retail of approximately $65.

Gold CRV: $600

Rhodium CRV: $550

Pillbox

7506 NR 050
Designer: Team
Size: 2"/50mm
Trademark: SC

The *Pillbox* was issued in the late 1970s. This 50mm size was made in both gold and rhodium finishes. It was retired in 1983 at a suggested retail of approximately $80.

Gold CRV: $700

Rhodium CRV: $600

Pineapple, Giant—Gold

7507 260 001/010 116
Designer: Max Schreck
Size: 9-3/4"/260mm
Trademark: SC or Swan

The *Giant Pineapple* was issued in 1981, and is notable with gold leaves. It is still produced and sells for the suggested retail of $3250.

SC CRV: $4500

Swan CRV: $3250

Pineapple, Giant—Rhodium

7507 NR 260 002/7507 260 002
Designer: Max Schreck
Size: 9-3/4"/260mm
Trademark: SC

The *Giant Pineapple* was issued in rhodium in 1981. It is notable with its rhodium-colored leaves. It was retired in 1986 at the suggested retail of $2000.

CRV: $5750

Pineapple, Large—Gold

7507 NR 105 001/010 044 001
Designer: Max Schreck
Size: 4-1/8"/105mm
Trademark: SC or Swan

The *Large Pineapple* in gold was issued in 1981 and has several variations. The gold leaves can be found in smooth or textured, and a third version that has a more tapered body near the fruit's top. The current more tapered version sells for the suggested retail of $260.

SC, Gold Textured CRV: $350

Swan, Gold Textured CRV: $300

SC, Gold Smooth CRV: $700

Swan, Gold Current CRV: $260

Pineapple, Large—Rhodium

7507 NR 105 002/7507 105 002
Designer: Max Schreck
Size: 4-1/8"/105mm
Trademark: SC

The *Large Pineapple* in rhodium was issued in 1981. There are two known variations: one with textured rhodium leaves and the other with smooth rhodium leaves. It was retired in December 1986 at the suggested retail of $150.

SC, Textured CRV: $600

SC, Smooth CRV: $750

Pineapple, Small—Gold

7507 060 001/012 726
Designer: Max Schreck
Size: 2-1/2"/64mm
Trademark: SC or Swan

The *Small Pineapple* in gold was issued in 1986 with smooth gold leaves. It is still in production and sells for the suggested retail of $90.

SC CRV: $125

Swan CRV: $90

Pineapple, Small—Rhodium

7507 NR 060 002/7507 060 002
Designer: Max Schreck
Size: 2-1/2" 64mm
Trademark: SC or Swan

The *Small Pineapple* in rhodium was issued in 1983. Two variations exist, one with smooth leaves, and the other with textured leaves. It was retired in Europe in 1990, but retired four years earlier in the U.S. in December 1986. The suggested retail at retirement in the U.S. was $55.

SC, Smooth CRV: $250
SC, Textured CRV: $250
Swan, Smooth CRV: $200
Swan, Textured CRV: $200

Pin, Stick—1987 Membership Pin

SCS 87 Member
Designer: Team
Size: 2"/50mm
Trademark: SCS

The *1987 Membership Stick Pin* was given to Swarovski Collectors Society members as part of the charter membership package. It is notable with a large "C" with "S" to each side of the "C." It was only produced for one year.

CRV: $60-$75

Pin, Stick—1987 Membership

SCS 1987 Member
Designer: Team
Size: 2"/50mm
Trademark: SC

The *1987 Member Stick Pin* bears the SC logo and was given as a gift to members joining the Collectors Society during 1987.

CRV: $60-$75

Pin, Stick—1988-1991 Membership

SCS 1988-1991 Member
Designer: Team
Size: 2"/50mm
Trademark: Swan/SCS

The *1988-1991 Membership Stick Pin* was the second in the series of membership pins. It is notable with the swan logo in a silver color on a blue background. It was retired in December 1991.

CRV: $60

Pin, Stick—1992-1995 Membership

SCS 1992-1995 Member
Designer: Team
Size: 2"/50mm
Trademark: Swan/SCS

The *1992-1995 Membership Stick Pin* was the third in the series of membership pins, and was given to members from 1992 to 1995. It features a black swan on a silver background. It was retired in December 1995.

CRV: $40-$50

Planet, Crystal Millennium

(See Crystal Planet)

COLLECTING DEALER DISPLAY PLAQUES

One of the most interesting and exciting aspects of collecting involves searching for items that are not generally issued for sale to the general public. This has always been the mystique of the "Limited Edition." Secondary market values typically increase in proportion to the limited availability of an item to the general public.

The fact that Dealer's Plaques were never produced for retail sale makes them very intriguing to collectors. First of all, only one is produced for each retailer in a given region of the world. Secondly, many of the early plaques were discarded or taken back by sales representatives when the newer-style plaque was issued. Therefore, some of those earliest issued crystal display plaques are very difficult to find.

The search becomes a great deal of fun when you begin to find out what the retailer considers the value to be. Many retailers would often give the plaque to a good customer who had purchased many pieces over a period of time.

There are now about sixty known dealer display plaques that have been located by collectors and added to their collections. We have listed some of the earliest and most valuable pieces in this section. Many of the additional finds and examples have been resold on the secondary market for prices ranging from $50 to $2000.

Explore, search, bargain and add a special display piece to your own personal collection. I guarantee you, the search will be rewarding and add a touch of adventure to your collecting experience.

PLAQUES (By Numerical Designation)

Octagonal Dealer's Plaque

SCDPNR1
Designer: Team
Size: 4"/100mm
Trademark: SC

The *Octagonal Dealer's Plaque* was produced exclusively for the European market. It was used as a display piece, and only one piece was issued per European dealer. It is very rare and highly sought after by worldwide collectors.

CRV: $1500-$2250

"Emerald Cut" Style Dealer's Plaque

SCDPNR2
Designer: Team
Size: 2-3/4"/70mm
Trademark: SC

Issued in the late 1970s, the *"Emerald Cut" Dealer Plaque* was the first display plaque issued to U.S. retailers. Three distinctly different variations have been noted. One variation has blue print, one has black print, and the other has a gray surface with a Bermuda Blue backside. It was retired when plaque-style number three was issued.

Blue CRV: $600
Black CRV: $800
Silver CRV: $2000

Tall Crystal Iceberg Dealer's Plaque

SCDPNR3
Designer: Team
Size: 3-5/8"/90mm
Trademark: SC

The *Tall Crystal Iceberg Dealer's Plaque* was the second display plaque issued to U.S. dealers. The Swarovski Company usually removed this plaque from the dealer's display when a new style was issued. There is very high demand for this item by worldwide collectors.

CRV: $500

"Square" Crystal Iceberg Dealer's Plaque

SCDPNR4
Designer: Team
Size: 4-1/8"/105mm
Trademark: SC

The *"Square" Crystal Iceberg Dealer's Plaque* was the third style issued to U.S. retailers as a display-only piece. It is very much in demand by worldwide collectors.

CRV: $550

Oval Crystal Iceberg Dealer's Plaque

SCDPNR5
Designer: Team
Size 4-1/8"/105mm
Trademark: SC

The *Oval Crystal Iceberg Dealer's Plaque* was the fourth display piece issued to U.S. retailers and is very limited in supply. It is in demand by worldwide collectors. The price on the secondary market has remained low due to the lack of knowledge about this plaque among worldwide collectors to date.

CRV: $400

"Script Swarovski" Crystal Dealer's Plaque

SCDPNR6
Designer: Team
Size: 4-3/8"/105mm
Trademark: Swarovski in script

The *"Script Swarovski" Crystal Dealer's Plaque* was issued to Swarovski Jewelry retailers in the U.S. It is both unique and very desirable to advanced collectors worldwide.

CRV: $500

"Shark Tooth" Crystal Dealer's Plaque

SCDPNR7
Designer: Team
Size: 5-1/4"/135mm
Trademark: Swarovski in script

The *"Shark Tooth" Crystal Dealer's Plaque* derives its nickname due to its appearance of a shark's tooth lying on its side. It was issued as an early crystal display plaque for the Swarovski Jewelry line, and is very difficult to obtain for worldwide collectors.

CRV: $750

Rectangular Plastic Dealer's Display Plaque

SCDPNR8
Designer: Team
Size: 2-3/4"/69mm
Trademark: SC

The *Rectangular Plastic Dealer's Display Plaque* was issued to retailers for display purposes at the point of retail display. It has a gray background with navy blue lettering. It was retired in 1988.

CRV: $50-$75

Large Rectangular Plastic Dealer's Display Plaque

SCDPNR9
Designer: Team
Size: 5"/75mm
Trademark: SC

The *Large Rectangular Plastic Dealer's Display Plaque* is gray with navy blue lettering. It was retired in 1988.

CRV: $75-$100

Rectangular Plastic Dealer's Display Plaque

SCDPNR10
Designer: Team
Size: 4-1/8"/104mm
Trademark: Swan

The *Rectangular Plastic Dealer's Display Plaque* is easily recognized with its gray background and black and silver raised lettering. It was issued to retailers beginning in 1988. It was retired in the early 1990s.

CRV: $60-$75

Premier Dealer's Crystal Display Plaque

SCDPNR11
Designer: Team
Size: 4-3/8"/110mm
Trademark: Swan

The *Premier Dealer's Crystal Display Plaque* was issued to Premier Retailers in the U.S., Canada and Great Britain in 1989. It is notable with its square base.

CRV: $500-$600

Premier Dealer's Crystal Display Plaque

SCDPNR12
Designer: Team
Size: 4-3/8"/110mm
Trademark: Swan

The *Premier Dealer's Crystal Display Plaque* was issued to Premier Retailers in the U.S., Canada, and Great Britain in 1993. It is very much in demand by worldwide collectors. The piece is notable by its two triangular feet.

CRV: $650-$800

Plaque, Caring And Sharing

SCPCSNR1
Designer: Team
Size: 2-3/4"/69mm
Trademark: SCS/Swan

The *Caring and Sharing Plaque* was issued in 1989 as a display companion to the Turtledoves Annual SCS edition. Originally issued at a suggested retail of $27.50.

CRV: $125

Plaque, Mother And Child

SCPCSNR2
Designer: Team
Size: 2-3/4"/69mm
Trademark: SCS/Swan

The Mother and Child Plaque was issued in 1992 as a display compainion to the Whales Annual SCS edition. Originally issued at a suggested retail of $27.50.

CRV: $100

Plaque, Inspirational Africa

SCPCSNR3
Designer: Team
Size: 2-3/4"/69mm
Trademark: SCS/Swan

The *Inspirational Africa Plaque* was issued in 1995 as a display companion to the *Lion* annual SCS edition. The piece was originally issued at a suggested retail of $27.50.

CRV: $90

Plaque, Fabulous Creatures

SCPCSNR4
Designer: Team
Size: 2-3/4"/69mm
Trademark: SCS/Swan

The *Fabulous Creatures Plaque* was issued in 1998 as a display companion to the *Pegasus* annual SCS edition. Originally issued at a suggested retail of $32.

CRV: $75

Poplar Trees

7474 NR 020 003/7474 020 003
Designer: Gabriele Stamey
Size: 1-1/4"/32mm
Trademark: Swan

The *Poplar Trees* were issued in 1990 as part of the "Silver Crystal City" grouping and were originally sold as a three-piece set. Due to being easily tipped over, damage to these pieces is occurring at rapid pace. This increases the secondary market values for perfect pieces. The Poplar Trees were retired in 1994 at a suggested retail of $49.50 for the three-piece set.

CRV: $150

Puffins

7621 000 008/261 643
Designer: Martin Zendron
Size: 3"/75mm
Trademark: Swan

The *Puffins* were issued in 2001. There are no known variations. The current suggested retail is $160.

CRV: $160

Puppet

7550 000 003/217207
Designer: Gabriele Stamey
Size: 2-1/4"/56mm
Trademark: Swan

The *Puppet* was issued in 1997. Notable with colored stones for the hat and front of body as well as the eyes. The head is frosted crystal.

CRV: $125

Rabbit, Bunny

7678 000 001/208 326
Designer: Edith Mair
Size: 1-3/8"/43mm
Trademark: Swan

The *Bunny Rabbit* was issued in 1997, and is notable with its extremely long ears. It was retired in December 2000 at a suggested retail of $55.

CRV: $75

Rabbit, Large

7652 NR 45/7652 045 000
Designer: Max Schreck
Size: 1-1/2"/38mm
Trademark: SC or Swan

The *Large Rabbit* was issued in 1983 exclusively in the U.S. and Canada. There are no known variations. It was retired in 1988 at the suggested retail of $40.

SC CRV: $500
Swan CRV: $450

Rabbit, Mini

7652 NR 20/7652 020 000
Designer: Max Schreck
Size: 1"/25mm
Trademark: SC or Swan

The *Mini Rabbit* was issued in 1979, and was retired in December 1988 at a suggested retail of $25.

SC CRV: $125
Swan CRV: $100

Rabbit, Mini Lying

7678 NR 030/7678 030 000
Designer: Adi Stocker
Size: 1-3/8"/35mm
Trademark: SC or Swan

The *Mini Lying Rabbit* was issued in 1988, and there are no known variations. It was retired in December 1995 at a suggested retail of $45.

SC CRV: $125
Swan CRV: $100

Rabbit, Mini Sitting

7678 040 000/014 849
Designer: Adi Stocker
Size: 1-1/4"/32mm
Trademark: SC or Swan

The *Mini Sitting Rabbit* was issued in 1988. There are no known variations. The current suggested retail is $46.50.

SC CRV: $75
Swan CRV: $46.50

Rat, Zodiac

7693 000 001/275 436
Designer: Anton Hirzinger
Size: 1-3/4"/43mm
Trademark: Swan

The *Zodiac Rat* was issued in 2001. There are no known variations. The current suggested retail is $60.

CRV: $60

Reindeer

7475 000 602/214 821
Designer: Anton Hirzinger
Size: 3-1/4"/81mm
Trademark: Swan

The *Reindeer* was issued in 1997 with two mirrors to display with *Santa* and the *Sleigh*. There are no known variations. The current suggested retail is $190.

CRV: $190

Rhino

7610 000 006/622941
Designer: Anton Hirzinger
Size: 1-1/8"/29mm
Trademark: Swan

The *Rhino* was issued in 2003 at a suggested retail of $65. No known variations.

MSRP: $65

Rhinoceros, Large

7622 NR 70/7622 070 000
Designer: Adi Stocker
Size: 2-7/8"/73mm
Trademark: SC or Swan

The *Large Rhinoceros* was issued in 1988. There are no known variations. It was retired in December 1992 at the suggested retail of $95.

SC CRV: $175
Swan CRV: $150

Rhinoceros, Small

7622 NR 60/7622 060 000
Designer: Adi Stocker
Size: 2-3/8"/60mm
Trademark: Swan

The *Small Rhinoceros* was issued in 1990 and there are no known variations. It was retired in December 1995 at the suggested retail of $75.

CRV: $150

Rooster, Mini

7674 045 000/014 497
Designer: Gabriele Stamey
Size: 1-15/16"/49mm
Trademark: SC or Swan

The *Mini Rooster* was issued in 1987. There are no known variations. It was retired in December 2000 at a suggested retail of $55.

SC CRV: $95

Swan CRV: $75

Rooster, Zodiac

7693 000 010/625189
Designer: Anton Hirzinger
Size: 1-1/3"/33mm
Trademark: Swan

The *Zodiac Rooster* was issued in 2004 as part of the "Chinese Zodiacs" theme group. No known variations. Suggested retail at time of issue was $60.

CRV: $60

Rose, The

7478 000 001/174 956
Designer: Michael Stamey
Size: 3-1/4"/85mm
Trademark: Swan

The *Rose* was issued in 1993 as part of the "Exquisite Accents" grouping. It is notable with dewdrops on the leaves. There are no known variations. The current suggested retail is $155.

CRV: $155

Roses, Dozen Pink

7785 000 001/628343
Designer: Gabriele Stamey
Size: 2-9/16"/65mm
Trademark: Swan

The *Dozen Pink Roses* were issued in 2003 at an issue price of $125. No known variations.

CRV: $125

Sailboat

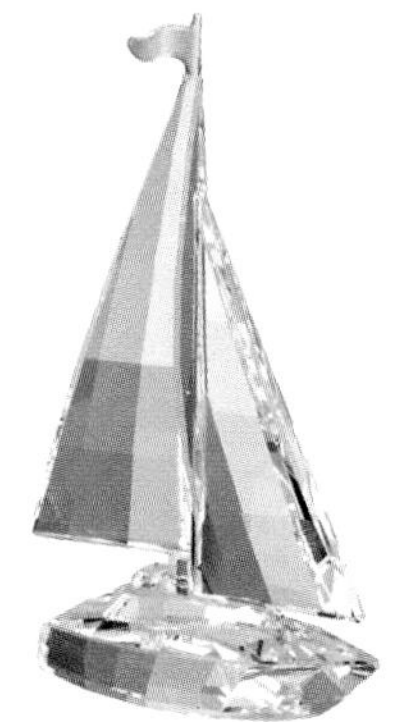

7473 000 004/183 269
Designer: Gabriele Stamey
Size: 3-3/4"/70mm
Trademark: Swan

The *Sailboat* was issued in 1994 and rests on a metal stand. There are no known variations. The current suggested retail is $215.

CRV: $215

St. Bernard

7619 000 006/201 111
Designer: Edith Mair
Size: 2"/50mm
Trademark: Swan

The *St. Bernard* was introduced in 1996 as part of the "Pet's Corner" grouping. This puppy features a separately attached crystal piece representing a keg around the puppy's neck.

CRV: $125

Sailing Legend

7473 000 006/619436
Designer: Hainz Tebertshofer
Size: 4-1/8"/104mm
Trademark: Swan

The *Sailing Legend* was issued in 2003 at a suggested retail of $300. No known variations.

CRV: $300

Salt And Pepper Set

7508 NR 068 034/7508 068 034
Designer: Team
Size: 2-3/8"/60mm
Trademark: SC and Swan

The *Salt and Pepper Set* was issued in 1982. Both pieces have rhodium tops and were sold separately in the European market. The set was retired in December 1988 at a suggested retail of $100.

SC CRV: $450
Swan CRV: $350

Santa Claus

7475 000 603/221 362
Designer: Martin Zendron
Size: 2-3/8"/60mm
Trademark: Swan

Santa Claus was issued in 1998, and displays with the *Sleigh* and *Reindeer* on two specially designed mirrors. There are no known variations of this piece. The current suggested retail is $160.

CRV: $160

Santa Maria

7473 000 003/162 882
Designer: Gabriele Stamey
Size: 4-5/8"/118mm
Trademark: Swan

The *Santa Maria* was issued in 1991, and rests on a blue mirror. The *Santa Maria* is one piece of the "When We Were Young" grouping. The current suggested retail is $385.

CRV: $385

Saxophone

7477 000 007/211 728
Designer: Martin Zendron
Size: 4-1/4"/105mm
Trademark: Swan

The *Saxophone* was issued in 1997, and rests on a metal stand. There are no known variations. It was retired in December 2003 at a suggested retail of $125.

CRV: $150

Schnapps Glasses

7468 NR 039 000/7468 039 00
Designer: Team
Size: 2-1/16"/53mm
Trademark: SC or Swan

The *Schnapps Glasses* were sold in the U.S. as a set of six and were issued in 1983. In the European and Canadian markets the Schnapps Glasses were sold in sets of three with the item number 7468 NR 039 055. They were retired in December 1990 at a suggested retail of $180 for the six-piece set.

SC CRV: $400
Swan CRV: $350

Sea Horse

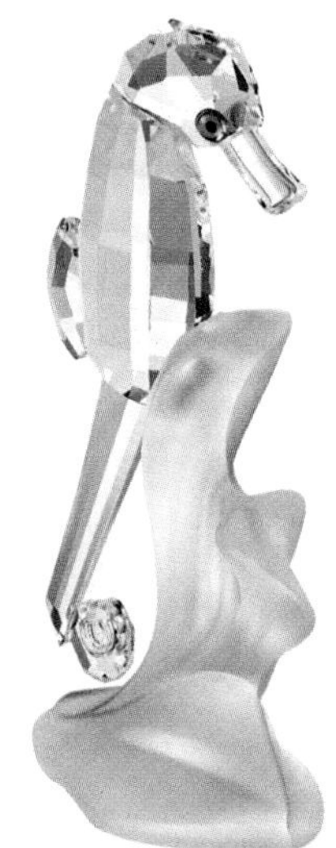

7614 080 000/168 683
Designer: Michael Stamey
Size: 3-1/8"/80mm
Trademark: Swan

The *Sea Horse* was issued in 1993. There are no known variations. The current suggested retail is $95.

CRV: $95

Sea Shell, South

7624 NR 072 000/7624 072 000
Designer: Michael Stamey
Size: 2-3/4"/70mm
Trademark: Swan

The *South Sea Shell* was issued in 1991. There are no known variations. It was retired in December 1994 at a suggested retail of $120.

CRV: $175

Seal, Large

7646 NR 85/7646 085 000
Designer: Max Schreck
Size: 3-1/2"/89mm
Trademark: SC or Swan

The *Large Seal* was issued in 1985. There are five different known variations. It was retired in December 1995 at the suggested retail of $85.

SC (Black Nose European Variation) CRV: $275
Swan (Black Nose European Variation) CRV: $250
SC (Silver Whiskers U.S. Release) CRV: $200
Swan (Silver Whiskers U.S. Release) CRV: $175
SC (Black Whiskers Euro, then Worldwide) CRV: $190
Swan (Black Whiskers Euro, then Worldwide) CRV: $175
SC (Black Whiskers, looking left or right) CRV: $250
Swan (Black Whiskers, looking left or right) CRV: $150

Seal, Mini

7663 046 000/012 530
Designer: Adi Stocker
Size: 1-1/2"/38mm
Trademark: SC or Swan

The *Mini Seal* was issued in 1986 and has a current suggested retail of $46.50. There are three known variations.

SC (no whiskers) CRV: $400
Swan (no whiskers) CRV: $375
SC (silver whiskers) CRV: $300
Swan (silver whiskers) CRV: $200
SC (black whiskers) CRV: $250
Swan (black whiskers: CRV: $200

Seals, Member

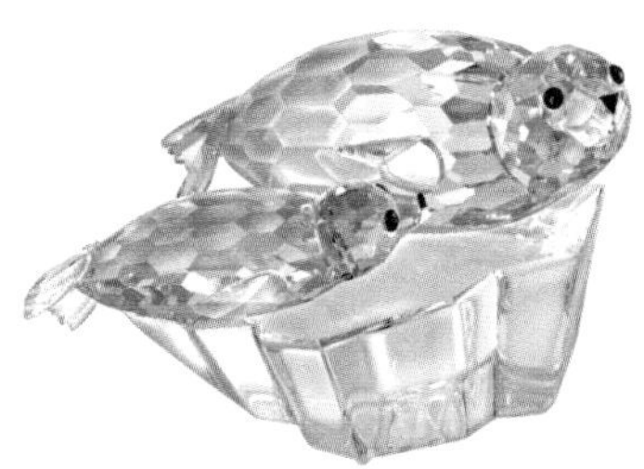

DO1X911/158 872
Designer: Michael Stamey
Size: 4"/102mm
Trademark: Swan/SCS

The *Seals* were issued as the second annual Swarovski Collectors Society Member redemption piece in 1991. The retail price at the time of issue was $225.

CRV: $600

Shell

7624 000 003/191 692
Designer: Michael Stamey
Size: 1-1/4"/31mm
Trademark: Swan

The *Shell* was issued in 1995, and features a small crystal piece representing a pearl within the open shell. This piece is part of the "Maritime Trio" set. The current suggested retail is $46.50.

CRV: $46.50

Shepherd

7475 NR 000 007/7475 000 007
Designer: Team
Size: 1-7/8"/48mm
Trademark: Swan

The *Shepherd* was issued in 1992 as part of the "Nativity Scene." It was only produced for one year and was retired in December 1993. The suggested retail at its retirement was $65. There are no known variations, and the short production period makes it very limited on the secondary market.

CRV: $125

Siamese Fighting Fish—Blue

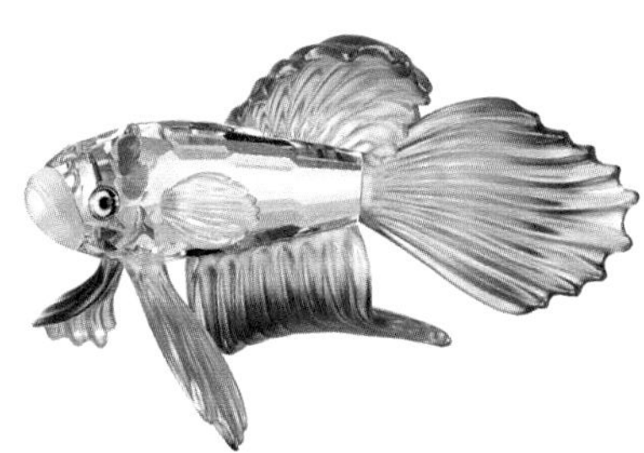

7644 000 005/ 236 718
Designer: Heinz Tabertshofer
Size: 3-1/4"/82 mm
Trademark: Swan

The *Siamese Fighting Fish* was issued in blue in 1999 as part of the "South Sea" grouping. Also available in green.

CRV: $125

Siamese Fighting Fish—Green

7644 000 006/261 259
Designer: Hainz Tabertshofer
Size: 3-1/4"/82mm
Trademark: Swan

The *Siamese Fighting Fish* was issued in green in 2000 as part of the "South Sea" grouping. Also available in blue.

CRV: $125

Siamese Fighting Fish—Red

7644 000 013/660941
Designer: Heinz Tebertshofer
Size: 2-2/3"/66mm
Trademark: Swan

The *Red Siamese Fighting Fish* was issued in 2004 as part of the "South Sea" theme group. Notable with red fins, crystal Sahara eyes, and clear crystal body. No known variations. Sugggested retail at the time of issue was $125.

CRV: $125

Sleigh

7475 000 601/205 165
Designer: Martin Zendron
Size: 4-1/4"/106mm
Trademark: Swan

The *Sleigh* was issued in 1996, and is usually displayed with the *Santa* and the *Reindeer*. It is sold with two packages and a small sisal tree. The current suggested retail is $295.

CRV: $295

Snail

7648 NR 030/7648 030 000
Designer: Michael Stamey
Size: 1-1/2"/38mm
Trademark: SC or Swan

The *Snail* was issued in 1986. There are several variations possible relating to the width of the snail's mouth and the antennae diameter. It was retired in December 1995 at the suggested retail of $55.

SC CRV: $125
Swan CRV: $100

Snail On Vine-Leaf

7615 000 005/196 501
Designer: Edith Mair
Size: 1-3/4"
Trademark: Swan

The *Snail on Vine-Leaf* was issued in 1996, and is notable with silver-colored antennae. The current suggested retail is $65.

CRV: $65

Snake, Zodiac

7693 000 011/625190
Designer: Anton Hirzinger
Size: 1-1/8"/28mm
Trademark: Swan

The *Zodiac Snake* was issued in 2004 as part of the "Chinese Zodiac" theme group. No known variations. The suggested retail at time of issue was $60.

DVR: $60

Snowman

7475 000 605/250 229
Designer: Edith Mair
Size: 2-1/4"
Trademark: Swan

The Snowman was issued in 2000. There are no known variations to date. The current suggested retail is $99.

CRV: $99

Sparrow

7650 NR 000 001/7650 000 001
Designer: Claudia Schneiderbauer
Size: 1-1/2"/38mm
Trademark: Swan

The Sparrow was issued in 1992, and there are no known variations. It was retired in December 1997 at the suggested retail of $29.50.

CRV: $75

Sparrow, Large

7650 NR 32/7650 032 000
Designer: Max Schreck
Size: 1-1/4"/32mm
Trademark: SC or Swan

The *Large Sparrow* was issued in 1983 exclusively in the U.S. and Canada. There are no known variations. It was retired in 1988 at the suggested retail of $40.

SC CRV: $275
Swan CRV: $225

Sparrow, Mini

7650 NR 20/7650 020 000
Designer: Max Schreck
Size: 3/4"/19mm
Trademark: SC or Swan

The *Mini Sparrow* was issued in 1979. There are no known variations. It was retired in December 1991 at the suggested retail of $27.50.

SC CRV: $90
Swan CRV: $75

Squirrel

7662 042 000/011 871
Designer: Max Schreck
Size: 1-3/4"/44mm
Trademark: SC or Swan

The *Squirrel* was issued in 1985. Three variations exist. The original European-only design has become distributed worldwide. This version has taller pointed ears. The U.S. version has small round ears. The third, and most scarce version, is the "Squirrel with Black Nut" version. The current retail is $55.

SC (U.S. small ears) CRV: $150
Swan (U.S. small ears) CRV: $125
SC (Black Nut) CRV: $850
Swan (Black Nut) CRV: $750

Stag

7608 000 004/291 431
Designer: Adi Stocker
Size: 5-1/2"/137mm
Trademark: Swan

The *Stag* was issued in 2002, and is notable with silver-colored metal antlers. There are no known variations. The current suggested retail is $385.

CRV: $385

Starfish

7624 000 001/191 690
Designer: Michael Stamey
Size: 1-3/4"/45mm
Trademark: Swan

The *Starfish* was issued in 1995. This piece is also part of the three-piece set entitled "Maritime Trio." It was retired in December 2003 at a suggested retail of $29.50. There are no known variations.

CRV: $40

Starter Set

7606 100 000/187 512
Designer: Team
Size: 3-7/8"/100mm (total display diameter)
Trademark: Swan

These three mini pieces (*Mini Cat, Mini Hedgehog, Mini Mouse*) were issued as a starter set in 1994. All three pieces are sold individually without the mirror that comes with the set. It was retired in December 2003 at the suggested retail of $112.

CRV: $125

Swan, 1995 Renewal

003-003802
Designer: Anton Hirzinger
Size: 1-1/4"/32mm
Trademark: Swan

The *1995 Renewal Swan* was produced only for one year, and was given to renewing members of the Swarovski Collectors Society. Limited edition closed at year-end in 1995.

CRV: $75

Swan, Brooch

7855 001 B
Designer: Team
Size: 5/8"/16mm
Trademark: Swan

The *Swan Brooch* was issued as a gift to Swarovski Collectors Society members when they attended special Swarovski-sponsored events, oftentimes as a gift with purchases. This *Swan Brooch* was retired in 1995, and currently is sold at retail as part of the Swarovski Jeweler's Collection.

CRV: $75

Swan, Centenary

7633 NR 100 000
Designer: Anton Hirzinger
Size: 2"/50mm
Trademark: Swan

Notable with 100 individual stones representing water on the swan's feathers. Issued in 1995 to commemorate the 100th anniversary of the Swarovski company. Price at time of issue was $115.

CRV: $175

Swan Family

7550 000 006/243 373
Designer: Adi Stocker
Size: 3"/75mm
Trademark: Swan

The *Swan Family* was issued in 2000. There are no known variations. The current suggested retail is $190.

CRV: $190

Swan Large

7633 063 000/010 005
Designer: Max Schreck
Size: 2-7/8"/73mm
Trademark: SC or Swan

The *Large Swan* was issued in 1977. There are three known variations relating to the neck curvature and the body flatness, which rests on a flat surface. The most valuable is the variation with the most outstretched neck. The current suggested retail is $99.

SC CRV: $195

SC (stretched neck) CRV: $295

SC (current style) CRV: $150

Swan (current style) CRV: $99

Swans, Large (Set Of 2)

7633 000 063 P/283 616
Designer: Max Schreck
Size: 3"/76mm
Trademark: Swan

The *Large Swans* were issued in 1994 as a set of two. These swans are intended for use as a wedding cake topper. The current suggested retail is $198.

CRV: $198

Swan, Maxi

7633 160 000/189 254
Designer: Anton Hirzinger
Size: 6-1/2"/150mm
Trademark: Swan

The *Maxi Swan* was issued in 1995. There are no known variations. The current suggested retail is $4900.

CRV: $4900

Swan, Medium

7633 050 000/010 006
Designer: Max Schreck
Size: 2-1/8"/54mm
Trademark: SC or Swan

The *Medium Swan* was issued in 1977. There are two known variations. The older style has a flatter body and a longer neck and a greater arch. The SC trademark is only found on the older variation.

SC CRV: $325

Swan CRV: $95

Swan, Mini

7658 NR 27/7658 027 000
Designer: Max Schreck
Size: 15/16"/24mm
Trademark: SC or Swan

The *Mini Swan* was issued in 1982. Only a few pieces received the Swan trademark, therefore, the trademark on this piece brings the highest secondary market premium. There are no known variations. It was retired in December 1988 at a suggested retail of $25.

SC CRV: $125
Swan CRV: $200

Swan, Necklace

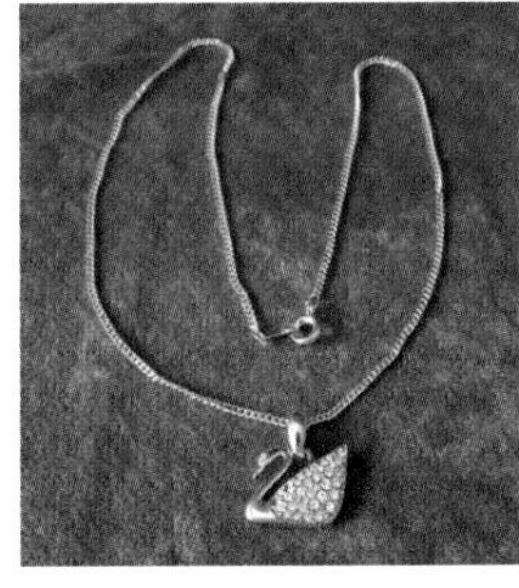

7855 001
Designer: Team
Size: 5/8"/16mm
Trademark: SCS/Swan

The *Swan Necklace* was issued as a gift to members of the Swarovski Collectors Society when attending special events. Retired in 1995, it can now be found as part of the Swarovski Jeweler's Collection.

CRV: $90

Swan, New Member

900 314 200 4579
Designer: Anton Hirzinger
Size: 1-1/2"/38mm
Trademark: Swan

This swan was produced and given to renewing members of the Swarovski Collectors Society beginning in 1996. No known variations.

CRV: $75

Swan, Small

7633 038 000/015 152
Designer: Max Schreck
Size: 1-1/2"/38mm
Trademark: SC or Swan

The *Small Swan* was issued in 1982, originally only in the U.S., until going worldwide in 1989. There are three known variations. The current suggested retail is $60.

SC CRV: $200
Swan (newer style, flatter body) CRV: $95
Swan (current model) CRV: $60

Sweet Heart

7480 000 001/210 035
Designer: Edith Mair
Size: 2"/50mm
Trademark: Swan

The *Sweet Heart* was issued in 1997 as a part of the "Exquisite Accents" grouping. It features a frosted ribbon and bow running across the heart. There are no known variations. The suggested retail is $125.

CRV: $125

Tank Wagon

7471 000 006/215 170
Designer: Gabriele Stamey
Size: 1-5/8"/41mm
Trademark: Swan

The *Tank Wagon* was issued in 1998 as part of the "When We Were Young" train grouping and was retired in December 2003 at a suggested retail of $95. There are no known variations.

CRV: $110

Tender Car

7471 000 002/015 147
Designer: Gabriele Stamey
Size: 1-1/4"/32mm
Trademark: SC or Swan

The *Tender Car* was issued in 1988 as part of the "When We Were Young" train grouping and was retired in December 2003. There are no known variations. The suggested retail at its retirement was $55.

SC CRV: $75
Swan CRV: $60

Terrier

7619 NR 000 002/7619 000 002
Designer: Adi Stocker
Size: 1-3/4"/44mm
Trademark: Swan

The *Terrier* was issued in 1990. There are no known variations. It was retired in December 1996 at the suggested retail of $75.

CRV: $125

Tiger

7610 000 003/220 470
Designer: Michael Stamey
Size: 3-1/8"/80mm
Trademark: Swan

The *Tiger* was issued in 1998 and there are no known variations. It was retired in December 2002 at a suggested retail of $275.

CRV: $275

Tigger

14012004
Designer: Arribas Collection
Size: 2-1/8"/44mm
Trademark: Swan

Tigger was issued in 2001 by the Arribas stores at the Disney Theme Parks. Only 5000 pieces were produced in an exclusive limited edition. The suggested retail at the time of issue was $350.

CRV: $400

Tinkerbell

14012001
Designer: Arribas Collection
Size: 3-1/4"/80mm
Trademark: ©Disney

Tinkerbell was issued in 2000 by the Arribas stores at the Disney Theme Parks. Only 10,000 pieces were produced in an exclusive limited edition. The suggested retail at the time of issue was $325.

CRV: $500

Tipping Wagon

7471 000 005/171 233
Designer: Gabriele Stamey
Size: 1-5/8"/41mm
Trademark: Swan

The *Tipping Wagon* was issued in 1993 as part of the "When We Were Young" train grouping. It was retired in December 2003 at a suggested retail of $95.

CRV: $125

Toucan

7621 NR 000 002/7621 000 002
Designer: Michael Stamey
Size: 2-3/8"/60mm
Trademark: Swan

The *Toucan* was issued in 1989 as part of the "Up In The Trees" grouping. There are no known variations. It was retired in December 1992 at a suggested retail of $85. It was then reissued in a new design with a new number in 1999.

CRV: $175

Toucan

7621 000 006/234 311
Designer: Michael Stamey
Size: 3"/76mm
Trademark: Swan

The *Toucan* numbered 7621 000 006 was issued in 1999 as part of the "Feathered Friends" grouping. There are no known variations. The current suggested retail is $155.

CRV: $155

Tortoise

7632 000 001/210 085
Designer: Edith Mair
Size: 2"/50mm
Trademark: Swan

The *Tortoise* was issued in 1997 and has a current suggested retail of $60.

CRV: $60

Town Hall

7474 NR 000 027/7474 000 027
Designer: Gabriele Stamey
Size: 2-3/8"/65mm
Trademark: Swan

The *Town Hall* was issued in 1993 as part of the "Silver Crystal City." It was retired in December 1994 at a suggested retail of $135. The short length of production makes it a little difficult to find on the secondary market.

CRV: $225

Train, Mini

7471 400 000/193 014
Designer: Gabriele Stamey
Size: 3-1/4"/85mm
Trademark: Swan

The *Mini Train* was issued in 1995 with a mirror decorated with train tracks, and consists of four pieces. There are no known variations. The current suggested retail is $125.

CRV: $125

Train (Set Of 3)

7471 NR 100/7471 100 000
Designer: Gabriele Stamey
Size: 5-3/8"/140mm
Trademark: SC or Swan

The *Train, Set of 3* was issued in 1988 and included the *Locomotive, Tender Car,* and a *Wagon Carriage*. It was discontinued when the fourth piece was issued in 1990. The suggested retail when it was discontinued was $305.

SC CRV: $350
Swan CRV: $325

Train (Set Of 4)

7471 NR 1001/7471 100 001
Designer: Gabriele Stamey
Size: 6-3/8"/175mm
Trademark: SC or Swan

The *Train, Set of 4* was issued in 1990 and included the *Locomotive, Tender Car, Wagon Carriage,* and the *Petrol Wagon*. The suggested retail when the set was discontinued was $400.

SC CRV: $500
Swan CRV: $475

Treasure Box, Butterfly (Heart)

7465 NR 52/100/7465 052 100
Designer: Max Schreck
Size: 1-15/16"/49mm
Trademark: SC or Swan

The *Treasure Box, Butterfly* in the heart shape was issued in 1981. It was retired in December 1990 at a suggested retail of $95. There are no known variations.

SC CRV: $350
Swan CRV: $325

Treasure Box, Butterfly (Oval)

7466 NR 063 100/7466 063 100
Designer: Max Schreck
Size: 2-1/2"/64mm
Trademark: SC

The *Treasure Box, Butterfly* in the oval shape was issued in 1981. It was retired in December 1988 at a suggested retail of $95. There are no known variations.

SC CRV: $400
Swan CRV: $375

Treasure Box, Butterfly (Round)

7464 NR 50/100/7464 050 100
Designer: Max Schreck
Size: 1-15/16"/49mm
Trademark: SC

The *Round Butterfly Treasure Box* was issued in 1981. It is notable with its frosted butterfly, which is the handle for the lid. There are no known variations. It was retired in December 1988 at a suggested retail of $95.

CRV: $275

Treasure Box, Flower (Heart)

7465 NR 52/7465 052 000
Designer: Max Schreck
Size: 1-15/16"/49mm
Trademark: SC

The heart-shaped *Treasure Box with Flower* was issued in 1981, and is notable with its flower, which is the handle for the lid. There are no known variations. It was retired in December 1988 at a suggested retail of $95.

CRV: $400

Treasure Box, Flower (Oval)

7466 NR 063 000/7466 063 000
Designer: Max Schreck
Size: 2-1/2"/64mm
Trademark: SC or Swan

The *Oval Treasure Box with Flower* was issued in 1981, and is notable with its frosted flower, which is the lid handle. There are no known variations. It was retired in December 1990 at a suggested retail of $95.

CRV: $375

Treasure Box, Flower (Round)

7464 NR 50/7464 050 000
Designer: Max Schreck
Size: 1-15/16"/49mm
Trademark: SC or Swan

The *Round Treasure Box with Flower* was issued in 1981, and is notable with its frosted flower, which is the lid handle. There are no known variations. It was retired in December 1990 at a suggested retail of $95.

CRV: $325

Tree Topper, Chrome

632784
Designer: Team
Size: 6-1/8"/153mm
Trademark: Swan

The *Chrome Tree Topper* was issued in 2003 as a functional Christmas Tree ornamental topper. Features a center star surrounded by six smaller stars and six spikes. Suggested retail at time of issue was $145.

CRV: $145

Tree Topper, Gold

632785
Designer: Team
Size: 6-1/8"/153mm
Trademark: Swan

The *Gold Tree Topper* was issued in 2003 as a functional Christmas Tree ornamental topper. Features a center star surrounded by six smaller stars and six spikes. Suggested retail at time of issue was $145.

CRV: $145

Tulip, Blue

606 546
Designer: Team
Size: 3-1/2"/87mm
Trademark: Swan

The *Blue Tulip* was issued in 2002 as a limited edition renewal gift for members of the Swarovski Collectors Society renewing their membership during 2002. It was retired December 2002.

CRV: $75

Tulip, Red

626 481
Designer: Team
Size: 3-1/2"/87mm
Trademark: Swan

The *Red Tulip* was issued in 2003 as a limited edition renewal gift for members of the Swarovski Collectors Society renewing their membership during 2003. It was retired December 2003.

CRV: $50

Tulips (Bag Of)

606 546 R
Designer: Team
Size: 1-1/4"/30mm
Trademark: Swan/SCS

The *Bag of Tulips* was issued in 2002 as a limited edition renewal gift. Members who renewed for multiple years received this limited edition offering. *The Bag of Tulips* contained nine tulips: three red, three blue and three yellow.

CRV: $75

Turtle, Giant

7632 240 000/010 101
Designer: Max Schreck
Size: 9-1/2"/240mm
Trademark: SC or Swan

The *Giant Turtle* was issued in 1981. With a total length of 9-1/2", or 240mm, this giant piece is very impressive. There are no known variations.

SC CRV: $5500
Swan CRV: $4900

Turtle, King

7632 NR 75/7632 075 000
Designer: Max Schreck
Size: 3"/76mm
Trademark: SC or Swan

The *King Turtle* was issued in 1983, and features dark green eyes. It was issued only in the U.S. and Canada. It was retired in June 1988 at a suggested retail of $80. There are no known variations.

SC CRV: $775
Swan CRV: $675

Turtle, Large

7632 NR 45/7632 045 000
Designer: Max Schreck
Size: 2-1/4"/57mm
Trademark: SC or Swan

The *Large Turtle* was issued in 1977. It features green eyes and a clear crystal body. There are no known variations. It was retired in December 1998 at a suggested retail of $75.

SC CRV: $125
Swan CRV: $85

Turtle, Small

7632 NR 30/7632 030 000
Designer: Max Schreck
Size: 1-1/2"/38mm
Trademark: SC or Swan

The *Small Turtle* was issued in 1977, and its features include black eyes with a clear crystal body. There are no known variations. It was retired in December 1996 at a suggested retail of $49.50.

SC CRV: $100
Swan CRV: $75

Turtledoves

DO1X891/117 895
Designer: Adi Stocker
Size: 3-1/2"/89mm
Trademark: Swan/SCS

The *Turtledoves* were issued as a limited annual edition to members of the Swarovski Collectors Society during the 1989 membership year at a suggested retail of $195. Variations exist regarding the positions of the birds on the branch/base.

Swan/SCS CRV: $1000

Unicorn

DO1X961/191 727
Designer: Martin Zendron
Size: 4-3/8"/111mm
Trademark: Swan/Swarovski

The *Unicorn* was issued in 1996 to members of the Swarovski Collectors Society. Each piece has an etched date of "96" and "MZ," representing the initials of the designer Martin Zendron. There are no known variations. The issue price was $325, and was produced for only one year.

Swan/Swarovski CRV: $650

Unicorn (2004)

7550 000 013/630119
Designer: Anton Hirzinger
Size: 4-1/8"/103mm
Trademark: Swan

The *Unicorn* was issued in 2004 as part of the "Fairy Tales" theme group. The swan trademark is usually found under the right hind hoof. Suggested retail at time of issue was $285.

CRV: $285

Vase

7511 NR 70/7511 070 000
Designer: Team
Size: 2-7/8"/73mm
Trademark: SC or Swan

The *Vase* was issued in 1985. It features a trio of small frosted flower blossoms at the vase's neck. There are no known variations. The suggested retail when the *Vase* was retired in December 1990 was $70.

SC CRV: $225
Swan CRV: $175

Vase Of Roses

7400 200 204/293 394
Designer: Gabriele Stamey
Size: 2-3/4"
Trademark: Swan

Vase of Roses was issued as a special edition to members of the Swarovski Collectors Society to commemorate the society's 15th anniversary. It features 15 ruby-red roses with silver stems fitting into a clear, crystal round vase. It was retired in December 2002 at an issue price of $140. It was produced for only one year.

CRV: $175

Violin

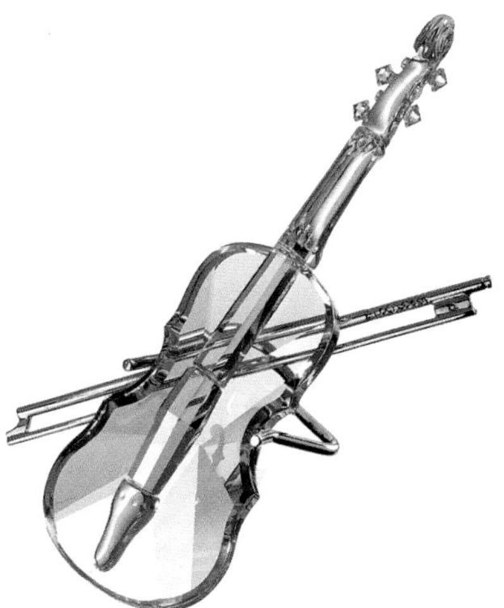

7477 000 002/203 056
Designer: Gabriele Stamey
Size: 4-1/4"/105mm
Trademark: Swan

The *Violin* was issued in 1996 as part of the "Crystal Melodies" grouping, and comes with a metal bow and stand. There are no known variations. The current suggested retail is $145.

CRV: $145

Walrus

7620 NR 100 000/7620 100 000
Designer: Michael Stamey
Size: 4"/102mm
Trademark: Swan

The *Walrus* was issued in 1989, and features frosted tusks, a clear crystal body, and black eyes. There are no known variations. It was retired in December 1993 at a suggested retail of $135.

CRV: $225

Whale

7628 NR 80/7628 080 000
Designer: Michael Stamey
Size: 3-1/4"/83mm
Trademark: SC or Swan

The *Whale* was issued in 1987. Some variations have been noted regarding the mouth size. It was retired in December 1991 at a suggested retail of $85.

SC CRV: $350
Swan CRV: $275

Whales

DO1X921/164 614
Designer: Michael Stamey
Size: 4-1/8"/105mm
Trademark: Swan/SCS

The *Whales* were issued as a limited edition annual offering to members of the Swarovski Collectors Society in 1992. There are no known variations. The suggested retail when it was retired in December 1992 was $265.

CRV: $600

Wild Horses

7607 000 003/236 720
Designer: Martin Zendron
Size: 13-1/4"/330mm
Trademark: Swan

The *Wild Horses* were issued in 2001 as a limited edition of 10,000 pieces. Each piece has the edition number etched into the crystal base. The *Wild Horses* were released during the 25th anniversary of the production of Swarovski Silver Crystal. The designer's initials and the year of issue are found on the black wooden base. It was retired in December 2001 at the issue price of $4000.

CRV: $6000

Winnie The Pooh

SDW 004/14012005
Designer: Arribas Stores
Size: 1-3/4"/44mm
Trademark: © Disney

The Arribas Stores issued *Winnie The Pooh* as an exclusive edition at the Disney Theme Parks. This exclusive edition consists of 5,000 pieces, which were issued in 1999. Beautifully encrusted with Swarovski stones and issued at a suggested retail of $350.

CRV: $400

Wise Men

7475 NR 200 000/7475 200 000
Designer: Team
Size: 1-3/4"/45mm
Trademark: Swan

The *Wise Men* were issued in 1992 as a three-piece set, and are scarce due to one year of production. There are no known variations. It was retired in December 1993 at a suggested retail of $175. It was produced to be part of the "Nativity Scene."

CRV: $300

Wolf

7550 000 002/207 549
Designer: Edith Mair
Size: 2-1/2"/62mm
Trademark: Swan

The *Wolf* was issued in 1996. There are no known variations. The current suggested retail is $155.

CRV: $155

Woodpeckers

DO1X881/014 745
Designer: Adi Stocker
Size: 4-1/8"/105mm
Trademark: Swan/SCS

The *Woodpeckers* were issued as an annual limited edition for members of the Swarovski Collectors Society in 1988. Some pieces have been noted with a clear base on the underside of the tree base. It was issued with an octagonal mirror bearing the SCS logo.

Swan (clear base variation)
CRV: $2750
Swan CRV: $2000

GALLERY

Alligator, MSRP ***$75***

Angel, MSRP ***$215***

Anniversary Birthday Cake, CRV ***$300***

Anniversary Squirrel, CRV ***$150***

*Anniversary Vase of Roses, CRV **$150***

*Antonio, CRV **$400***

*Anteater, MSRP **$60***

Apple Photo Stand, King, gold, CRV **$675**

Apple Photo Stand, King, rhodium, CRV **$600**

Apple Photo Stand, small, gold, CRV **$195**

Apple Photo Stand, small, rhodium, CRV **$275**

Baby Beaver, Sitting, CRV ***$85***

Baby Frog, CRV ***$29.50***

Baby Giraffe, CRV ***$265***

Baby Lovebirds, CRV ***$160***

Baby Panda, CRV ***$27.50***

Baby Penguins, set of three, CRV ***$75***

Baby Sea Lion, CRV ***$49.50***

Baby Shark, CRV ***$160***

Baby Snails on Vine Leaf, CRV ***$49.50***

Baby Tortoises, CRV ***$46.50***

Bald Eagle, CRV ***$280***

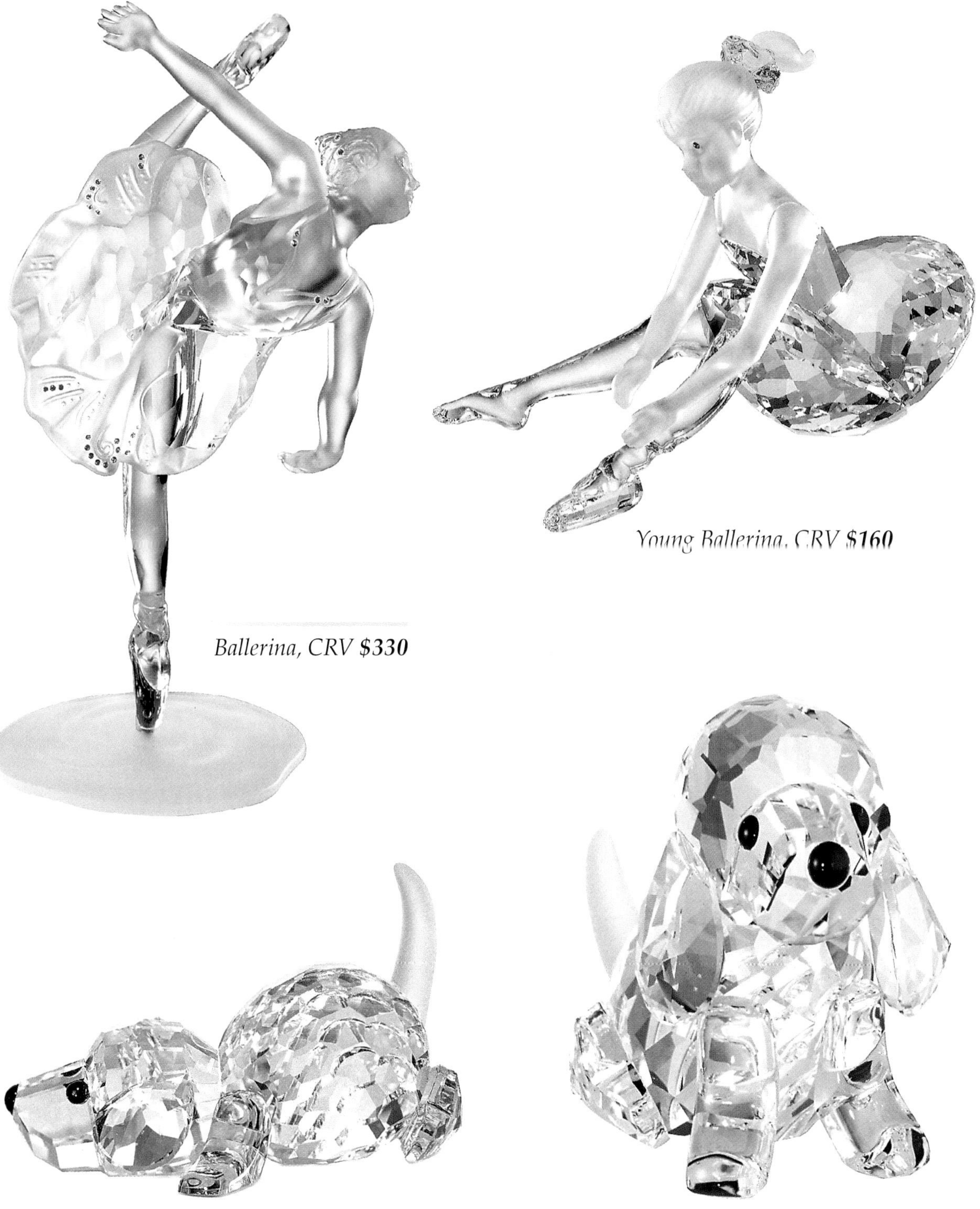

Young Ballerina, CRV **$160**

Ballerina, CRV **$330**

Playing Beagle, CRV **$49.50**

Beagle Puppy, CRV **$50**

Giant Bear, CRV **$3000**

King Bear, CRV **$2000**

Koala Bear, left facing, MSRP **$75**

Kris Bear with Honey Pot, CRV **$85**

*Celebration Kris Bear, CRV **$85***

*Kris Bear on Skates, **$85***

*Kris Bear with Skis, with base, CRV **$85***

*Large Bear, CRV **$99***

Mini Bear (current), CRV ***$55***

Mini Bear (retired), CRV ***$300***

Mother Panda Bear, CRV ***$125***

Rhodium Bee on Lily, CRV **$5750**

Gold Bee on Lily, CRV **$2000**

Gold Beetle Bottle Opener, CRV **$1400-$1800**

Rhodium Beetle Bottle Opener, CRV **$1400-$1600**

Bird Bath, CRV **$215**

Birthday Cake, CRV **$300**

Mini Blowfish, CRV **$29.50**

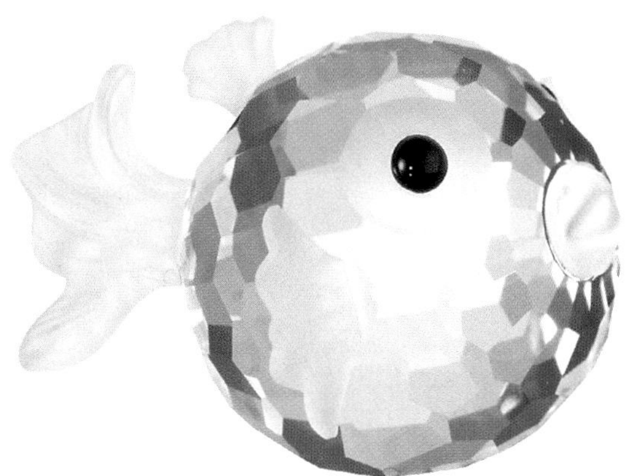

Small Blowfish, CRV **$55**

Blush Brush, CRV **$1500**

Butterfly, version 3, CRV **$90**

Mini Butterfly, CRV **$65**

Gold Butterfly, CRV ***$1395***

Butterfly on Leaf, CRV ***$90***

Rhodium Butterfly, CRV ***$3750***

Flowering Cactus, CRV ***$160***

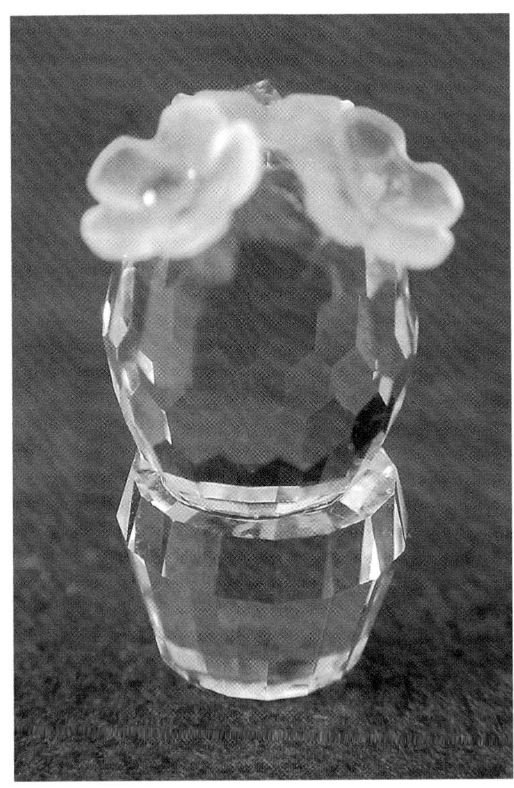

*Member Renewal Cactus, CRV **$295***

*Camel, CRV **$380***

*Candleholder 101, SC CRV **$190**, Swan **$100***

*Candleholder 108, CRV **$750***

*Candleholder 109, pin style, CRV **$195***

*Candleholder 110, hole style, CRV **$300***

*Candleholder 111, hole style, CRV **$900***

*Candleholder 114, pin style, CRV **$400***

*Candleholder 116, hole style, CRV **$3500***

Candleholder 126, CRV ***$750***

Candleholder 130, hole style, CRV ***$3500***

Candleholder 131, set of six, SC CRV ***$400****, Swan CRV* ***$250***

Candleholder 134, SC CRV ***$150****, Swan CRV* ***$125***

Gold Candleholder 136, CRV ***$595***

Rhodium Candleholder 136, CRV ***$750***

Candleholder 141, SC CRV ***$950****, Swan CRV* ***$750***

Candleholder 142, SC CRV ***$425****, Swan CRV* ***$375***

Candleholder 143, SC CRV ***$450****, Swan CRV* ***$400***

Train Carriage, SC CRV ***$175****, Swan CRV* ***$150***

Mini Cat, SC CRV ***$50****, Swan CRV* ***$27.50***

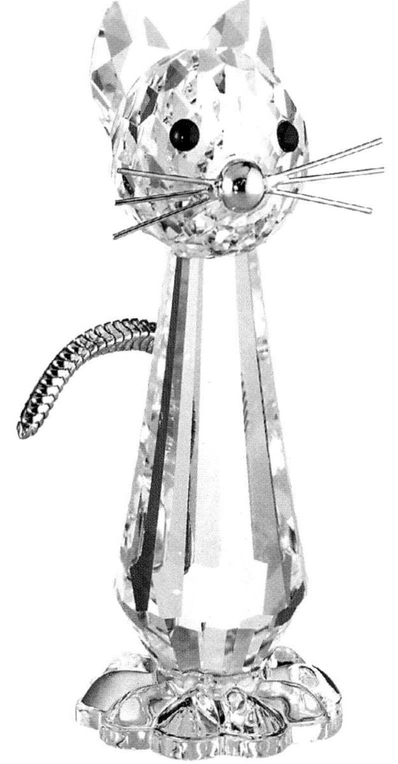

Replica Cat, CRV ***$42.50***

Sitting Cat, CRV ***$90***

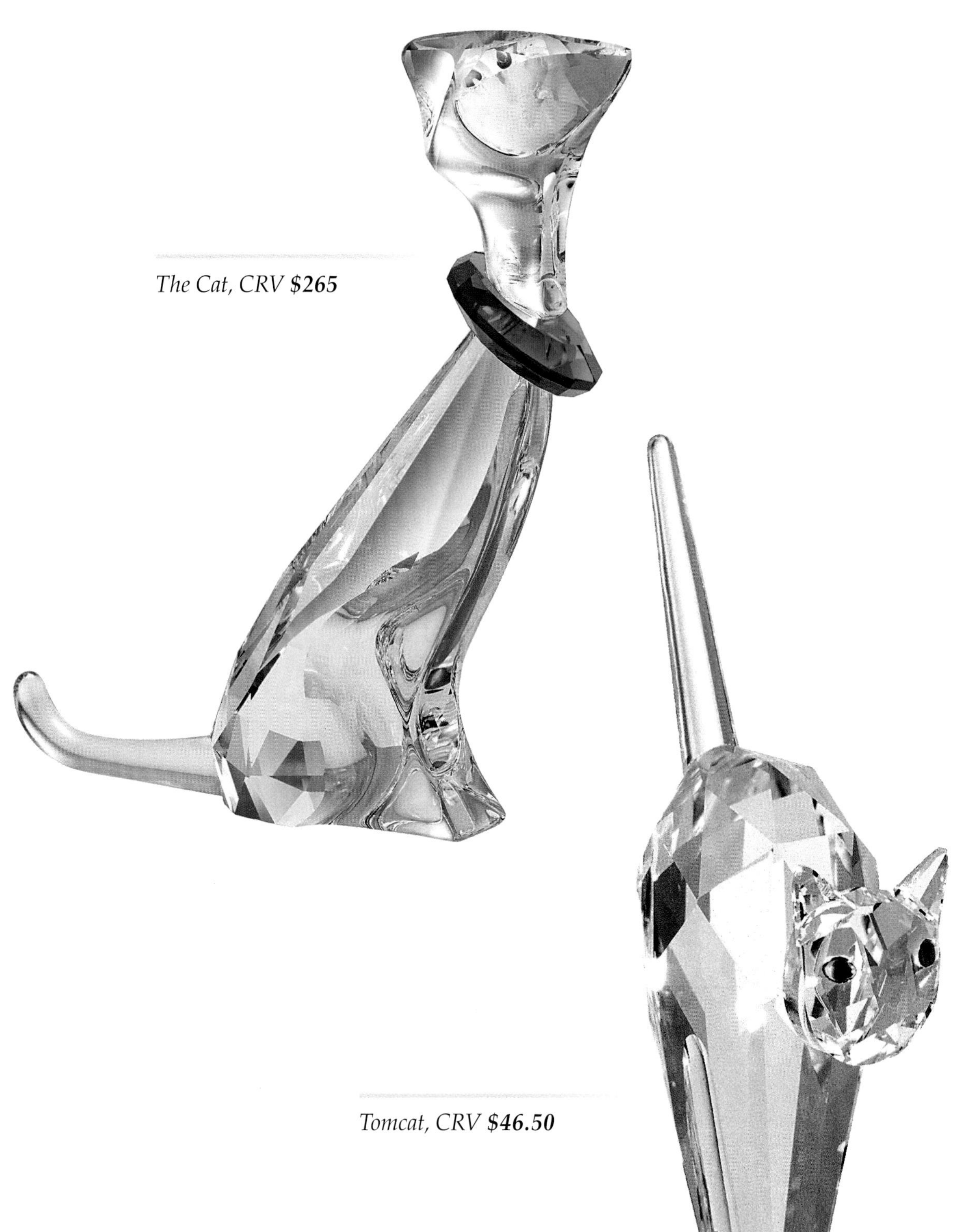

The Cat, CRV **$265**

Tomcat, CRV **$46.50**

Centenar, CRV ***$750***

Cheetah, current style, CRV ***$280***

Wooden Chess Set, CRV ***$2750***

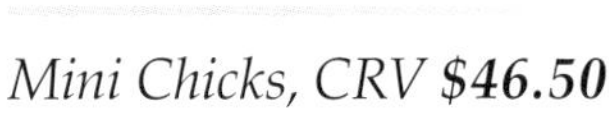
Mini Chicks, CRV ***$46.50***

*Chimpanzee, CRV **$125***

*Christmas Tree, CRV **$130***

*Rhodium Ashtray, CRV **$850***

*Cinderella, CRV **$330***

Belle Epoque Clock, CRV ***$900***

Colosseum Clock, CRV ***$950***

Four Leaf Clover, CRV ***$49.50***

Cobra, CRV ***$145***

*Cockatoo, CRV **$145***

*Cockerel, CRV **$75***

*Columbine, CRV **$400***

*Conch, CRV **$40***

The Cross of Light, CRV **$385**

Mini Crab, CRV **$65**

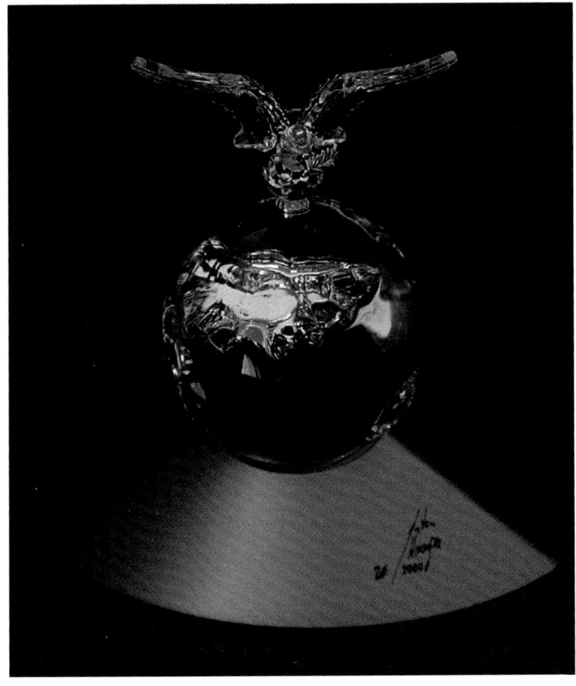

Crystal Planet, CRV **$300**

Dino, CRV **$130**

Doe, CRV ***$215***

The Dog, CRV ***$300***

Dolphin, CRV ***$215***

Dolphin Brooch, CRV ***$150***

Member Dolphins, CRV **$1250**

Maxi Dolphin, CRV **$895**

Donald Duck, CRV **$295**

Dove, CRV ***$60***

Dragon, 5-3/4", CRV ***$330***

Dragon, 5-1/2", CRV ***$750***

Dragonfly, CRV ***$85***

Mini Drake, SC CRV ***$60****, Swan CRV* ***$46.50***

Giant Mallard Duck, SC CRV ***$6000****, Swan CRV* ***$4600***

Large Duck, CRV ***$695***

Mini Standing Duck, SC CRV ***$60****,*
Swan CRV ***$42.50***

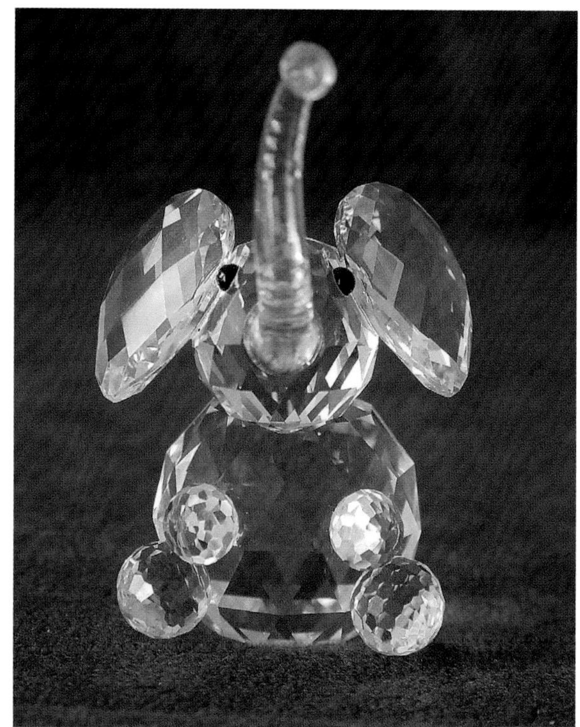

Dumbo, two examples of the many ear and tusk variations, CRV ***$4000-$5000***

*Dumbo, Arribus Stores version, CRV **$375***

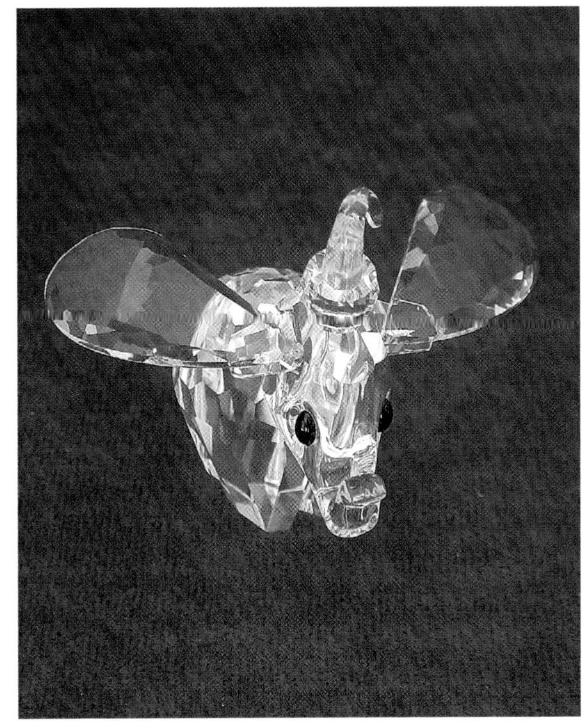

*Dumbo, 1990, CRV **$1200***

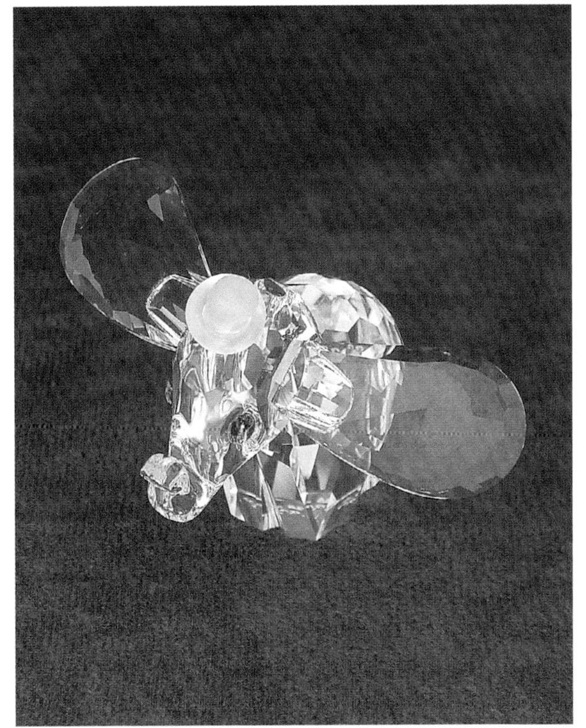

*Dumbo 1993, CRV **$500***

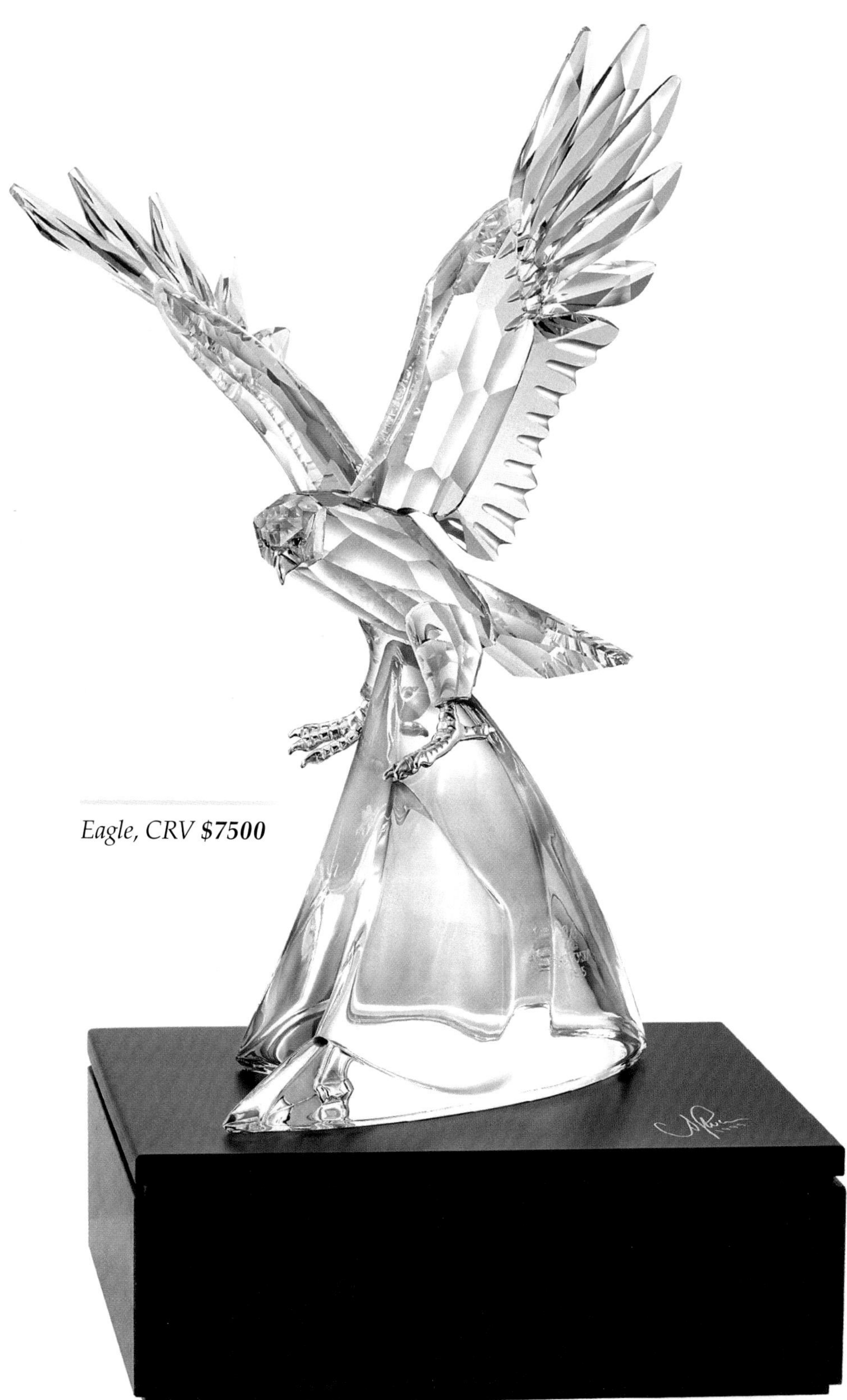

Eagle, CRV ***$7500***

*Elephant Baby, CRV **$160***

*Elephant Brooch, CRV **$100***

*Club Member Annual Elephant, CRV **$1500***

Small Elephant, CRV $65

Two examples of the Large Falcon Head, one with the V base and one with the smooth base, SC CRV ***$3250***, *Swan CRV* ***$2800***

Fawn, CRV ***$125***

Set of Three Field Mice, CRV ***$46.50***

Flamingo, CRV **$265**

Mini Running Fox, SC CRV **$80**, *Swan CRV* **$70**

Maxi flower Arrangement, CRV **$540**

Frog, CRV **$49.50**

German Shepherd, CRV **$145**

Zodiac Goat, CRV **$60**

Mother Goose, **$95**

Young Gorilla, CRV **$145**

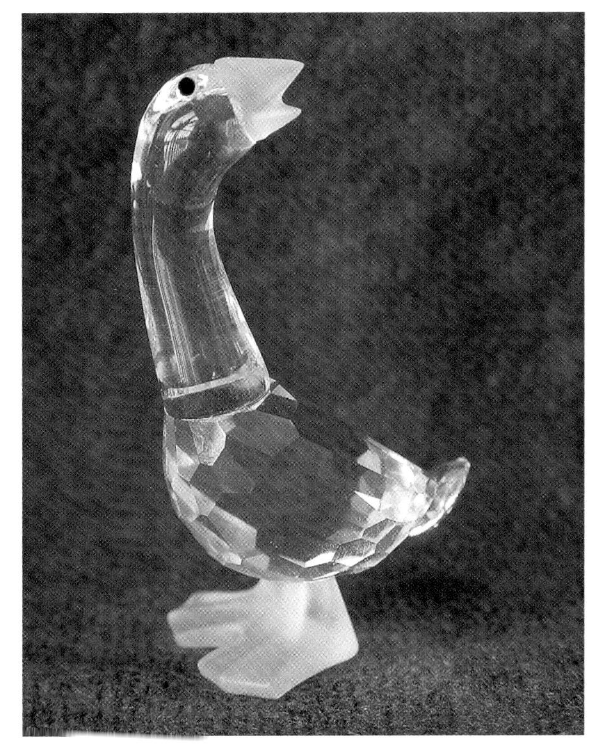

Dick Gosling, CRV **$75**

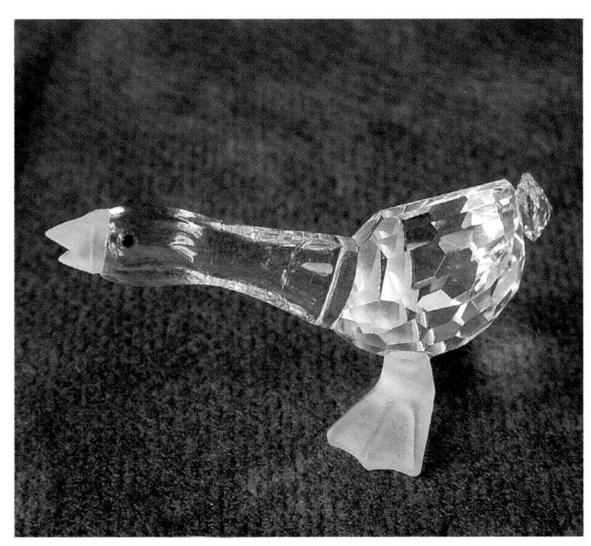

Harry Gosling, CRV **$75**

Tom Gosling, CRV **$75**

Grand Piano & Stool, CRV ***$280***

Large Grapes, gold leaves and stem, CRV ***$2500***

Small Grapes, gold leaves & stem, CRV **$325**

Small Grapes, gold leaves & stem, CRV **$325**

Grizzly, CRV **$330**

Grizzly Cub, CRV **$99**

Harlequin, CRV **$400**

1996 Renewal Heart, CRV **$125**

1997 Renewal Heart, CRV **$110**

1998 Renewal Heart, CRV **$80**

*Large Hedgehog, 2-3/4", SC CRV **$500**, Swan CRV **$200***

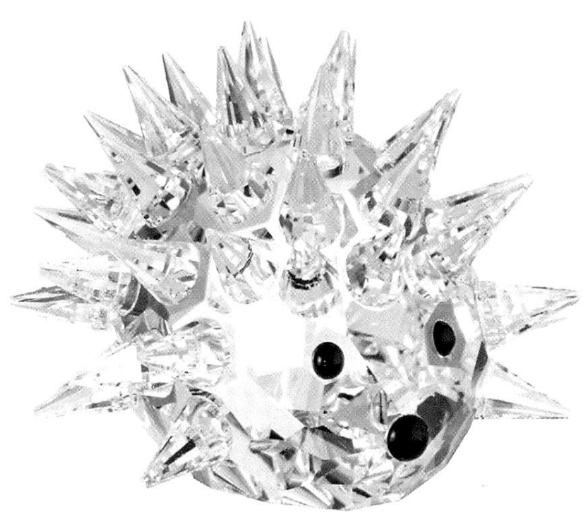

*Medium Hedgehog number 045, SC CRV **$125**, Swan CRV **$90***

*Replica Hedgehog, CRV **$42.50***

*Small Hedgehog, CRV **$500***

*Small Hedgehog, 1-1/2", SC CRV **$100**, Swan CRV **$60***

*Hen, MSRP **$75***

*Silver Heron, CRV **$280***

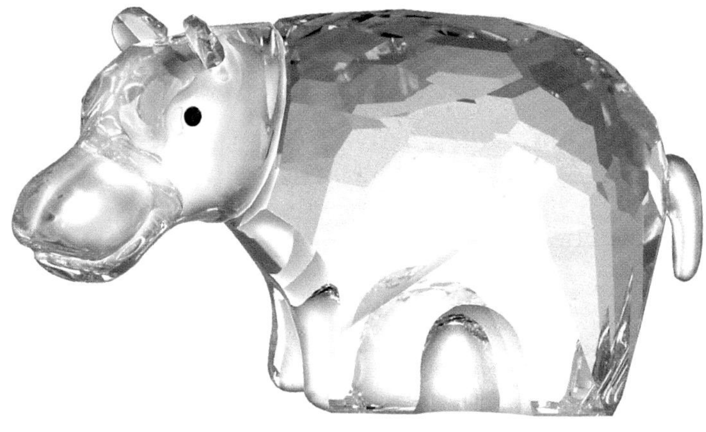

*Hippo, MSRP: **$65***

*Arabian Stallion, CRV **$265***

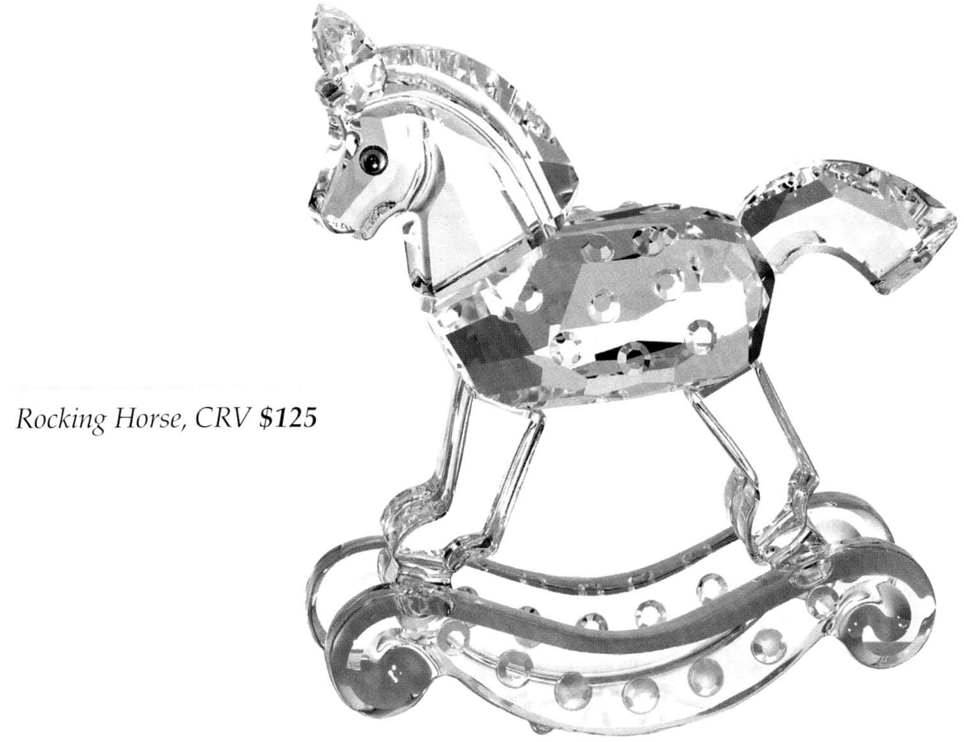

*Rocking Horse, CRV **$125***

White Stallion, CRV **$265**

Zodiac Horse, CRV $65

Hummingbird, CRV ***$215***

Gold Hummingbird, SC CRV ***$1500****,*
Swan CRV ***$1250***

Rhodium Hummingbird, CRV ***$6500***

Ibex, CRV ***$215***

*Isadora, CRV **$450***

*Mother Kangaroo with Baby Joey, CRV **$99***

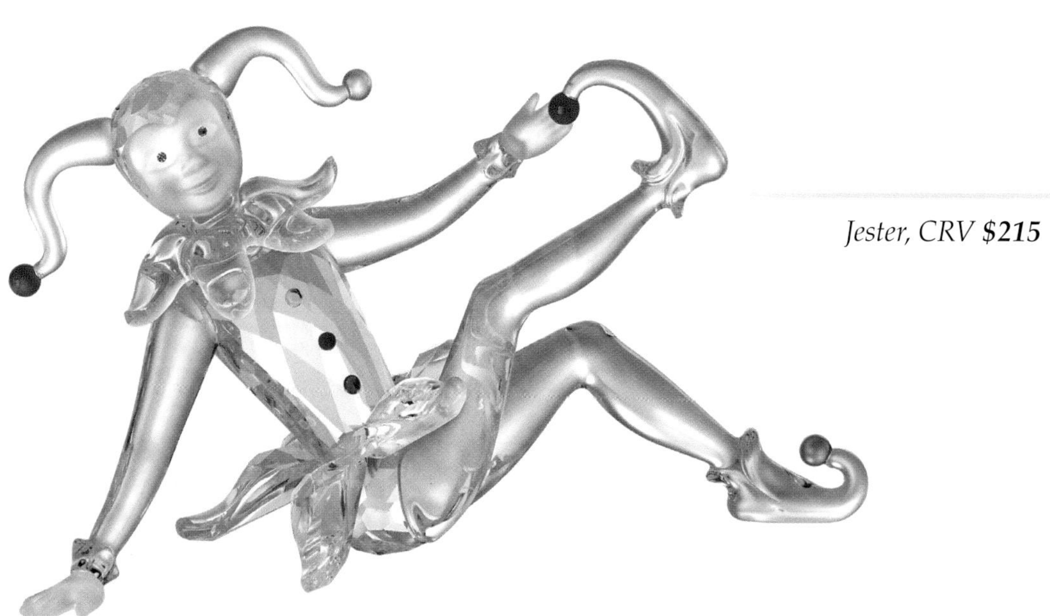

*Jester, CRV **$215***

*Kitten, CRV **$110***

*Malachite Kingfishers, MSRP **$160***

*Kristallwelton Wall, CRV **$400***

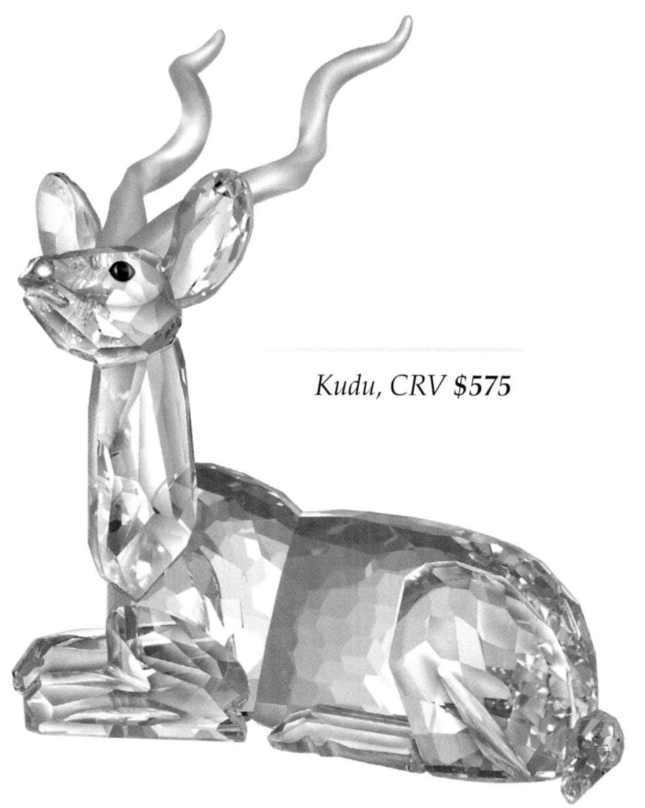

Kudu, CRV **$575**

Ladybug, CRV **$29.50**

Leopard, CRV **$265**

*Lion, 4-3/4", CRV **$330***

*Lion Cub, CRV **$125***

*Lion Fish, CRV **$145***

*Lion, CRV **$600***

*Little Red Riding Hood, CRV **$190***

*Locomotive, SC CRV **$200**, Swan CRV **$170***

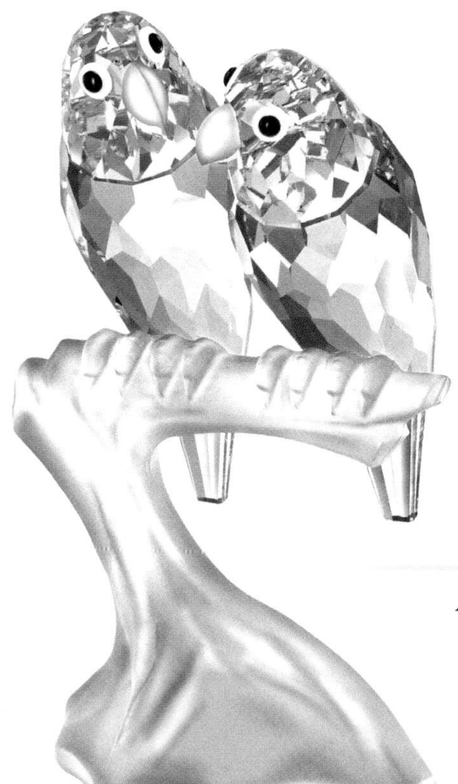

*Annual edition Lovebirds, CRV **$4000-$5000***

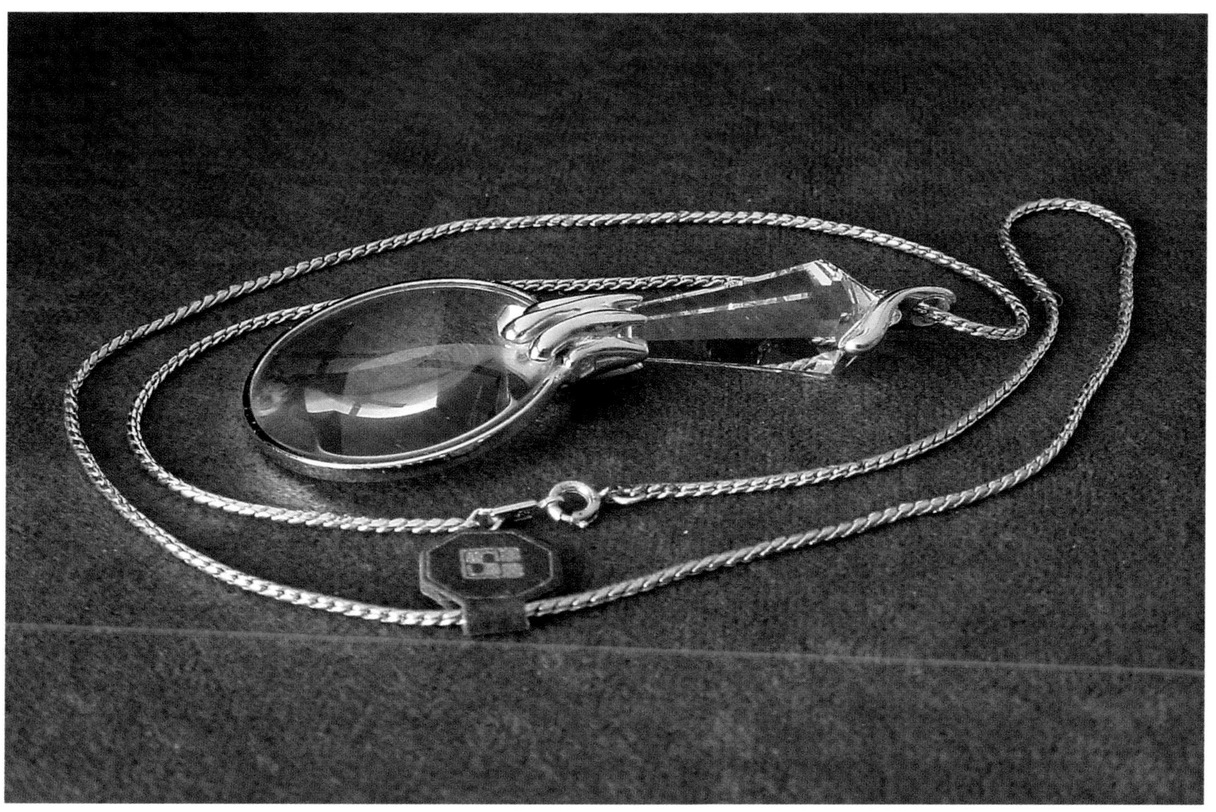

*Rhodium, Chain-style Magnifier, CRV **$1500***

*Gold Table Magnifier, CRV **$1350***

*Rhodium Table Magnifier, CRV **$1250***

1999 Renewal Marguerite, CRV ***$60-$75***

2000 Renewal Marguerite, CRV ***$50-$60***

2001 Renewal Marguerite, CRV ***$60-$75***

Maritime Trio, CRV **$125**

Marmot, CRV **$75**

Minnie Mouse, CRV **$325**

Zodiac Monkey, CRV **$60**

Replica Mouse, CRV **$42.50**

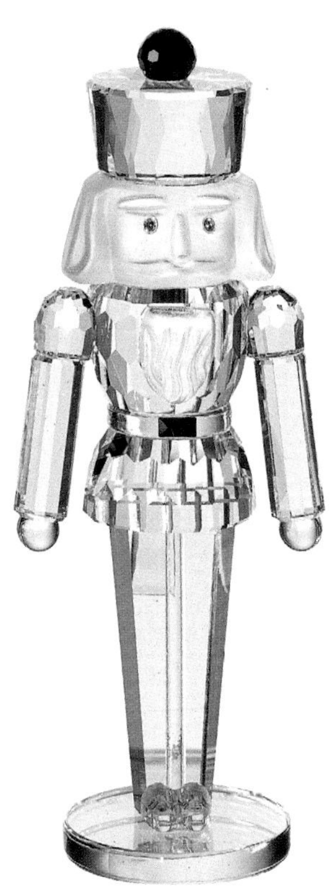

Nutcracker, CRV **$175**

Open Shell with Pearl, SC CRV ***$200,***
Swan CRV **$175**

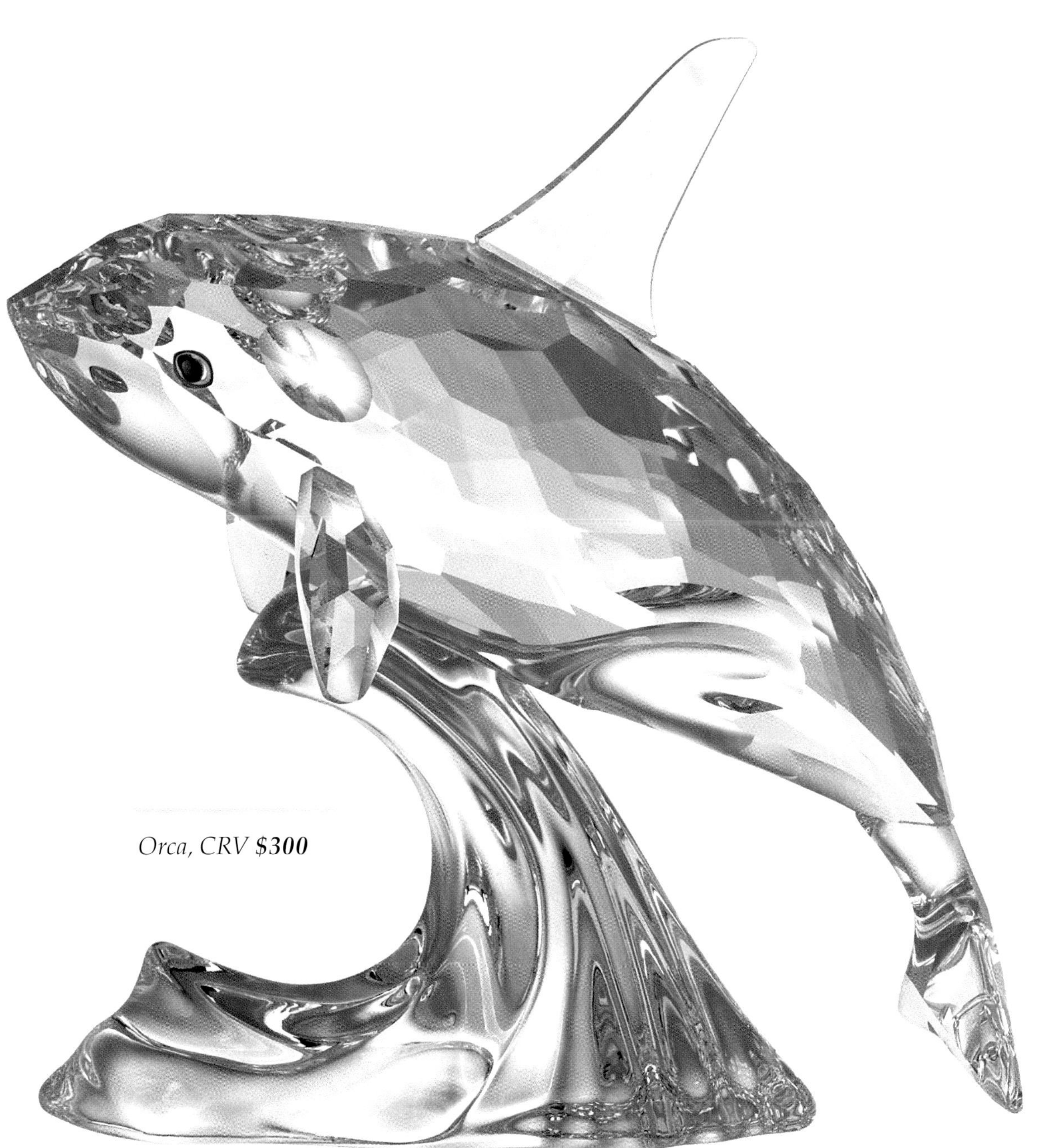

Orca, CRV ***$300***

Pink Orchid, depending on shade
CRV ***$145-$300***

1981 Christmas Ornament, CRV ***$450***

1986 Christmas Ornament, CRV ***$400***

1987 Christmas Ornament, CRV **$400**

1988 Christmas Ornament, **$125**

1989 Christmas Ornament, CRV **$400**

1990 Christmas Ornament, CRV **$325**

*1991 Christmas Ornament, European CRV **$500***

*1992 Christmas Ornament, CRV **$225***

*1993 Christmas Ornament, CRV **$450***

*1994 Christmas Ornament, CRV **$250***

1995 Christmas Ornament, CRV ***$200***

1996 Christmas Ornament, CRV ***$100***

1997 Christmas Ornament, CRV ***$100***

1998 Christmas Ornament, CRV ***$95***

1999 Christmas Ornament, CRV ***$150***

2000 Christmas Ornament, CRV ***$175***

Christmas Ornament 2001, CRV ***$100***

2002 Christmas Ornament, CRV ***$100***

Large Owl, SC CRV ***$175****, Swan CRV* ***$130***

Giant Owl, SC CRV ***$3000****, Swan CRV* ***$2055***

Mini Owl, SC CRV ***$50****, Swan* ***$29.50***

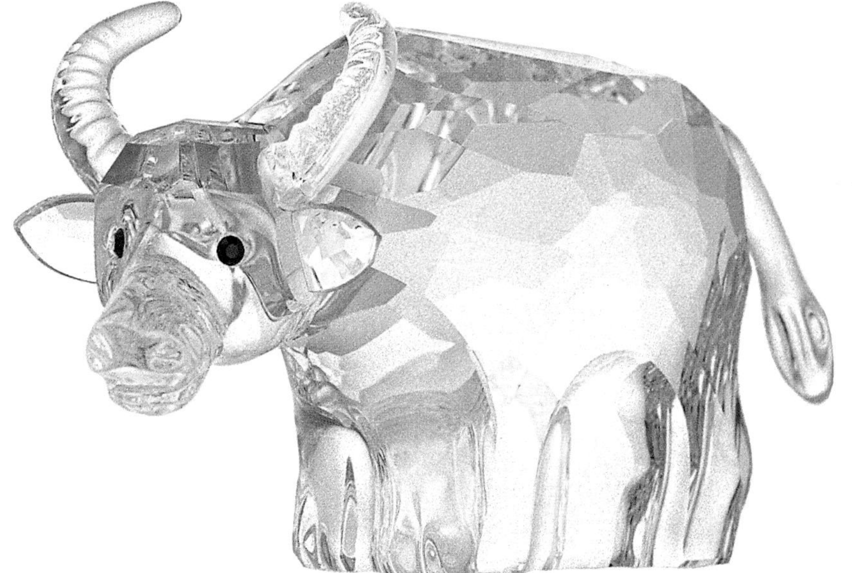

Zodiac Ox, CRV **$65**

Vitrail Medium Atomic Paperweight, CRV **$1500**

Vitrail Medium Carousel Paperweight, CRV **$1400**

Member renewal Chaton, CRV ***$175***

Giant Chaton, CRV ***$4500***

Large Chaton, CRV ***$275***

Bermuda Blue Cone Paperweight, SC CRV ***$1200****, Swan CRV* ***$900***

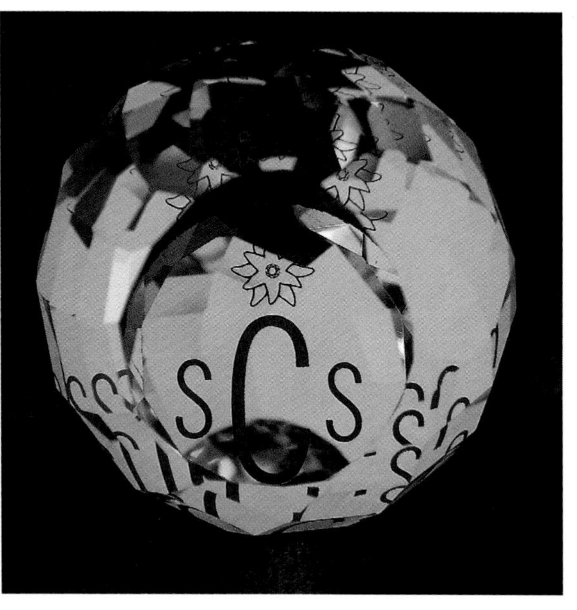

1987-1988 round Dealer Paperweight, CRV **$500**

1989-1991 round Dealer Paperweight, CRV **$400**

Member Paperweight, CRV **$90**

Member Paperweight, CRV **$75**

Crystal Cal Octron Paperweight, SC CRV **$225**,
Swan CRV **$200**

Crystal Cal Round Paperweight, SC CRV **$175**,
Swan CRV **$150**

Parrot, issued 2002, CRV **$225**

Pear, CRV **$195**

Peacock, CRV **$5000-$6000**

Pegasus, CRV **$375**

1994 Lancome Tresor Perfume Bottle, CRV **$500**

1995 Lancome Tresor Perfume Bottle, CRV **$350**

*1994 Renewal Picture Frame, CRV **$45***

*Oval Picture Frame, SC CRV **$600**, Swan CRV **$500***

*Square Picture Frame, gold European, CRV **$375***

Pierrot, CRV ***$500***

Mini Pig, crystal tail, European version, CRV ***$250***

Mini Pig, wire tail, U.S. version, CRV ***$29.50***

Zodiac Pig, CRV ***$60***

Giant Pineapple, gold, SC CRV **$4500**, *Swan CRV* **$3250**

Rhodium Giant Pineapple, CRV **$5750**

Rhodium Large Pineapple, textured, CRV **$600**

Octagonal Dealer's Plaque, CRV **$1500-$2250**

Emerald cut-style Dealer's Plaque, blue lettering, CRV ***$600***

Oval Crystal Iceberg Dealer's Plaque, CRV ***$400***

Premier Dealer's Crystal Display Plaque, CRV ***$500-$600***

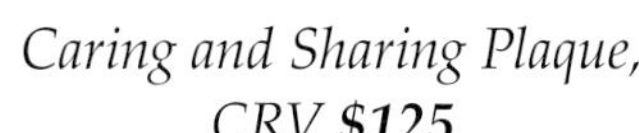

Caring and Sharing Plaque, CRV ***$125***

Mother and Child Plaque, CRV ***$100***

Inspirational Africa Plaque, CRV ***$90***

Fabulous Creatures Plaque, CRV ***$75***

Poplar Trees, CRV **$150**

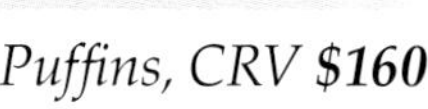

Puffins, CRV **$160**

Puppet, CRV **$125**

Mini Sitting Rabbit, SC CRV **$75**, *Swan CRV* **$46.50**

Zodiac Rat, CRV ***$60***

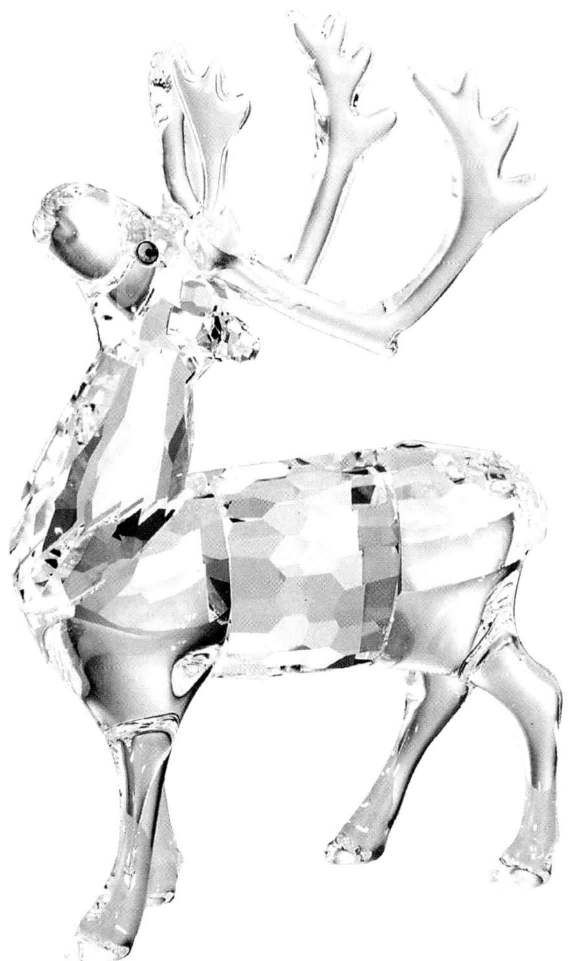

Rhino, MSRP ***$65***

Reindeer, CRV ***$190***

Mini Rooster, SC CRV **$95**, *Swan CRV* **$75**

The Rose, CRV **$155**

Dozen Pink Roses, CRV **$125**

St. Bernard, CRV **$125**

Sailboat, CRV **$215**

Sailing Legend, CRV **$300**

Santa Claus, CRV **$160**

Santa Maria, CRV **$385**

Saxophone, CRV ***$150***

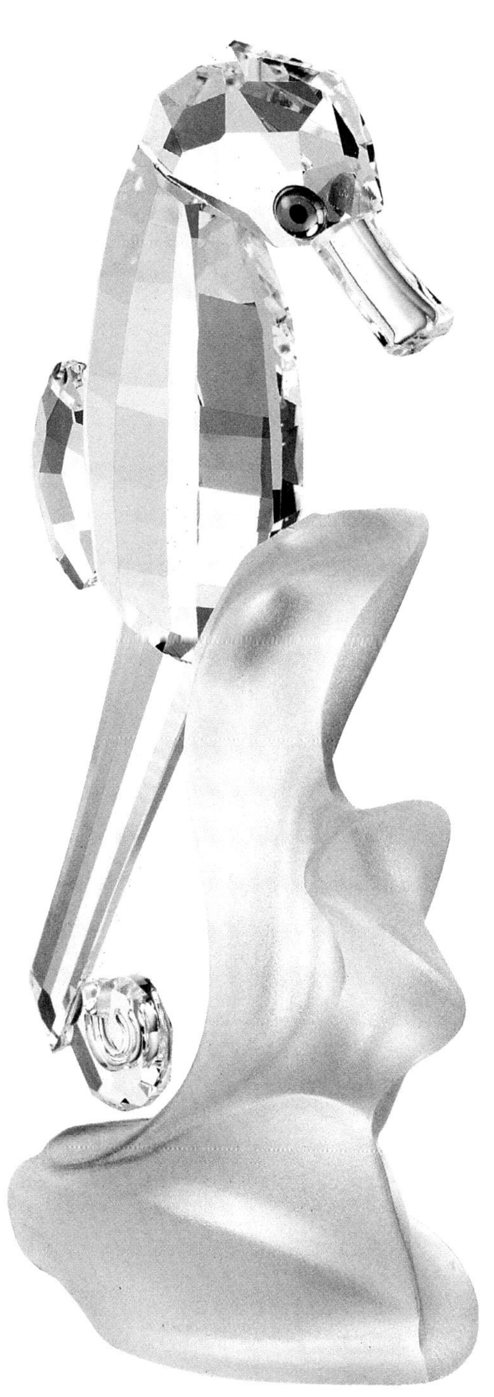

Sea Horse, CRV ***$95***

*Mini Seal, black whiskers, SC CRV **$250**, Swan CRV **$200***

*Member Seals, CRV **$600***

*Shell, CRV **$46.50***

Siamese Fighting Fish, blue, CRV **$125**

Siamese Fighting Fish, green, CRV **$125**

Sleigh, CRV **$295**

Snail on Vine-Leaf, CRV **$65**

Snowman, CRV **$99**

Mini Sparrow, SC CRV **$90**, *Swan* **$75**

Squirrel, U.S., small ears, SC CRV ***$150,***
Swan ***$125***

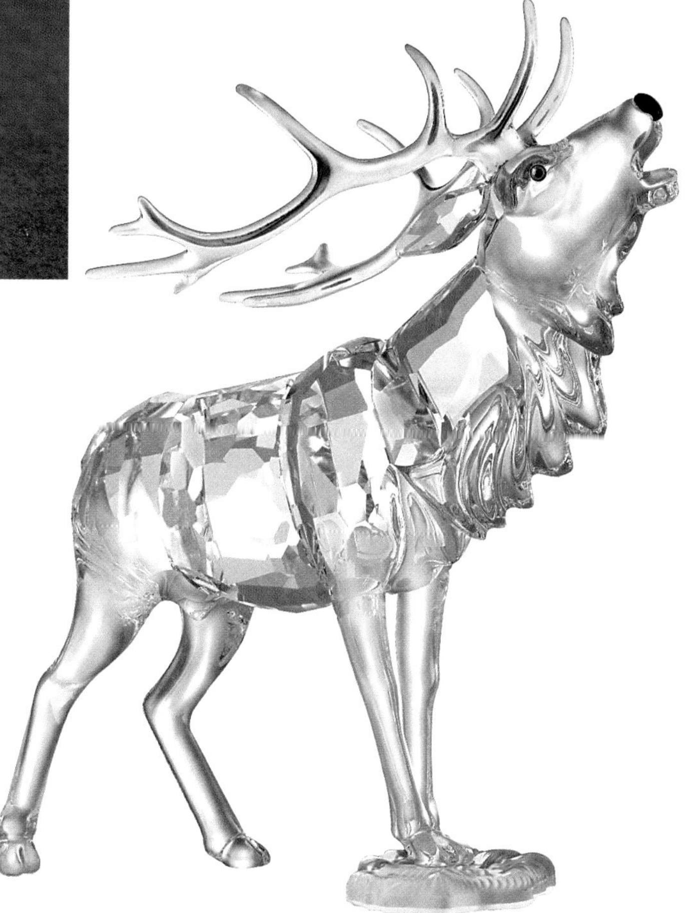

Stag, CRV ***$385***

Starfish, CRV ***$40***

Starter Set, CRV **$125**

1995 Renewal Swan, CRV **$75**

Swan Brooch, CRV **$75**

*Centenary Swan, CRV **$175***

*Swan Family, CRV **$190***

*Large Swan, current style, SC mark, CRV **$150***

*Maxi Swan, CRV **$4900***

*Medium Swan, SC CRV **$325**, Swan CRV **$95***

*Mini Swan, SC CRV **$125**, Swan CRV **$200***

Swan Necklace, CRV ***$90***

New Member Swan, CRV ***$75***

Small Swan, current model CRV ***$60***

Sweet Heart, CRV ***$125***

Tank Wagon, CRV ***$125***

Tender Car, SC CRV ***$75****, Swan CRV* ***$60***

Tipping Wagon, CRV ***$125***

Tigger, CRV ***$400***

Toucan, 3", CRV ***$155***

Tortoise, CRV ***$60***

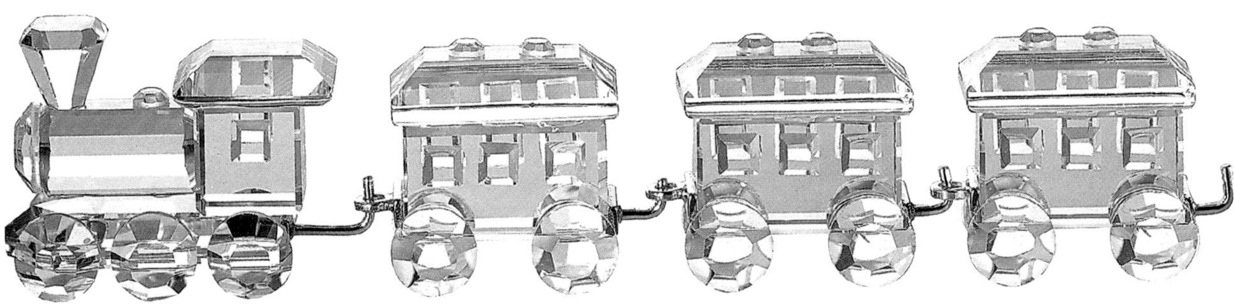

Mini Train, CRV ***$125***

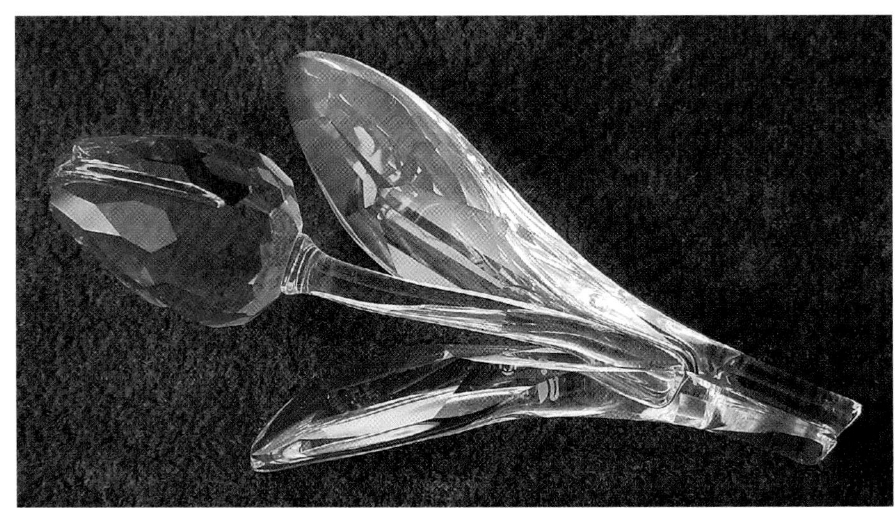

Blue Tulip, CRV ***$75***

*Giant Turtle, SC CRV **$5500**, Swan CRV **$4900***

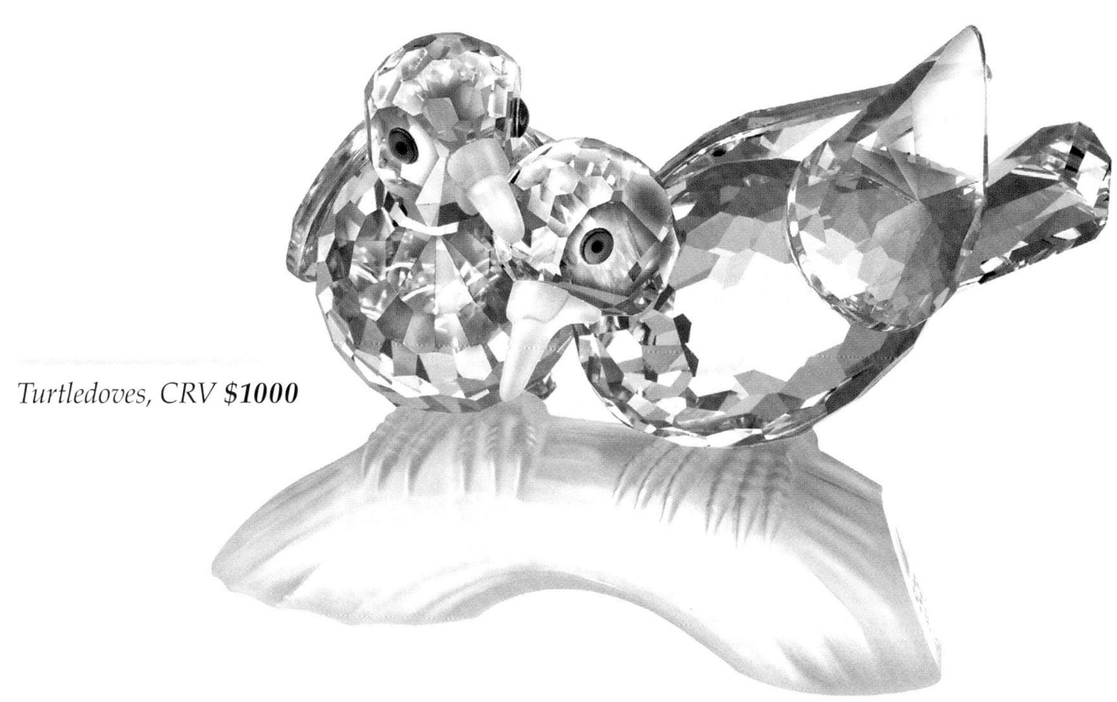

*Turtledoves, CRV **$1000***

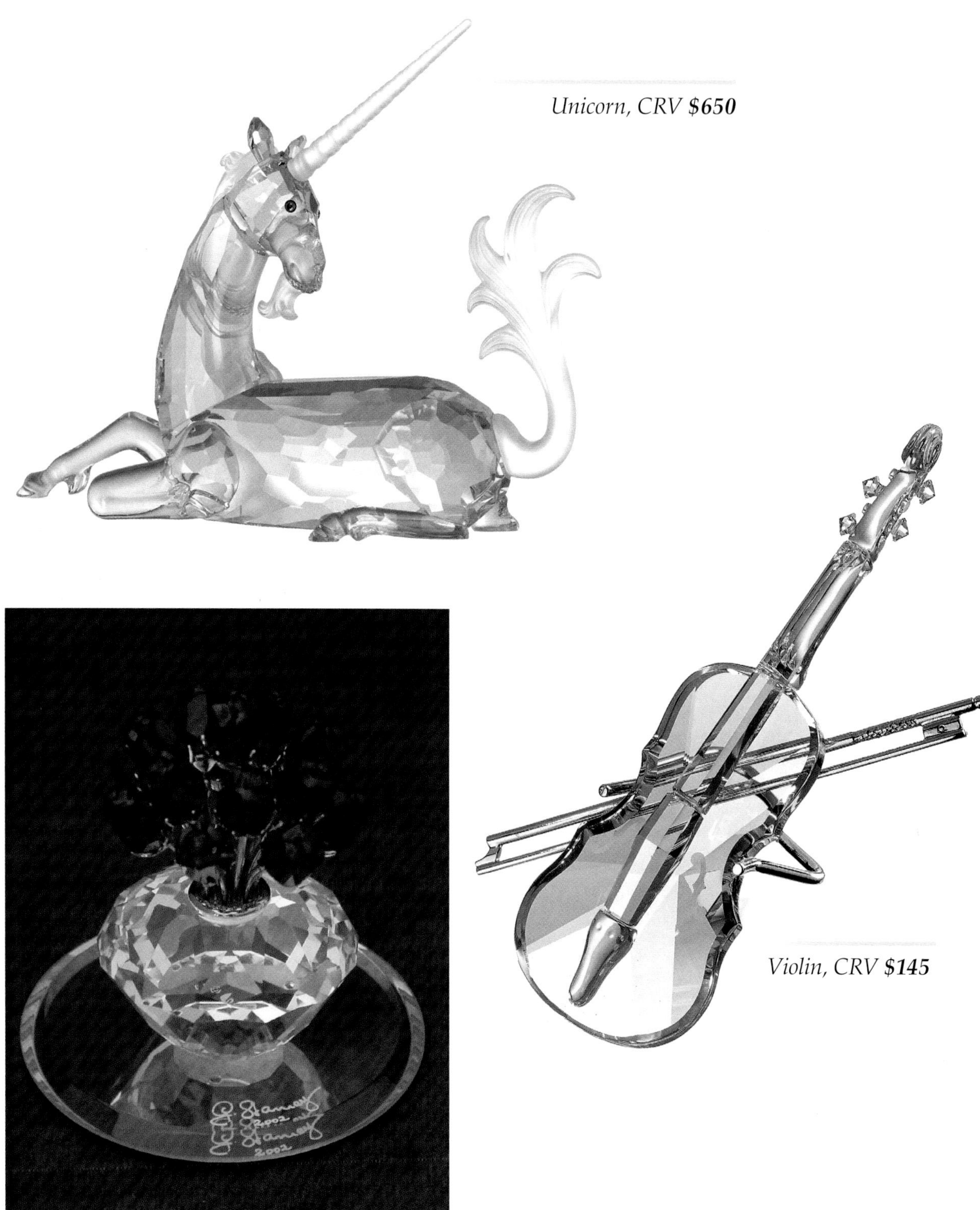

Unicorn, CRV **$650**

Violin, CRV **$145**

Vase of Roses, CRV **$175**

Whales, ***$600***

Wild Horses, CRV ***$6000***

Winnie The Pooh, CRV ***$400***

Wolf, CRV ***$155***

Woodpeckers, CRV ***$2750***

GLOSSARY OF TERMS

Anniversary Exclusives: Swarovski Silver Crystal items that are offered exclusively to members of the Swarovski Collectors Society to commemorate significant anniversaries of the member or Society.

Artist's Signature: Some pieces are signed by the Silver Crystal Designers at special events. At selected special events the designers use an etching tool to hand-sign the crystal.

Chip: This term is used to describe a flaw in a piece of crystal. A chip is usually rough to the touch and makes the crystal less desirable to collectors.

Clear: The term used to describe the Swarovski Silver Crystal items that are transparent and allow the ability to see through them.

Closed Edition: Often used as another term to describe a retired Swarovski Silver Crystal item. These closed or retired items will never again be produced.

Club Year: The club year for the Swarovski Collectors Society runs from January 1 through December 31 each year.

Club Exclusive: This refers to the products made for membership premiums, and sold exclusively to members of the Swarovski Collectors Society. Each of these items bears a special SCS backstamp to identify it as such.

Collector's Plaque: Special plaques produced especially for the collector to display with a particular piece. An example of this type plaque would be the special plaques produced for display with the Annual Editions.

Current Production: Term used to describe Swarovski Silver Crystal items that are being produced at the present time. These are the items available at Authorized Swarovski Retailers at the manufacturer's suggested retail prices.

Current Trademark: Term used to describe the symbol presently being used on the Swarovski Silver Crystal that represents the company's trademark.

Dealer's Plaque: A plaque made and distributed by the Swarovski Company to Authorized Retailers for the purpose of advertising the fact that they are authorized dealers in Swarovski Silver Crystal. These plaques have taken on various shapes and forms through the years.

Discontinued: Designates an item that has been changed in design from the original, but modified production still carries the same production number.

Final Year of Issue: Term used to describe an item that has been announced for retirement, but is still available until the end of the year, or as soon as authorized retailers' stocks have been exhausted.

Flocked Base: This term refers to the small piece of felt on the bottom of the paperweights, for example, to protect the color-giving coating.

Frosted: The description of Swarovski Silver Crystal that has received a special treatment to make it translucent, rather than clear.

Gold: The application of a gold plating to give a Swarovski piece, with accompanying metal, a look of solid gold.

Hammered Metal: The term used to describe the technique used to give texture to metal. An example would be the textured leaves on some Swarovski Silver Crystal Pineapples.

GLOSSARY OF TERMS

Limited Edition: Those items that are manufactured with a designated numerical limitation. These Swarovski Silver Crystal items can be limited also by a specific period of time. Sometimes limited or exclusive editions are made to be sold by a single distributor.

Manufacturer's Suggested Retail Price (MSRP): This is the Swarovski Company's suggested retail price, at which current items are to be sold by authorized product retailers.

Measurement: The listing of each piece, as to size, is taken from factory measurements of the standard piece. In this publication, it is stated in both inches and millimeters. Items are listed with measurements of the greatest height, width or diameter.

Nickel: One of the metals used in the production of adornments to the Silver Crystal. Nickel is silver in color and appearance.

Prototype: Term used to describe a one-of-a-kind first sample of a newly designed Swarovski Silver Crystal item. Often times, modifications are made to these original prototypes.

Renewal Gifts: Renewal Gifts are those items produced by Swarovski especially for the members who renew their memberships in the Swarovski Collectors Society for another year.

Retired: Retirement announcements are made periodically. As of a certain date, Swarovski Silver Crystal items are discontinued permanently. These items usually are quickly purchased by collectors who wish to avoid paying higher prices later on the secondary market.

Rhodium: This metal is used as part of the adornment for Swarovski Silver Crystal items, and is silver in color.

Sample Model: A prototype piece modeled for the production approval. May, or may not, have gained approval.

Secondary Market: When an item is bought or sold after its initial purchase, it is said to be traded on the secondary market.

Smooth Leaves: Term used to describe leaves on the Pineapple that are smooth and shiny, rather than textured.

Swarovski: Name of the crystal produced by the Swarovski Company of Wattens, Austria. When giving lectures on Swarovski, I tell my audiences to think of the proper pronunciation in this way: Just say "I swore off skiing", and then say Swore OFF Ski—say it faster, and you have Swarovski (swore-off-ski).

Transparent: Term used to describe crystal that is clear or has some color, but is unfrosted. It is a clear crystal, or colored crystal, that you can see through.

Translucent: Term used to describe Swarovski Silver Crystal with color added, and a frosted finish.

Variations: Term used to describe a Swarovski Silver Crystal piece that is different than the standard issued items. A variation can include a change of facet style, number, or position of additional pieces (eyes, nose, and whiskers). Hand assembly of Swarovski Silver Crystal through the years has allowed for many interesting and highly valuable collectibles.

LISTING

A

Airplane..7473 000 002
Alligator 7661 000 005/221 629
Angel (Nativity) 7475 000 009
Angel..7474 000 600/194 761
Anniversary
  Birthday Cake.............................. 003-0169678/169 678
  Squirrel.......................................7400 097 001/208 433
  The Vase of Roses........................7400 200 204/293 394
Anteater...7680 000 001/271 460
Antonio..7400 200 300/606 441
Antonio Plaque...626 472
Apple
  Apple... 7476 000 001
  Apple Photo Stand
    King—Gold...7504 060 000 G
    King—Rhodium..................................7504 060 000 R
    Medium—Gold ....7504 050 000 G
    Medium—Rhodium.............................7504 050 000 R
    Small—Gold.......................................7504 030 000 G
    Small—Rhodium................................7504 030 000 R
Arabian Stallion 7612 000 002/221 609
Arch (Nativity) 7475 000 010
Ashtray
  Ashtray (new) 7461 100 000
  Ashtray V. 1 (old).......................................7501 061 000
  Ashtray V. 3 (old).......................................7501 061 000
Atomic Paperweight....................................7454 060 000
Athena Clock .... 9280 NR 102
Automobile, Old Timer 7473 000 001

B

Baby
  Baby Beaver, Lying 7616 000 003
  Baby Beaver, Sitting.................................. 7616 000 002
  Baby Carp.................................... 7644 000 003/211 743
  Baby Carriage 7473 000 005
  Baby Frog 7642 000 002/286 313
  Baby Giraffe................................7603 000 002/236 717
  Baby Lovebirds.......................... 7621 000 005/199 123
  Baby Panda ....7611 NR 000 002/181 081
  Baby Penguins (set of 3)............. 7661 000 003/209588
  Baby Sea Lion .... 7661 NR 000 004/221 120
  Baby Shark 7644 000 007/269 236
  Baby Snails on Vine Leaf.... 7550 NR 000 009/268 196
  Baby Tortoises (set of 2)............ 7632 000 002/220 960
Bag of Hearts SCMR10
Bag of Marguerites..SCMR11
Bag of Tulips 606546R
Bald Eagle.......................................7670 000 002/248 003
Ballerina 7550 000 005/236 715
Ballerina, Young............................7550 000 004/254 960
Barrel Paperweight 7453 060 000
Beagle
  Playing Beagle .... 7619 NR 000 004/172 296
  Puppy, Beagle 7619 000 001/158 418
Bear
  Giant Bear.. 7637 112 000
  King Bear V. 1 .... 7637 092 000
  King Bear V. 2 .... 7637 092 000
  Koala Bear
    Koala, Large 7673 040 000/014 366
    Koala, Mini....................... 7673 NR 030 000/119 172
  Kris Bear
    Kris Bear 7637 000 001/174 957
    Kris Bear/Honey Pot 7637 000 003/213 068
    Kris Bear/Celebration.............7637 000 005/238 168
    Kris Bear Clock........................ 7481 000 001/212 687
    Kris Bear on Skates 7637 000 002/193 011
    Kris Bear on Skis 7637 000 004/234 710
    Kris Bear Pict. Frame 7506 000 002/214 805
  Large Bear 7637 075 000/010 009
  Mini Bear (current)....................7664 044 000/012 262
  Mini Bear (retired).................................... 7670 032 000
  Panda Bear, Baby.........................7611 000 002/181 081
  Panda Bear, Mother 7611 000 001/181 080
  Polar Bear 7649 085 000
  Small Bear 7637 054 000
Beaver
  Lying Baby Beaver 7616 000 003
  Mother Beaver 7616 000 001
  Sitting Baby Beaver.................................. 7616 000 002
Bee
  Bee on Flower (Bumblebee)..................... 7615 000 002
  Bee on Lily, Gold 7553 100 000
  Bee on Lily, Rhodium 7553 200 000

- Beetle Bottle Opener
  - Opener—Gold ... 7505 076 001
  - Opener—Rhodium ... 7505 076 002
- Bell
  - Bell, Table, Large ... 7467 071 000
  - Bell, Table, Medium ... 7467 054 000
  - Bell, Table, Small ... 7467 039 000
  - Bell, Solaris ... 7467 000 001/235 526
- Bird Bath ... 7460 108 000/010 029
- Birds' Nest ... 7470 050 000
- Birthday Cake ... 003-0169678/169 678
- Blowfish
  - Blowfish, Large ... 7644 041 000
  - Blowfish, Mini ... 7644 020 000/013 960
  - Blowfish, Small ... 7644 030 000/012 724
- Blush Brush ... SCBB 000 001 Prototype
- Boats
  - Sailboat ... 7473 000 004/183 269
  - Santa Maria ... 7473 000 003/162 882
- Bottle Openers (Beetle) ... 7505 076 000
- Box
  - Coin, SCS Member ... 7400/090/000
  - Pillbox ... 7506 030 000
  - Pillbox ... 7506 050 000
- Box, Treasure
  - Jewel Box ... 7464 000 001/207 886
  - Sweet Heart Jewel Box ... 7480 000 002/219 966
- Brooch, Member
  - Brooch, Small ... SCBNR99
  - Brooch, Small ... SCBNR101
  - Brooch, Small ... SCBNR102
  - Centenary Swan ... 003-0004418
  - Dolphin, Member ... SCBNR1
  - Elephant, Member ... SCBNR2
  - Kristallwelten Brooch ... 9005617861007
  - Mask Brooch, Green ... SCBNR2001
  - Mask Brooch, Red ... SCBNR2000
  - Mask Brooch, Tabac ... SCBNR1999
  - SCS Member Brooch ... SCMR91
  - Small Wattens Brooch ... SCBNR8
  - Swan, Member, 1995 ... 003-0004418
  - Swan, Member ... 7855001B
  - Swan, Blue ... 1807234
  - Swan, Mini Swan ... SCBNR6
  - Swan, Multi-color ... SCBNR3
- Brush
  - Brush, Blush ... SCBBNR1 Prototype
  - Brush, Shaving ... SCSBNR2 Prototype
- Buffalo, The ... 624598
- Bumblebee ... 7615 000 002
- Bunch of Grapes ... 7509 150 070/01164
- Bunny, Rabbit ... 7678 000 001/208 326
- Butterfly
  - Butterfly, Large ... 7639 055 000/010 002
  - Butterfly, Gold ... 7551 100 000
  - Butterfly, Mini ... 7667 035 000/012 774
  - Butterfly, Mini ... 7671 030 000
  - Butterfly, Rhodium ... 7551 200 000
  - Butterfly Fish ... 7644 077 000
  - Butterfly on Leaf ... 7615 000 003/182 920

C

- Cactus, Flowering ... 7484 000 001/291 549
- Cactus, Member, Ren ... SCMR88
- Cake, Birthday ... 003-0169678
- Camel ... 7607 000 004/247 683
- Candleholders
  - 101 Snowflake ... 7600 101 000
  - 102 ... 7600 102 000
  - 102 (Smoked Topaz) ... 7600 102 000
  - 103 U.S. ... 7600 103 000 United States
  - 103 European ... 7600 103 000 European
  - 104 U.S. ... 7600 104 000 United States
  - 104 European ... 7600 104 000 European
  - 106 ... 7600 106 000
  - 107 ... 7600 107 000
  - 108 European ... 7600 108 000 European
  - 109 ... 7600 109 000
  - 110 ... 7600 110 000
  - 111 ... 7600 111 000
  - 112 ... 7600 112 000
  - 112 Smoked Topaz ... 7600 112 000
  - 113 European ... 7600 113 000 European
  - 114 U.S. ... 7600 114 000
  - 115 ... 7600 115 000
  - 116 ... 7600 116 000
  - 118 European ... 7600 118 000 European

D

E

Eagle
- Eagle 7607 000 001/184 872
- Eagle, Bald 7670 000 002/248 003
- Eagle, The 624599

Egg
- Egg, Paperweight 7458 063 069
- Egg, Paperweight, Bermuda Blue .... 7458 NR 063 088/7458 063 088
- Egg, Paperweight, Crystal Cal .... 7458 NR 063 095/7458 063 095
- Egg, Paperweight, Vitrail Medium .... 7458 NR 063 087/7458 063 087

El Dorado Clock .... 9280 NR 106

Elephant
- Disney Dumbo .... 7640 NR 35
- Elephant Brooch, Mem. 003-8902448
- Elephant, Baby 7640 000 001/191 371
- Elephant, Member DO1X931/169 970
- Elephant, Large .... 7640 NR 55/7610 055 000
- Elephant, Large 7640 060 000
- Elephant, Small 7640 040 000

F

Falcon Head
- Falcon Head, Large 7645 100 000
- Falcon Head, Small 7645 045 000

Fawn 7608 000 001

Field Mouse 7631 025 000/162 886

Field Mice, Set of three 7631 015 000/181 513

Fish
- Fish, Butterfly 7644 077 000
- Fish, Mini Telescope 7644 000 010/631103
- Fish, Siamese Fighting—Blue ... 7624 000 005/236 718
- Fish, Siamese Fighting—Green 7624 000 006/261 259
- Fish, Siamese Fighting—Red 7644 000 013/660941
- Fish, Three South Sea 7644057 00

Flacon
- Flacon, Oriental 7482 000 001/217 826
- Flacon, Rose 7482 000 002/236 693
- Flacon, Napoleon 7482 000 003/265 518

Flamingo 7670 000 003/289 733

Flower Arrangement, Maxi 7478 000 004/252 976

Flowering Cactus 7484 000 001/291 549

Foals 627637

Four Leaf Clover 7483 000 001/212 101

Fox
- Fox, Large 7629 070 000
- Fox, Mini Running 7677 055 000
- Fox, Mini Sitting 7677 045 000/014 955

Frog
- Frog 7642 000 001/183 113
- Frog, Baby 7642 000 002/286 313
- Frog, Prince, Black Eyes 7642 048 000
- Frog, Prince, Clear Eyes 7642 048 000

G

Games of Kings
- Chess Set, Glass 7550 432 032 G/155 753
- Chess Set, Wooden 7550 432 032

German Shepherd 7619 000 007

Geometric Paperweight 7432 057 002

Giraffe, Baby 7603 000 002/236 717

Glasses, Schnapps 7468 039 000

Goat, Zodiac 7693 000 003/275 438

Goldfish, Miniature 7644 000 002/202 103

Goose, Mother 7613 000 001

Gorilla, Young 7618 000 002/2733394

Goslings
- Gosling, Dick 7613 000 004
- Gosling, Harry 7613 000 003
- Gosling, Tom 7613 000 002

Grand Piano/Stool 7477 000 006/174 506

Grapes, Bunch of,
- Grape, Gold 7509 150 070/011 864
- Grapes, Large, Gold & Rhod. 7550 030 015
- Grapes, Medium, Gold & Rhod. 7550 020 029
- Grapes, Small, Gold & Rhod. 7550 020 015

Grizzly 7637 000 006/243 880

Grizzly Cub 7637 000 007/261 925

H

Harlequin
- Harlequin 7400 200 100/254 044
- Harlequin Paperweight 27871460M6306
- Harlequin Paperweight 27871440M6306

- Harlequin Plaque 276 870
- Harp 7477 000 003
- Heart, Renewal 96 9003141991306
- Heart, Renewal 97 9003141991307
- Heart, Renewal 98 9003141991308
- Heart, Sweet 7480 000 001
- Hedgehog
  - Hedgehog, King 7630 060 000
  - Hedgehog, Large .... 7630 050 000 (old)
  - Hedgehog, Large 7630 070 000
  - Hedgehog, Medium 7630 040 000
  - Hedgehog, Medium 7630 045 000/013 265
  - Hedgehog, Replica 7606 000 002/183 273
  - Hedgehog, Small .... 7630 030 000 (old)
  - Hedgehog, Small 7669 035 000/013 989
- Hen, Mini 7675 030 000/014 492
- Heron, Silver 7670 000 001
- Hippopotamus
  - Hippopotamus, Large 7626 065 000
  - Hippopotamus, Small 7626 055 000
- Holy Family
  - Holy Family/Arch (Nativity) .... 7475 NR 000 001
  - Holy Family/Set of 3 (Nativity) .... 7475 NR 100 000
- Horse
  - Horse, Arabian Stallion 7612 000 002/221 609
  - Horse, Rocking 7479 000 001/183 270
  - Horse, White Stallion 7612 000 001/174 958
  - Horse, Zodiac 7693 000 005/289 908
- Houses
  - House, Set I & II 7474 100 000
  - House, Set III & IV 7474 200 000
- Hummingbird
  - Hummingbird 7615 000 001/166 184
  - Hummingbird, Gold 7552 100 000
  - Hummingbird, Rhodium 7552 200 000

I

- Ibex 7618 000 001/275 439
- Isadora 7400 200 200/279 648
- Isadora Paperweight 7400 200 060/602 838/M6550
- Isadora Paperweight 7400 200 040/608 238/M6550
- Isadora Plaque 602 383

J

- Jester 7550 000 011/275 555
- Jewel Box, Blue Flower 7464 000 001/207 886
- Jewel Box, Sweet Heart 7480 000 002/219 966
- Jubilee Vase of Roses 7400 200 204/293 394

K

- Kangaroo Mother/Joey 7609 000 001/181 756
- Key Chain Mem. Ren. SCMR89
- Kingfisher 7621 000 001
- Kitten 7634 028 000
- Kitten, Lying 631857
- Kitten, Standing 631856
- Kiwi 7617 043 000
- Koala Bear
  - Koala, Large 7673 040 000/014 366
  - Koala, Mini 767 030 000/119 472
- Kris Bear
  - Kris Bear 7637 000 001/174 957
  - Kris Bear/Honey Pot 7637 000 003/213 068
  - Kris Bear/Celebration 7637 000 005/238 168
  - Kris Bear/Clock 7481 000 001/212 687
  - Kris Bear on Skates 7637 000 002/193 011
  - Kris Bear on Skis 7637 000 004/234 710
  - Kris Bear Picture Frame 7506 000 002/214 805
- Kristallwelten Brooch 9005617861007
- Kristallwelten Key Ring 90033142110546
- Kristallwelten Necklace 9005617861006
- Kristallwelten Paperweight .... 9990 NR 000 005
- Kristallwelten Wall .... 9990 NR 000 006
- Kudu, Member DO1X941/175 703

L

- Ladybug 7604 000 001/190 858
- Ladybug Picture Frame 7506 000 003/211 739
- Leopard 7610 000 002
- Lighter
  - Lighter, V. 1 .... 7462 062 000
  - Lighter, V. 2 .... 7462 062 000
  - Lighter, V. 1 .... 7500 NR 062 (old polished)
  - Lighter, V. 2 .... 7500 NR 062 (old brushed)

Lighter, V. 3 .... 7500 NR 062 (old polished, gold)
Lion 7610 000 004/269 377
Lion, Cub 760 300 001/210 460
Lion, Member DO1X951/185 410
Lion, Baby Sea Lion 7661 000 004/221 120
Lionfish... 7644 000 008/604 011
Little Red Riding Hood................. 7550 000 001/191 695
Locomotive, Train 7471 000 001/015 145
Lovebirds, Baby.............................. 7621 000 005/199 123
Lovebirds, Member..............................DO1X861/013 560
Luggage Tag, Mem. Ren.................................... SCMR93
Lute...7477 000 004

M

Madame Penguin...................................7661 NR 000 002
Magnifier
Chain Magnifier
Chain Mag., Gold 7800 026 001
Chain Mag., Rhodium..............................7800 026 002
Table Mag., Gold...7510 001 001
Table Mag., Rhodium ....7510 NR 01/7510 001 002
Mallard
Mallard 7647 080 000
Mallard, Giant 7647 250 000/014 438
Marguerite
Marguerite, 1999 Renewal 9003140086126
Marguerite, 2000 Renewal 9003140086127
Marguerite, 2001 Renewal 227 537
Maritime Trio...................................7624 100 000/191 697
Marmot..7608 000 005/289 305
Maxi Pieces
Dolphin, Maxi............................7644 000 004/221 628
Flower Arrangement, Maxi 7478 000 004/252 976
Swan, Maxi...7633 160 000
Member Pieces
Boxes ....
New Member Gifts ....
Renewal Gifts ....
Mice, Field, Set of 3 ....7631 015 000/181 513
Mouse, Field.................................... 7631 025 000/162 886
Millennium Crystal Planet...........7607 000 004/238 985
Minnie Mouse 14012002
Mickey Mouse 14012000
Mini Train 7471 400 000/193 014

Mini Zoo..7656 006 000
Miniature, Goldfish 7644 000 002/202 103
Monkey, Zodiac.............................. 7693 000 004/289 901
Mother
Mother Goose 7613 000 001
Mother Kangaroo/Baby............. 7609 000 001/181756
Mother Panda 7611 000 001/181 080
Mother Rabbit............................ 7623 055 000/014 850
Mouse
Mice, Field, Set of 3 ....7631 015 000/181 513
Mickey Mouse 14012000
Minnie Mouse 140120002
Mouse, Field............................... 7631 025 000/162 886
Mouse, King...7631 060 000
Mouse, Large 7631 050 000
Mouse, Medium 7631 040 000
Mouse, Mini..7655 023 000
Mouse, Replica 7606 000 001/183 272
Mushrooms 7472 030 000

N

Napoleon Clock.. 9280 NR 101
Napoleon Flacon 7482 000 003/265 518
Necklace
Necklace, Swan, Member............................7855/001N
Night Owl..7636 000 002/206 138
Nutcracker...................................... 7475 000 604/236 714

O

Octron
Octron Paperweight 7456 041 000
Octron, Giant Paperweight...................... 7456 090 000
Octron Penholder..................................... 7457 041 000
Old Timer Automobile 7473 000 001
Open Shell With Pearl 7624 055 000/014 389
Orca 7644 000 009/622939
Orchid
Orchid, Pink................................7478 000 003/200 087
Orchid, Yellow............................7478 000 002/200 280
Oriental, Flacon 7482 000 001/217 826
Ornaments, Christmas
Year 1981 1981

P

Black Swan SCDPWNR3
Blue Swan SCDPWNR2
Paperweight, Employee Commemorative (No Number Assigned)
Paperweight, Egg
Egg, New Style.. 7458 063 069
Egg, Old Style... 7458 NR 63
Bermuda Blue.. 7458 063 088
Crystal Cal... 7458 063 095
Vitrail Medium 7458 063 087
Paperweight, Geometric 7432 057 002
Paperweight, Member SCMPWNR1
Paperweight, Member SCMPWNR2
Paperweight, Member SCMPWNR3
Paperweight, Octron................................ 7456 041 000
Bermuda Blue.. 7456 041 088
Clear 7456 041 000
Crystal Cal... 7456 041 095
Helio 7456 041 000
Inn Green 7456 041 000
Large.. 7456 090 090
Sahara.. 7456 041 000
Seal 7456 041 000
Tabac.. 7456 041 000
Vitrail Light 7456 041 000
Vitrail Medium 7456 041 000
Volcano.. 7456 041 000
Paperweight, One Ton 7459 065 000
Paperweight, Pegasus.................. 9409 060 000/M5714
Paperweight, Pyramid, Large 7450 050 000
Bermuda Blue.. 7450 050 088
Crystal Cal... 7450 050 095
Helio 7450 050 000
Inn Green... 7450 050 090
Sahara.. 7450 050 000
Seal 7450 050 000
Tabac.. 7450 050 000
Vitrail Light 7450 050 000
Vitrail Medium 7450 050 087
Volcano.. 7450 050 000
Pyramid, Small 7450 040 000
Bermuda Blue.. 7450 040 088
Crystal Cal... 7450 040 095
Helio 7450 040 000
Inn Green... 7450 040 090
Sahara.. 7450 040 000
Seal 7450 040 000
Tabac.. 7450 040 000
Vitrail Light 7450 040 000
Vitrail Medium 7450 040 087
Volcano.. 7450 040 000
Round 30mm 7404 030 000
Bermuda Blue.. 7404 030 088
Crystal Cal... 7404 030 095
Inn Green... 7404 030 090
Sahara.. 7404 030 000
Vitrail Medium 7404 030 087
Round 40mm 7404 040 000
Bermuda Blue.. 7404 040 088
Crystal Cal... 7404 040 095
Inn Green... 7404 040 090
Sahara.. 7404 040 000
Vitrail Medium 7404 040 087
Volcano.. 7404 040 000
Round 50mm 7404 050 000
Bermuda Blue.. 7404 050 088
Crystal Cal... 7404 050 095
Helio 7404 050 000
Inn Green... 7404 050 090
Sahara.. 7404 050 000
Vitrail Medium 7404 050 087
Volcano.. 7404 050 000
Round 60mm 7404 060 000
Bermuda Blue.. 7404 060 088
Crystal Cal... 7404 060 095
Helio 7404 060 000
Inn Green... 7404 060 090
Sahara.. 7404 060 000
Vitrail Medium 7404 060 087
Volcano.. 7404 060 000
Paperweight, Columbine 7400 200 060
Paperweight, Harlequin 27871440
Paperweight, Isadora 7400 200 060/602 838/M6550
Paperweight, Pierrot............. 9409 040 000/9409 060 000
Paperweight, Wild Horses 283 324/M6414
Parrot 7621 000 004
Parrot 7621 000 009/294 047
Partridge... 7625 050 000

- Pear ... 7476 000 002
- Peacock ... 7607 000 002/218 123
- Pegasus, member ... 7400 098 000/216 327
- Pelican ... 7679 000 001/171 899
- Pen, Writing, Renewal ... SCMR92
- Penholder, Octron ... 7457 041 000
- Penguin
  - Penguin, Father ... 627068
  - Penguin, Large ... 7643 085 000
  - Penguin, Madame ... 7661 000 002
  - Penguin, Mini ... 7661 033 000/010 027
  - Penguin, Mother With Babies ... 627 067
  - Penguin, Sir ... 7661 000 001/191 448
  - Penguins, Baby (set of 3) ... 7661 000 003/209 588
- Petrol Wagon ... 7471 000 004/015 151
- Piano with Stool ... 7477 000 006/174 506
- Picture Frame
  - Picture Frame, Butterfly ... 7506 000 004/211 742
  - Picture Frame, Blue Flower ... 7506 000 001/207 892
  - Picture Frame, Kris Bear ... 7506 000 002/214 805
  - Picture Frame, Ladybug ... 7506 000 003/211 739
  - Picture Frame, Leather ... SCMR93
  - Picture Frame, Oval ... 7505 NR 075G/7505 075 000G
  - Picture Frame, Square
    - Square, Gold, U.S. ... 7506 NR 60 G/7506 060 000G
    - Square, Gold, Euro. ... 7506 NR 060 001/7506 060 001G
    - Square, Rhod., Euro. ... 7506 NR 060 002R/7506 060 002R
- Pierrot Member ... 7400 099 000/230 586
- Pig
  - Pig, Large ... 7638 NR 65/7638 065 000
  - Pig, Medium ... 7638 050 000
  - Pig, Med., Glass Tail, V.1 ... 7638 050 000
  - Pig, Med., Wire Tail, V.2 ... 7638 050 000/010 031
  - Pig, Mini
    - Pig, Mini, Wire Tail, V.1 ... 7657 027 000
    - Pig, Mini, Glass Tail, V.2 ... 7657 027 000/010 028
    - Pig, Mini, Glass Tail, V.3 ... 7657 027 000
  - Pig, Zodiac ... 7693 000 006/289 914
- Pillbox
  - Pillbox ... 7506 030 000
  - Pillbox ... 7506 050 000
- Pineapple
  - Pineapple, Giant
    - Pineapple, Giant, Gold ... 7507 260 001/010 116
    - Pineapple, Giant, Rhodium ... 7507 260 002
  - Pineapple, Large
    - Pineapple, Large, Gold ... 7507 NR 105 001/010 044
    - Pineapple, Large, Rhodium ... 7507 105 002
  - Pineapple, Small
    - Pineapple, Small, Gold ... 7507 060 001/012 726
    - Pineapple, Small, Rhodium ... 7507 060 002
- Pins
  - Pin, Member
  - Pin, Stick, Member ... 1987 Charter
  - Pin, Stick, Member ... 1987 Membership
  - Pin, Stick, Member ... 1988—1991 Membership
  - Pin, Stick, Member ... 1992—1995 Membership
- Planet, Crystal Millennium ... 7607 000 004/238 985 ... (see Crystal Planet)
- Plaques, Dealer (in numerical order)
  - Octagonal ... SCDPNR1
  - Emerald Cut ... SCDPNR2
  - Tall Crystal Iceberg ... SCDPNR3
  - Square ... SCDPNR4
  - Oval Crystal Iceberg ... SCDPNR5
  - Script Swarovski Crystal ... SCDPNR6
  - Shark Tooth ... SCDPNR7
  - Rectangular Plastic ... SCDPNR8
  - Large Rectangular Plastic ... SCDPNR9
  - Rectangular Plastic ... SCDPNR10
  - Premier Dealer ... SCDPNR11
  - Premier Dealer ... SCDPNR12
  - Caring and Sharing ... SCPCSNR1
  - Mother and Child ... SCPCSNR2
  - Inspiration Africa ... SCPCSNR3
  - Fabulous Creatures ... SCPCSNR4
- Pluto, Dog ... 7635 070 000
- Polar Bear ... 7649 085 000
- Polar Star Clock ... 9280 NR 103
- Poodle
  - Poodle, Sitting ... 7619 000 005/181 317
  - Poodle, Standing ... 7619 000 003
- Poplar Trees ... 7474 020 003
- Puffins ... 7621 000 008/261 643
- Puppet ... 7550 000 003/217 207

T

U

V

W

Y

Z

INDEX

A

B

INDEX

C

D

E

F

G

H

I

J

K

P

Q

R

S

T

U

V

W

Z